MBLEx STUDY GUIDE 2017

MBLEx Test Prep and Practice Test Questions for the Massage & Bodywork Licensing Exam

TABLE OF CONTENTS

INTRODUCTION: BECOMING A LICENSED MASSAGE THERAPIST

Congratulations! You are one step closer to becoming a certified massage therapist. The end of examinations is in sight, and soon your practice will be in full swing.

Before you can begin your practice as a professional massage therapist, there are a few more steps to complete following massage school graduation. The MBLEx (Massage and Bodywork Licensing Examination) is one of them. After you receive confirmation that you have passed the exam, you can begin the process to become licensed to practice in your state. The licensing process varies from state to state. The best information can be found with your state's regulatory board—either online or in person, via phone or at the office.

This book is designed to help you succeed in the examination and beyond. In this introductory chapter, you will learn what you can expect in preparing to take the MBLEx and what steps to take once you pass.

This book as a whole will review material you can expect to see on the examination, as well as information that will be useful to you in starting your own practice, whether on your own as an independent business owner or as an employee at a spa.

Some advice in using this guide: find a peaceful place to study, free from distractions from the outside world. Sprinkle breaks in throughout your study sessions, allowing time for your brain to process the information. Be mindful that sleep is necessary in order for your brain to categorize and process information, and to be alert come test day.

What is a Massage Therapist?

A **massage therapist** is a professional trained in the manipulation of soft tissues of the body by stroking, rubbing, kneading, and using other techniques to encourage relaxation and healing in the client's body.

There are many different types, or modalities, of massage that massage therapists can incorporate into their practice and treatments—typically massage therapists will use a blend of their knowledge and skills to create their own treatment style. Just like other professionals, massage therapists can use their unique brand to build a client base; whether you are known for your gentle, relaxing work or your deep, therapeutic work, or perhaps a mixture of both, clients will seek you out based on your style in addition to things like your personality, work ethic, and practice space.

To become a professional massage therapist working in the United States, an individual will have to fulfill a number of requirements as described below.

QUALIFICATIONS

Requirements to become a professional massage therapist vary from state to state, and sometimes even from county to county within a state. It is very important that you know and understand the rules where you live, or where you want to practice, to ensure you have met all the requirements to practice professionally. If you have questions about requirements, you can find specific resources at your school, or you can contact the regulatory oversight body/registrar of your state.

While students entering a massage school program are encouraged to have some secondary education or some degree of professional experience, a GED or high school diploma is all that most schools require.

Most massage schools offer programs that meet, if not exceed, hours and education required by their state for licensure, in addition to providing students with the knowledge to pass the MBLEx. Hours for general massage programs can vary from 350 hours to 1,000, depending on the state. Most programs only offer the bare minimum in regards to massage education, and often certifications like prenatal and postnatal massage or hot stone massage are obtained through continuing education after a massage therapist is a practicing professional.

In addition to classroom learning, most massage schools will offer on-the-job training with externships in sports offices or spas, student clinics, and other events outside school. Students can be observed by instructors and other professionals—allowing them to get some "real world" experience while still receiving coaching from the experts. Stay organized with the following checklist:

> **Becoming a Professional Massage Therapist: Checklist**
>
> ☐ Complete massage school program.
>
> ☐ Study for the MBLEx.
>
> ☐ Pass the MBLEx.
>
> ☐ Register with the state and pay fees.
>
> ☐ Receive your license in the mail.
>
> ☐ Begin your professional practice!

COMMON ROLES AND RESPONSIBILITIES OF MASSAGE THERAPISTS

Being a professional massage therapist is an incredibly rewarding line of work. You get to help people who are stressed or in pain return to a more relaxed state of mind, teach them about their muscular anatomy and show them how to stretch to relieve chronically tight muscle groups, and become a constant sign of strength and peace in people's lives. It feels good!

As rewarding as the field of massage therapy can be, it also has challenges. Sometimes schedules are not right, or a person might forget his appointment; you might have a client who was not completely truthful on her intake form, or you may have a client who is inappropriate or difficult to deal with. While we always hope all clients will come fifteen minutes before their appointment, be honest with their health history, and behave kindly, we have to be prepared to deal professionally with the worst—just in case.

Excellent communication skills are of the utmost importance. You will not only appear professional, but you will also earn respect from your clients by setting boundaries. Keeping things professional can sometimes be difficult with very friendly clients who want to know more about you—where you grew up, where you live now, who you vote for, if you're seeing anyone . . . The slope can get slippery pretty quickly. Being an excellent communicator, though, you can put a stop to these comments and questions by encouraging clients to focus on their breathing, or, if that does not work, by asking them to stop or warning them you will have to stop the treatment if their prying continues.

The above is an example of being professional and keeping yourself safe. Other safety concerns may be physical; to avoid risking injury, make sure equipment is in working order and cords and other hazards are out of the way of both the client and the therapist. Communication protects clients by keeping them informed as long as you, as the therapist, describe the treatment specifically. (Please note this information is covered more in depth in chapter 3 of this review book.)

Not to be dismissed is hygiene, which is also of the utmost importance. You should maintain short, unpainted nails; keep hair out of your face; clean your body regularly; and wash your hands frequently throughout your shift, especially after each client. Also, keep in mind that what you eat emits smells from your body; if garlic chicken gives you gas, it is probably best to save that meal for after your shift is over.

> 🔍 Think about it. A client is waiting for her massage therapist and sees him picking his nose or eating. Without washing his hands, the therapist greets her and takes her to the treatment room. Then, during the massage he blows his nose without washing his hands. Not only is that disgusting, but it also puts her at risk of catching a cold. She will probably complain to management and get the therapist scolded, suspended, or worse; she may even leave a negative review on social media. Either of those actions could cost the therapist not only his reputation, but also his career. You do not want to be that therapist.

The best way to deal with clients is to try to put yourself in their shoes. Yes, the client may be acting like a jerk, but on her intake form she said she has had lower back and neck pain for three months. You would probably be a little grumpy too if you were in pain that long. If all else fails, remain professional and know that after the treatment, you can suggest another therapist for her next massage.

Massage Therapy Settings

A number of people still view massage as a luxury that occurs in a high-end spa. While that can be the case, there are many different settings where massage takes place.

Yes, massage can take place in a high-priced, luxury spa. Typically, these massage treatments come with flourishes, or extras, such as body wraps or facials, or hot stone treatments. Because of the setting, the experience of the therapist, and additions to the treatment, these massages are often expensive, being upward of $150 per treatment. Not only can you work in spas on land, but cruise ships also have spas—you can see the world while working.

As you are currently studying massage therapy or have just completed your training, you know that massage is much more than a relaxing treatment at a spa. Massage can also take place in a rehabilitation clinic, for clients recovering from a physical injury or an addiction. As discussed in chapter 6, compassionate touch can promote healing and serenity within the body.

Massage can also supplement chiropractic and physical therapy as part of a monthly maintenance regimen or as a temporary measure during recovering from an injury or surgery. In addition, professional and collegiate sports teams often have massage therapists on staff to ensure their players are in top-notch condition both before and after sporting events.

Sports massage, deep tissue, clinical/medical massage, oncology (cancer) massage—all of these specific, different types of massage are needed in a number of settings. Massage therapy is a growing field with a wide range of opportunity and advancement in a number of different areas.

In addition to the physical practice of performing massage, there are plenty of other jobs within massage, from teaching general massage courses or continuing education classes to writing about massage for magazines or even test preparation books like this one. The world of massage is rich with possibilities!

THE FUTURE OF MASSAGE THERAPY

The world of massage is far reaching and ever expanding. As the field gains more credibility with national certification standards like the MBLEx and state licensing, opportunities for therapists grow. Some insurance carriers even cover massage therapy in clinical settings; due to the affordability of such coverage, more people are being drawn to massage as clients. Additionally, many clients are looking for a holistic health approach, using massage along with a healthy diet and exercise to maintain a balanced lifestyle.

Furthermore, medical professionals are increasingly looking to massage therapists to help their patients with pain management or in palliative care, though there are some out there who still view massage as a luxury.

While it is great news for you as a therapist that the world of massage therapy is growing and advancing, it also means that with the change and growth will come new challenges. Therapists are responsible for individual professional development. More reputable institutions are turning out massage therapists ready to grow and advance the industry. Massage therapists must uphold a high level of professionalism to maintain and increase the respect and validity paid to the field and their work.

National Certification

Massage, like any other trade profession, needs to have rules, regulations, and standards of education that can be measured to ensure that individual professionalism is maintained. The MBLEx is the national certification that measures these standards in the world of massage.

WHAT IS THE MBLEx?

The MBLEx is maintained and administered by the Federation of State Massage Therapy Boards (FSMTB). The FSMTB's mission is to support member boards in the work so that the practice of massage therapy is provided to the public in a safe and effective manner. The FSMTB developed the MBLEx to "offer the first standardized licensing exam for the massage and bodywork profession; to facilitate professional mobility; to give the regulatory community oversight over exam content, organizational policies and procedures pertaining to the exam; and to significantly speed up the process between application and examination to avoid unnecessary delays in licensure."

Think of it like this: passing the MBLEx and getting licensed establishes your credibility as a massage therapist in your community. Your clients will see your credentials and be confident that you know what you are doing in providing their treatment.

There are two different ways to sign up to take the MBLEx: through the FSMTB or through your state's licensing board or agency. To go through the FSMTB, sign up for the exam at the official website: https://www.fsmtb.org/mblex/application-process/. After you verify that you have completed all the necessary education, agree to the test's policies in writing, and pay the fee of $195, you'll receive an "Authorization to Test" (ATT) via email. You must sign up to take the test within ninety days at Pearson Vue: http://www.pearsonvue.com/fsmtb/. If you need to change locations or your testing date, you can contact Pearson Vue as well.

Should you go through your state's licensing board or agency, you must first be approved by that organization; the same steps as above apply in terms of signing off on the test, paying the fee, and scheduling the exam.

Each multiple-choice question is worth one raw point. The total number of questions you answer correctly is added up to obtain your raw score, which is then converted to a number on a scale of 300 – 900. In order to pass the MBLEx, you must receive at least a score of 630.

The score will be kept electronically, but you can request a physical copy for a twenty-dollar fee.

Either route you take will allow you to move toward being a licensed professional therapist after you pass—it really just depends on how your school or state does things. One option is no better than the other; what you choose may be based on preference and availability of services in your area.

What You Need to Learn to Pass the MBLEx

This guide will help you prepare to take the MBLEx exam. Each chapter is designed with you passing the exam in mind. You will find tools, study tips, and plenty of practice questions to cover each topic found on the MBLEx.

The breakdown of the exam follows in the table below. While it may seem like an overwhelming amount of information, there are only 100 questions to be answered in two hours. Think back to your days in massage school, and use this test prep as a road map for your success.

Everything from muscle actions, origins, and insertions to asking your clients about their health history will be on the exam. Remember to breathe.

What's on the MBLEx?

Topic	Content	Percentage	Number of Questions*
Body Systems	Anatomy and Physiology	12%	11 – 13
	Kinesiology	11%	10 – 12
Pathology	Pathology, Contraindications, Special Populations, Areas of Caution	13%	12 – 15
Application	Benefits and Physiological Effects of Techniques That Manipulate Soft Tissue	14%	13 – 16
Assessment	Client Assessment, Reassessment, and Treatment Planning	17%	16 – 18
CAM (Complimentary and Alternative Medicines)	Overview of Massage and Bodywork Modalities/ Culture/History	5%	4 – 6
Professional	Ethics, Boundaries, Laws, Regulations	15%	14 – 17
	Guidelines for Professional Practice	13%	12 – 15

*numbers are approximate

WHAT TO EXPECT ON TESTING DAY

You do not have to dread test day anymore! You have put hours, days, weeks, and months into preparing for this exam, and this book is designed to make sure you know your stuff—which you do!

Now that you know you have the material down, here is what you need to know for the logistical side of taking this exam:

+ Arrive at least thirty minutes early in the event there is a delay, and to ensure you are not feeling rushed before the start of the exam.

+ Bring only what you need. Most things, such as a watch, phone, chewing gum, etc., will not be allowed into the exam room. Lockers will be provided for keys or jackets.

+ Two forms of valid identification are required. Check https://www .fsmtb.org/ to be sure you have the most up-to-date information.

You will not be able to flag questions for review at a later time. If you need to use the bathroom, you may raise your hand, but it is better to go before the exam begins as the time does not stop for your breaks.

Since the test is computerized, it will base your questions on how well you are doing in the exam. If you answer a question correctly, then the next question will be of the same or higher difficulty level, but if you answer a question incorrectly, the following question will be easier. This pattern continues throughout the test.

After answering 100 questions in (under) two hours, you can notify the official that you are finished with the exam, and your score will be waiting for you at the front where you checked in.

After You Pass the MBLEx

You did it! You are now a CMT, or certified massage therapist. Now you have to register with your state licensing board so you can practice professionally. Most states require licenses to be renewed every two years, for a fee, in addition to a certain number of continuing education (CE) hours. As always, it is important to check with your state licensing board to make sure you have everything necessary for the initial license and then for the following renewal years.

Continuing education courses allow you to build your skill set and open your practice to a new level of clientele. Also, it is good for professionals to constantly be learning and practicing their skills on other professionals to get productive feedback.

The world of professional massage therapy is now open to you! Go forth and prosper!

ONE: THE FOUNDATION OF MASSAGE

The concept of touch to heal and comfort dates back thousands of years. Touch is a natural response to pain and, while the term *massage* is relatively new in the history of therapeutic touch, it has existed as long as humans.

Before the scientific study of the human body and written research, shamanism existed. The idea of a **shaman** (healer) using ritual to manage illness and pain, and maintain healthy bodily functions, existed in most early cultures on all continents of the globe. Illness and disease were associated with evil, demons, and spirits, and a shaman's magical abilities were respected and honored. What can be learned from shamanic ritual is that humankind has always sought to heal. Shamans were male and female. Today, healers in these societies, tribes, and communities are still viewed with respect, and as a link to a rich cultural past that relied on a holistic concept of healing.

What people think of today as tools and techniques used in the healing arts include methods that date back to tribal shamanism and rituals. Examples are:

+ aromas and scents
+ baths
+ cold
+ energy flow
+ grains
+ heat
+ herbs

+ movement
+ observation
+ ointments and oils
+ practices to prepare and aid in childbirth
+ steam
+ teas
+ touch

The letters *BCE* are used to denote Before the Common Era. BCE years progress backward in time, as opposed to the time we live in, the Common Era, which progresses forward. For example, the first century BCE dates from 1 BCE to 100 BCE, the second century BCE dates from 101 BCE to 200 BCE, etc.

1000 900 800 700 600 500 400 300 200 100 0 100 200 300 400 500 600 700 800 900 1000

BCE   CE

The practice of what has become known as Traditional Chinese Medicine (TCM) is believed to date back to 3000 BCE. The first formal written record of Chinese medical practices, the **Nei Ching**, is considered to be the bible of TCM. It contains references to the use of practices related to touch for healing. This occurred during the time of the **Emperor Huang Ti** (2697 BCE – 2596 BCE). **Amma**, a system of manual and energy techniques, is considered the forerunner of the practice of massage and bodywork. This practice spread to Japan, where it was incorporated into the country's healing culture.

Ayurveda is a health and treatment system that was derived and developed within India's Vedic culture around 1800 BCE. *Ayurveda* literally means "life (*ayur*) knowledge (*veda*)." It is a holistic approach to maintaining health and healing. Included in this practice is the use of oils infused into the body using manual strokes for the purpose of balancing the recipient's body, mind, and spirit.

> Here is a list of key names in the history of massage and bodywork in the order in which they are presented. Note a key term or words to associate with each one that will jog your memory:

Asclepius	Celsus	Bright	Ling	Nissen
Herodicus	Avicenna	Borelli	Mezger	Graham
Asclepiades	Paré	Harvey	Taylor Bros.	Kellogg

Herodicus, a fifth-century BCE Greek doctor, is noted for his determination that combining diet and exercise is important for proper maintenance and functioning of the body. In his writings, he discussed the benefits of rubbing the body, the speed of the rubbing strokes, and the degree of pressure applied depending on the condition being addressed. Today, some view him as the **father of sports medicine**. Herodicus is believed to have been a tutor to Hippocrates, who will be discussed further below.

> The god of medicine and healing, **Asclepius**, was worshipped during the time of Greek mythology and ancient Greek religious practices. His symbol, the rod of Asclepius, a snake-entwined staff, is still the symbol of the modern medical profession.

During the Classical, or Hellenic, period in ancient Greece, new ways of studying human culture, referred to academically as the *humanities*, developed. This period saw a movement toward rational thinking based on observation and study. The physician **Hippocrates**, who became known historically as the **father of medicine**, theorized that disease is a natural occurrence related to imbalances in the body and that the body has the ability to heal itself. He believed in observation, logical thought, and systematic principles of diagnosis. His doctrines evolved into the theory known as the **four humors**. The four humors refer to bodily fluids classified as:

+ phlegm: cold and moist like water
+ blood: hot and moist like air
+ yellow bile: hot and dry like fire
+ black bile: cold and dry like earth

These fluids must be balanced to maintain health. While Hippocrates does not comment in depth on what we know today as massage, he did use the word *anatripsis* to refer to the technique of rubbing. He furthered the teachings of Herodicus on rubbing, believing that the strokes should move bodily fluids toward the heart and body center to benefit circulation and the excretory process. This concept, hundreds of years later, would reappear in the form of Swedish massage.

From Greece, these activities and treatments moved into Roman medical practices, where the Hippocratic model of treatment continued with **Asclepiades**, a Greek physician who settled in Rome, and **Aulus Cornelius Celsus**, a Roman physician who wrote *De Medicina* during the first century AD. They were important contributors to modern-day medicine and medical treatments. *De Medicina* was a medical guide that addressed diet, surgery, pharmacology, and the treatment of different illnesses and ailments. Celsus believed that the use of hydrotherapy, exercise, and rubbing were important contributors to health, healing, and well-being. It was during the time period between Hippocrates and Celsus when what we know today as massage emerged.

After the fall of the Roman Empire, much of what was gained in medical education returned to the realm of shamanic beliefs, but was controlled more by religion and religious dogma. Baths and gymnastics were viewed as glorification of the body and were soon banned. However, during this time, the concept of massage and touch was viewed as valuable to the Christian rituals of care for the sick and dying. These rituals were administered primarily by women who, under the authority of the church, continued to provide support and aid to those who were dying or suffered from disease and disorders that were not considered curable or treatable.

In Arabian societies, **Avicenna**, who lived from 980 to 1037 CE, wrote and contributed volumes in writing to medical history. Avicenna was greatly influenced by the Greeks and wrote about massage, exercise, and the value of hydrotherapies. He was a big endorser of the use of friction techniques after athletic events as well as the importance of touch and grooming applied to valued horses after their participation in physical activity.

Historically, during the period of the European Renaissance and Enlightenment in the fourteenth through sixteenth centuries, the foundations of what is now considered Western medicine (anatomy, chemical pharmacology, and surgical techniques) advanced rapidly. **Ambroise Paré**, a French military surgeon, discovered the orthopedic benefits of massage. **Timothy Bright**, a physician, wrote about the value of baths, exercise, and massage and began teaching his ideas at Cambridge University in England. Also, during the sixteenth century, the Chinese published works that discussed pediatric massage and the Japanese published works that discussed passive and active massage techniques.

By the end of the seventeenth century, an Italian, **Giovanni Alfonso Borelli**, learned about muscular contraction through dissection; **William Harvey**, an English physician, discovered how blood circulation is propelled by the beating of the heart. This discovery lent credence to the Greek belief, in the time of Hippocrates, of using motions to move bodily fluids in the direction of the heart. At this point in time, after all the advancement in scientific study, massage began to be recognized more and more by physicians in Europe as an acceptable and beneficial therapeutic treatment.

PRACTICE QUESTIONS

1. In ancient tribal societies, *shaman* was another name for what?

A) demon

B) doctor

C) healer

D) disease

Answers:

A) Incorrect. A demon was something that was associated with illness and disease.

B) Incorrect. The word *doctor* was not associated with shamanism.

C) Correct. A shaman was viewed as a healer.

D) Incorrect. A disease was something a shaman attempted to heal through ritual.

2. Which of the following methods were NOT used by shamans for healing?

A) herbs

B) surgery

C) touch

D) steam

Answers:

A) Incorrect. Herbs were used in shamanic healing.

B) Correct. Surgery, as we know it today, was not used by shamans.

C) Incorrect. Touch was used in shamanic healing.

D) Incorrect. Generating steam was used in shamanic healing.

3. The practice of amma began where?

A) China

B) Japan

C) India

D) Greece

Answers:

A) Correct. Amma is a system of manual and energy techniques that originated in China.

B) Incorrect. Amma spread to Japan from China.

C) Incorrect. Ayurveda is a health and treatment system developed in India.

D) Incorrect. Amma is not associated with Greece.

4. Who was the Greek god of medicine and healing?

A) Asclepius

B) Herodicus

C) Celsus

D) Hippocrates

Answers:

A) Correct. Asclepius is best known today by his symbol, the rod of Asclepius, a snake-entwined staff.

B) Incorrect. Herodicus was a Greek doctor.

C) Incorrect. Celsus was a Roman physician who wrote *De Medicina*.

D) Incorrect. Hippocrates is considered the father of medicine.

5. Anatripsis refers to what technique?

A) equine massage

B) rubbing

C) a technique used to balance bodily fluids

D) energy balancing used by shamans

Answers:

A) Incorrect. Avicenna believed in using friction techniques for grooming horses.

B) Correct. Hippocrates used the word *anatripsis* to describe rubbing.

C) Incorrect. Hippocrates believed that bodily fluids needed to be balanced; anatripsis was one technique used to accomplish this balance.

D) Incorrect. *Anatripsis* was a term that was not known to shamans.

6. Who learned about muscular contraction through dissection?

A) William Harvey

B) Ambroise Paré

C) Timothy Bright

D) Giovanni Alfonso Borelli

Answers:

A) Incorrect. William Harvey discovered how blood circulates.

B) Incorrect. Ambroise Paré, a military surgeon, found the orthopedic benefits of massage.

C) Incorrect. Timothy Bright wrote about the value of baths, exercise, and massage.

D) **Correct.** Giovanni Alfonso Borelli was an Italian physician.

State Licensing

Most individual states require licensure to work as a massage therapist, as do the District of Columbia, Puerto Rico, and the US Virgin Islands. State oversight will vary so it is extremely important that the massage therapist seeks out the rules and regulations related to practicing massage. In states that require licensure, a written scope of practice and definition of what constitutes massage will be laid out in some form to provide guidelines to a licensed therapist. While each state may define massage in varied terminology, in general, the following is a common description of basic massage and bodywork:

Massage is the manipulation and mobilization of soft tissue, including skin, fascia, tendons, ligaments, and muscles, to enhance muscle tone and circulation, promote relaxation and a general sense of well-being, and relieve stress and muscle tension.

Techniques used in the practice of massage may be described as:

+ compression
+ friction
+ gliding strokes/effleurage
+ kneading/petrissage
+ rocking
+ shaking
+ Swedish gymnastics (table stretches, joint mobilization, range of motion)
+ tapping/tapotement/percussion
+ vibration

Tools that may be used in the application of massage are:

+ elbows
+ feet
+ forearms
+ hands and handheld tools, both manual and motorized, that mimic and assist with approved techniques (i.e., hot stones, bamboo, vibration and kneading tools)

Massage treatment topical applications may include:

+ cold
+ heat
+ herbal
+ lubricants (i.e., oil, lotion, gel, warming and cooling agents)

+ salts and sugars for topical scrubs
+ water

Each state or jurisdiction will provide a list of approved massage and bodywork modalities beyond what would be considered Swedish or relaxation massage.

The History of Swedish Massage

In the early nineteenth century, **Pehr Henrik Ling**, born in 1776 in Sweden, became a teacher of fencing and gymnastics and a student of anatomy and physiology. He came to understand through his observations that physical movements were hindered by bad habits and abnormal body positioning. He found that by systematically retraining muscles, movements would be enhanced, defined, and more efficient. As a result, stress and strain on muscles and muscle joints were greatly reduced. This system—which became known as **Swedish gymnastics**—relied on a few active, passive, and assisted stretches with little to no mechanical apparatus involvement. Today, these movements may be referred to as table stretches, joint mobilization, and range-of-motion techniques. Ling went on to open the **Swedish Royal Central Institute of Gymnastics**, where he further developed his own system of medical gymnastics, exercise, and massage, known as the **Swedish movement cure**. While Ling was not a physician, medical doctors began to take seriously the value of his techniques and methodology. Ling died in 1839, but his program continued to spread throughout Europe and to the United States.

After Ling's death, the Dutch physician, **Johann Mezger** incorporated massage into physical rehabilitation. Since Mezger was a physician, his ability to promote massage to other physicians as an acceptable medical treatment gave him more credibility than Ling. As a result, scientific study was undertaken and published substantiating the medical benefits of massage. Mezger is considered the **founder of modern massage**.

The Swedish movement cure was introduced in the United States by **George Henry Taylor** and his brother, **Charles Fayette Taylor**, in 1856. After studying in Europe, they returned home to open an orthopedic practice using the newly learned techniques and went on to publish numerous papers on Ling's system, culminating in the publication of the first textbook on the subject. **Hartvig Nissen** opened the **Swedish Health Institute for the Treatment of Chronic Diseases by Swedish Movements and Massage** in Washington, DC, and wrote a paper entitled "Swedish Movement and Massage" in 1888 that was published in multiple medical journals. **Dr. Douglas O. Graham**, a practitioner of the Swedish movement cure, authored several writings on the history of massage. His most famous, *A Practical Treatise on Massage: Its History, Mode of Application and Effects, Indications & Contra-Indications*, was put into publication in 1902 and generated great public interest.

While the Taylor brothers, Nissen, and Graham were credited for introducing and convincing the medical community of the benefits of the Ling system, it was **John Harvey Kellogg** of Battle Creek, Michigan, who extended it to the general public through articles, books, and a wellness center. Kellogg, a medical doctor and health educator born in 1852, was a proponent of massage, hydrotherapy, and a vegetarian diet. He was also the medical superintendent of the popular **Battle Creek Sanitarium**, where early wellness techniques, including massage, were introduced to middle- and upper-class Americans. Kellogg did also believe in some controversial, discredited, and even discriminatory ideas and practices. Despite his controversial reputation, he is credited with writing *The Art of Massage*, published in 1895. This book discussed the history, physiological effects, and therapeutic applications of massage.

Swedish Massage: Skills and Modalities

Swedish massage is considered a systematic and scientific approach that relies on intent, touch, and pressure. It is a common feature on spa menus. Swedish massage is also the best-known type of massage in the United States—other countries may refer to it as *classic massage*. Its purpose is to rehabilitate, maintain, and relax using five basic Swedish massage strokes (which will be discussed in *Muscle Manipulation* later in this chapter): effleurage, petrissage, tapotement, friction, and vibration or shaking.

Often Swedish massage is applied with a lighter touch, while still using broad pressure, in order to achieve relaxation through increasing circulation and warming up superficial muscles. Sometimes the strokes can be long and slow; other times they can be short and quick. It all depends on what a client wants in his or her treatment, and how the therapist wants to go about achieving it. A lubricant, such as oil or lotion, is used to help the therapist perform the techniques in a fluid manner from one area to another area.

Swedish massage techniques are commonly used as a backbone for techniques applied in a range of other types of treatments, including deep pressure, sports, and more.

Muscle Manipulation

It is important for therapists to go back to their anatomy studies in muscle origination, insertion, and muscle fiber direction when working on clients. Although it is important to work out their clients' areas of complaint—typically trigger points and their referral patterns—therapists should keep in mind that a muscle runs from point A to point B, and sometimes C. Therefore their techniques should cover the entire muscle, at least in warming up and closing out their work in the area. (Anatomy is covered in depth in chapter 4.)

More specifically, there are four principles of massage when it comes to application. These principles are designed with the client's well-being in mind. Just like warming up before a workout, therapists need to move slowly into a client's tissue before their work becomes deep and specific.

The first principle is **general, specific, general**. For example, a therapist works the entire back, and then moves to the right lower back and right shoulder. The therapist finishes the right side, and moves to the left to repeat the treatment, before smoothing out the entire back.

The second principle is **superficial, deep, superficial**. A client has complained to his therapist of a knot (or trigger point) in the lower left gastrocnemius. Before the therapist can release the knot, she needs to warm up the tissue layer by layer, so that the muscle has enough blood flow to heal effectively.

The third principle is **peripheral, central, peripheral**. Two days before her massage, a client strains a muscle in her lower back. Before her therapist can work on the affected area, he must first work gently on the whole back, allowing the body to sink into the parasympathetic system and consequently relax into the treatment.

Finally, the fourth principle is **proximal, distal, proximal**. When working on the limbs, in order to provide centripetal (toward the heart) blood flow, a therapist must work the upper arm with strokes in the direction of the heart, then work into the lower arm with strokes toward the heart, and finish with the whole arm, stroking from the fingertips and wrist to the shoulder.

To achieve a relaxing effect, the massage strokes should be applied either gently or with the broad surfaces of the palms, forearms, and loose fists for deeper pressure. Additionally, the strokes should be applied slowly, matching the client's breath, and using an even rhythm.

For a more stimulating effect, the massage strokes should be brisk, erratic, and applied in less predictable patterns. This type of massage will stimulate the sympathetic nervous system. Deeper pressure in sensitive areas can also achieve this effect.

EFFLEURAGE

Effleurage comes from the French word *effleurer*, meaning to glide, stroke, or touch lightly. It is most commonly used at the beginning of the massage to spread lubricant and allow the client to become used to the therapist's touch. The effleurage stage is also used by the therapist to gather information through palpation, discovering temperature, tonicity, and texture of the tissue. The goal of effleurage is to prepare the tissue for deeper work to come. However, some massages that are more focused on relaxation and lighter work will maintain an effleurage focus throughout, using long strokes matching the client's breath.

> If an area of a limb is inflamed, injured, or infected, effleurage should not be used distal to the affected area. It should also not be performed repetitively on clients' limbs who have hypertension, heart disease, varicose veins, or edema from a thrombosis vein.

Effleurage is applied broadly and smoothly, typically with the hand using the palmar surface with the fingers together or on larger muscle groups such as the lower back and hamstrings, using the ulnar border of the forearm. Full contact is maintained with the client. The depth of the stroke depends upon a client's tolerance and tissue health. Therapists use a long stroke, covering the length of the muscle group, area, or limb.

The purpose of the first stroke is to distribute lubricant and assess muscle tone. Each stroke after should increase pressure slightly, stimulating venous blood flow. On the limbs, the strokes begin proximally on the thigh or upper arm, moving toward the heart. The pressure of each upward stroke should increase, while the return stroke should be gentle but maintain contact. The combination of strokes should move downward along the limb, until the strokes ultimately end up traveling the length of the limb from distal to proximal.

On the torso, effleurage strokes can be more circular or across muscle fiber. These strokes generally move from cervical to sacral, down the midline, and then up and around to return. The goal is to distribute lubricant, introduce touch to the body or body area, assess muscle tone and tightness, stimulate blood and lymph flow, warm the muscle, relax the body, calm and stimulate the nervous system, and flush metabolic waste.

Effleurage can be done using one hand, two hands, alternating hands, a forearm ironing stroke, knuckles, and fingers. Fingers can perform raking and nerve strokes that stimulate or relax and are often used to finish the massage treatment on a body area.

Effleurage can increase local circulation, reduce edema, and increase local venous and lymphatic return.

Petrissage (Kneading)

Petrissage is derived from the French word *petrir*, which means to knead. Kneading and other deeper techniques are used after the client's tissue is warmed up through effleurage. As petrissage is a more aggressive, deeper stroke, it is essential that the area has been adequately prepared with effleurage.

Petrissage uses the hands and fingers to lift, squeeze, and roll with the purpose of releasing soft tissue. This may also be referred to as *milking*. As opposed to gliding, petrissage focuses more locally on a muscle, muscle groups, and fascia.

The kneading technique can be used in a circular motion, where the skin and its underlying structures—muscles, tendons, and ligaments—are lifted up and moved away from the bone and then back toward it with a squeezing compression action. Tissue is rhythmically compressed and released. Kneading can be used on a muscle group, on an individual muscle, or, more specifically, on one particular area of a muscle. The pressure typically peaks during the middle of the technique. If a client is feeling too much pressure, the therapist should be sure to lessen his or her grasp.

Kneading affects local circulation. If a muscle has shortened and taut fibers, kneading can help to loosen adhesions and allow the fibers to lengthen; muscle hypertonicity can also decrease with kneading movements.

Kneading contraindications include acute trauma or injury; it should also not be performed on severely atrophied or atonic muscles, as the technique can cause further damage.

Kneading techniques are often used during sports massage to help athletes pre- or post-workout to minimize recovery time. These techniques maximize efficiency during a specified treatment time, allowing therapists to work more deeply than they could with effleurage strokes alone.

FRICTION

Friction strokes are similar to petrissage strokes but are usually even more localized, focusing more on muscle fibers, tendons, and ligaments. Strokes are performed in small, circular movements, targeting deeper layers of muscles bound with adhesions or trigger points. The friction technique involves moving superficial structures over deeper ones through precise pressure involving the therapist's fingers or thumbs.

This form of deep tissue massage uses techniques referred to as wringing, chucking, and cross fiber. **Wringing**, most often performed on the forearm, is done by grasping and moving one hand clockwise and the other counterclockwise, like wringing out a wet rag. **Chucking** is usually done along the gaps between the fingers and toes coming in contact with muscle, tendons, and ligaments.

The most common form of friction is **cross fiber**, with the intent of separating muscle fibers, breaking down adhesions and scar tissue, increasing circulation, and softening fascia. Therapists use the pressure and motion of their fingers or thumbs to move superficial tissues over deeper ones, causing the tissues to scrub against themselves.

Cross-fiber friction is different from basic friction techniques because it moves *across* the fiber rather than *with* the fiber. It is thought that cross-fiber friction works as a rolling pin to smooth out and break down any bumps in the "dough" of the muscle, tendon, or ligament.

Friction massage is intended to break up existing and forming adhesions in muscles, tendons, and ligaments—to mobilize tissue that has been feeling "stuck" due to adhesions preventing normal motion. It may be used specifically when a client is experiencing tendonitis—inflammation of a tendon.

This technique can be applied in all stages of injury from acute to chronic, but a client may find the work is too painful in the acute stage, as the tissue will most likely still be inflamed. Therapists should make sure to keep communication lines open as they perform friction massage, regardless of the client's stage of injury.

 The suffix –itis means *inflammation*. Whether a client is experiencing tonsillitis or plantar fasciitis, the tissue mentioned before the –itis is what is inflamed.

Friction massage is most commonly used in the subacute and chronic stages of injury. Its goal is to break down adhesions that prevent normal motion. The friction technique should be applied after ten to twenty minutes of effleurage and kneading to the area of injury. Friction massage will most likely cause inflammation due to its small, repetitive movements. A client will most likely experience discomfort with this treatment. It is important to perform friction work in one-to-two-minute intervals with effleurage strokes in between, so as to give the client a break from the intensity and allow the local blood flow being manipulated to do its job.

The specific work will *vasodilate* (bring local blood flow to) the area to help in the healing process. The therapist should ice the affected area between rounds of friction work; if ice is not available at the therapist's office, then the client should be instructed to apply ice soon after receiving the treatment. (Vasodilation and hot and cold therapy are discussed in more detail in chapter 6.)

Both friction and cross-fiber friction work to break down collagen in the tissues that forms with adhesions due to repetitive motions, injuries, or surgeries. In the late subacute stage, collagen fibers are more pliable; they are weaker and break down more easily. In the chronic stage, deeper and more vigorous friction is required to break down stronger collagen fibers.

Knowledge of anatomy is important in friction work. Sometimes a client experiences pain in an area that is not the location site of the injury, as is the case with secondary and satellite trigger points. An individual may experience a problem in one area or muscle, but the body might refer the pain to another location. Palpation is an important tool in the case of friction work, as is communication with the client.

TAPOTEMENT (PERCUSSION)

Tapotement is from the French word *tapoter*, meaning *to rap*, *drum*, or *pat*. As a result, it also goes by the name *percussion*. It is a rapid, rhythmic technique that uses the hands and fingers to stimulate nerve endings, increase circulation, loosen phlegm in the lungs, tone muscle, and desensitize hypersensitive areas. No lubrication is needed during tapotement. Tapotement ranges light to heavy; the technique is commonly used to loosen mucus in clients who have respiratory problems by hacking on the midback to loosen the mucus in the lungs.

Light tapotement includes pincement (*pincer* is French for *pinch* or *pluck*) and tapping, and helps to stimulate muscle firing and encourage blood flow to the area. Light tapotement is useful in stimulating muscles that are hypotrophied, either from paralysis or the removal of a cast. **Pincement** is performed by gently plucking the tissue between the thumbs and fingertips. **Tapping** is performed by tapping the tissue with the fingertips. In both techniques, the therapist's hands are light and springy, with the wrist relaxed; the technique is applied superficially.

Heavy tapotement includes hacking, clapping/cupping, and beating. Heavy tapotement can stimulate the stretch reflex of the muscles to which it is applied, temporarily increasing their tone. Additionally, it can reciprocally inhibit a muscle's antagonist. (For example, tapotement on the quadriceps can stretch the hamstrings.)

Hacking is performed with the ulnar border of the hands. For less force, the hands are relaxed; for more force, the hands are stiff. **Clapping/cupping** techniques are performed by holding the hands in a cupped position with the thumb and fingers held together; the wrists are pronated and the client's tissue is struck with alternating hands, resulting in a clopping noise. **Beating** is performed by holding the hands in a loose fist and using the knuckles, like knocking on a door, or using the ulnar surface of the palm, like pounding on a table.

When using tapotement, therapists should check with clients who may be unfamiliar with the technique to make sure they are comfortable. Smaller, bonier limbs like the arms and lower legs might not respond well to beating tapotement; therapists may be more successful with pincement, tapping, or maybe even hacking.

VIBRATION

Vibration, like tapotement, is rapid and rhythmical, but it differs in that the contact is constant. Vibration is used at any time during the massage and does not require lubrication. It can be slow, sustained, and nearly invisible to the untrained eye, or fast and vigorous.

Vibrations are typically used to distract the muscle being worked on from firing in a guarding type of manner. Distracting the muscle in this manner allows the therapist to access it more deeply, as vibrations applied for thirty seconds can decrease muscle tonicity.

Additionally, prolonged coarse vibrations, when applied to the thorax, can assist in mechanically loosening mucus that is present in respiratory conditions.

Vibrations are contraindicated when there are open or contagious skin lesions, as are any other types of hands-on treatments.

PRACTICE QUESTIONS

1. What deep, sustained technique's goal is to spread muscle fibers, soften tight muscles, and increase lymphatic flow and circulation in the area being treated?

    A) effleurage

    B) petrissage

    C) stroking

    D) compression

    Answers:

    A) Incorrect. Effleurage's long, fluid strokes are used to warm up superficial tissues.

    B) Incorrect. Petrissage focuses on deeper strokes based on effleurage-style techniques.

    C) Incorrect. Stroking is used to help the client get used to the therapist's touch, and for the therapist to move fluidly from area to area.

D) Correct. Compressions are long, sustained pressure techniques designed to slowly warm up and spread muscle fibers.

2. Which of the following is NOT a type of muscle manipulation technique?

   A) percussion

   B) effleurage

   C) petrissage

   D) punching

   Answers:

   A) Incorrect. Percussion is a type of muscle manipulation technique.

   B) Incorrect. Effleurage is a type of muscle manipulation technique.

   C) Incorrect. Petrissage is a type of muscle manipulation technique.

   D) Correct. Punching is not a type of muscle manipulation technique.

3. What is the difference between friction and cross-fiber friction work?

   A) There is no difference.

   B) Friction uses a heat tool and cross-fiber uses a therapist's hands.

   C) Friction is performed with the direction of muscle fibers and cross-fiber friction uses superficial tissues to scrub against deeper tissues.

   D) Friction uses superficial tissue to scrub against deeper tissues and cross-fiber friction is performed with the direction of muscle fibers.

   Answers:

   A) Incorrect. Friction is more superficial, using the therapist's fingers or thumbs; cross-fiber uses the therapist's digital pressure to move superficial structures against deeper ones.

   B) Incorrect. Friction and cross-fiber friction are both performed with a therapist's fingers and thumbs.

   C) Correct. Friction is a more superficial technique, while cross-fiber uses superficial tissues to scrub against deeper tissues.

   D) Incorrect. Friction is a more superficial technique, while cross-fiber uses superficial tissues to scrub against deeper tissues.

4. In massage, which of the following techniques is a Swedish gymnastic technique?

   A) kneading

   B) gliding

   C) vibration

   D) joint mobilization

Answers:

A) Incorrect. Kneading is a Swedish massage technique.

B) Incorrect. Gliding is a Swedish massage technique.

C) Incorrect. Vibration is a Swedish massage technique.

D) Correct. Joint mobilization is a Swedish gymnastic technique.

5. States will generally allow all of the following topical applications used during massage except one. Which one?

A) salt and sugar

B) hot wax for hair removal

C) water

D) herbal products

Answers:

A) Incorrect. Salt and sugar scrubs are common in spas.

B) Correct. Hot waxing is a practice performed by aestheticians.

C) Incorrect. Water used to prepare hot and cold treatments used in massage is acceptable.

D) Incorrect. Herbal products may be infused or incorporated into massage applications.

6. Who was Pehr Henrik Ling?

A) creator of the Swedish movement cure

B) a Dutch physician

C) a doctor who opened an orthopedic practice in the United States

D) the author of *A Practical Treatise on Massage*

Answers:

A) Correct. Ling created the Swedish movement cure.

B) Incorrect. Johann Mezger, a Dutch physician, incorporated massage into physical rehabilitation after Ling's death.

C) Incorrect. The Taylor brothers opened an orthopedic practice in the United States after studying the Swedish movement cure.

D) Incorrect. Douglas O. Graham wrote *A Practical Treatise on Massage*.

7. Who wrote the book *The Art of Massage*?

A) Hartvig Nissen

B) Charles Fayette Taylor

C) John Harvey Kellogg

D) Pehr Henrik Ling

A) Incorrect. Hartvig Nissen wrote a paper entitled "Swedish Movement and Massage."

B) Incorrect. Charles Fayette Taylor and his brother published the first textbook on Ling's Swedish movement cure.

C) Correct. *The Art of Massage* was published in 1896.

D) Incorrect. Ling developed The Swedish movement cure but did not publish a book.

8. Another word for *gliding* is which of the following?

A) petrissage

B) effleurage

C) champissage

D) lypossage

Answers:

A) Incorrect. Petrissage is a kneading stroke.

B) Correct. *Effleurage* is a French word that means to glide.

C) Incorrect. Champissage is a type of head massage.

D) Incorrect. Lypossage is a body-contouring technique.

9. Chucking is a type of what massage stroke?

A) friction

B) tapotement

C) vibration

D) cross fiber

Answers:

A) Correct. Chucking is a type of friction.

B) Incorrect. Tapotement is also known as tapping or percussion.

C) Incorrect. Vibration is constant contact that is rapid and rhythmic with the intent to stimulate or relax.

D) Incorrect. Cross fiber is also a type of friction.

TWO: ETHICS

The Role of Ethics

The study of ethics and what is morally right and wrong extends back thousands of years to Aristotle and Plato. Ethical behavior is a combination of *moral reasoning* that results in rules and principles and *character* that results in motivation and consequences. From a sociological perspective, community, family, education, religion, and government are structures through which ethical questions have been defined and challenged over time. The ethical treatment of an individual and groups, regardless of appearance, education, disability, politics, race, religion, sex, sexual orientation, and wealth, continually has an effect on global decision-making as well as on the domains of law, medicine, and business.

>  December is designated as Universal Human Rights Month, with the purpose of commemorating the adoption of the Universal Declaration of Human Rights by the United Nations.

A **profession** describes a group of individuals who share the same occupation and perform the functions of the occupation in a consistent, moral, legal, and ethical manner. What defines a particular profession and its professional standards is encompassed in a **code of ethics**.

A code of ethics establishes professional conduct, behavior, and acceptable application of services provided by the profession. The reputation of a profession and a professional organization relies on a code of ethics to define and sustain the services being offered and, in the eyes of the public, assure that recipients of the services are being treated in a legal, dignified, fair, and honest way.

In the practice of massage, a therapist will be expected to abide by a code of ethics that will generally include some form of the following concepts and terminology:

+ quality of care
+ honesty and integrity in practice and communication

- ✦ acknowledgment of, and adherence to, a defined scope of practice
- ✦ confidentiality of client information

In addition, massage therapists make a commitment to

- ✦ act to benefit the client.
- ✦ do no harm.
- ✦ avoid implying or promising unreasonable expectations.
- ✦ maintain a competent level of service.
- ✦ further professional education and skills.
- ✦ abide by laws and guidelines of governing bodies that oversee the profession.
- ✦ not unlawfully discriminate, regardless of a client's personal beliefs.
- ✦ treat only if service is agreed to voluntarily and with informed consent.
- ✦ ensure the safety, comfort, and privacy of the client.
- ✦ refrain from sexual conduct, whether verbal or physical, with a client.
- ✦ refuse to be intimidated, influenced, or coerced to behave unethically.

The Associated Bodywork & Massage Professionals (ABMP) and the American Massage Therapy Association (AMTA) are organizations of which readers of this study guide may become members. Summaries of each organization's codes of ethics follow; for more information, please check https://www.abmp.com/abmp-code-ethics and https://www.amtamassage.org/About-AMTA/Core-Documents/Code-of-Ethics .html. Members are expected to strictly adhere to these codes.

ABMP Code of Ethics

Members of the AMPB must promise to adhere to the following standards.

1. **Commitment to High-Quality Care**: Massage therapists recognize they are responsible for maintaining therapeutic relationships with their clients.

2. **Commitment to Do No Harm**: Massage therapists always conduct and evaluate a client's health history through an intake process to determine contraindications or necessary session adaptations. If a therapist suspects the client may have an undiagnosed condition and that a massage could be harmful, the therapist should refer the client to a healthcare professional, only conducting a massage after that professional has authorized it. Massage therapists should also understand ethical and therapeutic touch and intent; a session is intended only to benefit the client.

3. **Commitment to Honest Representation of Qualifications**: Massage therapists work within their scope of practice and only provide services for which they are fully trained and credentialed. They never falsely represent affiliation or association with any particular group or system. If the client has needs beyond the therapist's scope of practice, the therapist will refer the client accordingly; in general, massage therapists will acknowledge the limitations of massage and bodywork.

4. **Commitment to Uphold the Inherent Worth of All Individuals**: Massage therapists practice compassion, respect, tolerance, and nondiscrimination. Therapists will never deny service based on ethnicity, gender, sexual orientation, disability, religion, nationality, politics, socio-economic status, or physical build.

5. **Commitment to Respect Client Dignity and Basic Rights**: Massage therapists maintain a hygienic and accommodating space, ensuring client dignity, and offer clients a way to voice dissatisfaction with treatment. Therapists ensure the integrity of the therapeutic relationship.

6. **Commitment to Informed Consent**: Clients must remain fully informed of a therapist's choices regarding their care, and they have the right to decide against certain therapies or techniques. Therapists may not carry out a massage at all without a client's informed consent.

7. **Commitment to Confidentiality**: Therapists never share a client's personal information without that client's consent (within the limits of the law). Therapists respect a client's right to privacy.

8. **Commitment to Personal and Professional Boundaries**: Therapists maintain a nonsexual environment, including refraining from romantic and/or sexual relationships with clients and not tolerating sexual overtures from clients. Therapists recognize that failure to do so may result in loss of credentials and legal consequences.

9. **Commitment to Honesty in Business**: Therapists must be honest and fair in business, maintaining records, complying with regulations, and following tax law. They will use logos appropriately.

10. **Commitment to Professionalism**: Therapists must be honest and respectful in professional communication. They should not malign other professionals or seek to take someone else's clients. They must never use drugs or alcohol before or while giving a massage and behave and appear professionally. They should contribute to the profession by engaging in professional development.

AMTA Code of Ethics

According to the AMTA, the following Principles of Ethics are aspirational: massage therapists should aim to achieve them in their work. They should provide the highest quality service to clients, refrain from discrimination, carry out self-assessment and professional development, respect clients' right to privacy and safeguard personal information, maintain professionalism, and do no harm.

In contrast, following certain Rules of Ethics is required. Massage therapists should work within their scope of practice, remain honest in advertising and charging for services, and not engage in sexual conduct during massage sessions. They may also use the AMTA name and logo only with proper authorization and avoid violating the confidentiality and proprietary rights of the AMTA or other organizations or persons.

Relationship between Therapist and Client

In a therapist-client relationship, an important topic is the difference between discrimination and the right of refusal. If a new or returning client arrives for a scheduled massage, a therapist does have the right to refuse to massage for a limited number of reasons:

+ contraindications
+ improper hygiene
+ personal safety

Following are a few examples of circumstances that may cause the therapist to inform the client that he or she cannot proceed with a scheduled massage:

A client arrives for a scheduled massage and informs the therapist that she has just been diagnosed with cancer and needs to begin treatment. She decided to get a massage to help her relax. While the therapist may feel great empathy for the client and understand her reasoning, professional boundaries and codes of ethics cannot be ignored. The therapist informs the client that to perform a massage, a written clearance from her physician is required.

 A contraindication is a condition that affects the treatment plan of a massage therapist.

A client arrives for a massage with extremely bad body odor that clearly indicates he has not showered properly for quite some time. This is a situation that crosses a therapist's professional, personal, and physical boundaries, as well as presents a realistic concern of exposure to germs and contagions. Extremely poor personal hygiene can be an indicator of both mental and physical illness.

A client demonstrates physical or verbal intimidation; a client is in the throes of the flu and arrives sneezing and coughing; a client arrives clearly under the influence of alcohol. These are examples of threats to a therapist's personal safety and cross multiple boundaries.

A therapist cannot, under any circumstance, refuse to massage a client based on discrimination that is clearly defined by codes of ethics and conduct, standards of practice, and federal and state laws. On the other hand, a client may refuse massage and does not need to disclose the reasoning. However, a business owner does have an obligation to the business and staff to establish why the client is refusing the service. Depending on the business cancellation policy, the business owner may have the right to charge the client.

Most businesses that employ therapists of both sexes will inquire if a client is comfortable with a male or female therapist when the appointment is being scheduled. This is because the sex of the therapist may represent a boundary issue for some clients. Outside of this one distinction, a business should not specify personal information about the therapist or tolerate the refusal of a client based on discrimination—for example, if a male client states that the female therapist he is scheduled with is overweight or too old.

Two important components of a therapist-client relationship are **self-disclosure** and **confidentiality**. A client, especially once a sense of safety and comfort is established, may reveal to a therapist personal thoughts, feelings, emotions, ideas, opinions, and health-related concerns. A therapist is bound by confidentiality not to disclose information outside of the therapeutic session, unless a client gives the therapist permission to share information with another massage therapist who may be providing massage to the same client, a medical professional who provides care to the client, a family member, or an insurance provider. This will normally occur when a client is receiving massage by prescription, the client is a minor, or if the massages are covered by insurance.

Other exceptions to confidentiality include a client revealing illegal activity that may have been committed or may be committed, a client disclosing suicidal thoughts or behavior, a certainty or strong reasonable suspicion of abuse, and knowledge of a highly communicable disease that has not been reported or treated. In these cases, the therapist may contact authorities directly or seek out advice from a supervisor, trusted peer, mentor, or a state agency. Initially, the therapist may not need to disclose a name until determining the proper and legal course of action. However, becoming aware of a criminal act that may be committed or has been committed, or of a threat to the health and well-being of the client and others, does require the therapist to respond and act, not only legally but ethically. In some instances, the therapist may be approached with a court order requiring the release of documentation or disclosure of information.

The most important factor in a massage therapist-client relationship is that it must be **client-centered**. From the time the client arrives for a scheduled session to departure, the focus needs to be on the client. A client relies on the therapist to provide a service and, in return, the therapist receives a fee for that service.

As in relationships between parents and children, teachers and students, doctors and patients, and employers and employees, the massage therapist-client role presents a **role and power differential**. Clients view the therapist as a professional with skills and knowledge that exceed their own. When clients receive a massage, they disclose personal information, disrobe, and allow themselves to be positioned in a vulnerable manner. Even with appropriate draping protocol, the fact that the client is naked puts the client in an exposed position, both physically and emotionally. To put clients at ease with this differential, therapists need to offer a service within a level of competence that includes not harming or aggravating a physical condition, and allow clients to be part of the treatment plan by giving them options, encouraging their input, and respecting their right to change the treatment plan once the massage has commenced.

It is your responsibility as the therapist to be alert to **nonverbal cues**, respect and maintain boundaries, and look for signs of transference and countertransference.

Nonverbal cues may include flinching and grimacing, indicating discomfort; a deeper and more rhythmic breathing pattern or sudden exhale, indicating a movement toward deep relaxation; or weeping or tearing, indicating an emotional release.

The first few massages may be the easiest when it comes to maintaining boundaries. Once a client becomes comfortable with the therapist and the therapeutic relationship, then the therapist needs to be more on guard regarding boundaries. If boundaries become subtly blurred through conversation and rapport, therapists should self-assess. Examples can include a therapist revealing more personal information than professionally appropriate, asking a client for professional advice, or a client sharing personal details about a new boyfriend or girlfriend.

A good self-assessment technique is to go over in your mind or write down the following:

+ description: What occurred? What made you feel that a boundary was overstepped?
+ feelings: At that moment, what were you thinking and feeling?
+ evaluation: How did it happen? Was it positive or negative for you personally and professionally?
+ conclusion: What should you have done? What were your options?
+ action plan: If it were to happen again, what should you do? How should the situation be handled?

In the practice of massage, therapists can get busy and not allow themselves time to self-assess. However, just like taking continuing education classes and reading massage magazine articles to enhance your skills and increase your knowledge, it is important to focus attention inward, check in, and center yourself.

PRACTICE QUESTIONS

1. Why is self-assessment a valuable technique in massage?

   A) It allows a client to feel empowered when it comes to treatment.

   B) It allows a therapist to informally diagnose a client's condition.

   C) It gives the therapist the opportunity to recognize areas where boundaries are at risk.

   D) It indicates to a client when to schedule a massage.

   Answers:

   A) Incorrect. Voluntary and informed consent empower a client.

   B) Incorrect. A therapist may not formally or informally diagnose a client's condition.

   C) Correct. Self-assessment allows therapists to focus on their role as massage therapists.

   D) Incorrect. There is no formal tool used to help a client determine when to schedule a massage.

2. A therapist has a right to refuse to massage a client for all of the following reasons EXCEPT:

A) improper hygiene

B) personal safety

C) contraindications

D) sexual orientation

Answers:

A) Incorrect. Extremely poor personal hygiene can be an indicator of both mental and physical illness.

B) Incorrect. Therapists do not have to proceed if they have justifiable concerns that their health and wellness may be at risk.

C) Incorrect. Proceeding with a massage when it is contraindicated by information obtained from the client violates the healthcare practitioner's do no harm ethic.

D) Correct. Not massaging someone solely based on sexual orientation is discriminatory.

Scope of Practice

In the practice of massage, all practitioners are bound legally, professionally, publicly, and personally by a scope of practice.

In the United States, the federal role in education is limited. Most education policy is decided at the state and local levels. However, Federal Student Aid, an office of the US Department of Education, manages financial assistance by providing grants and loans to students. As a result, there is oversight and monitoring of schools to ensure compliance with the laws, regulations, and policies governing the federal student aid program. Hence, the relationship between scope of practice and education is monitored to a point by the federal government, by assuring that the massage school attended is providing the necessary standards of education and curriculum for the profession.

 The US Department of Labor provides the following definition for massage therapists:

Massage therapists treat clients by using touch to manipulate the muscles and other soft tissues of the body. With their touch, therapists relieve pain, help heal injuries, improve circulation, relieve stress, increase relaxation, and aid in the general wellness of clients.

Most individual states require licensure to work as a massage therapist, as do the District of Columbia, Puerto Rico, and the US Virgin Islands. State oversight varies, so it is important that the massage therapist knows the rules and regulations related to practicing massage. In states that require licensure, a written scope of practice and definition of what constitutes massage will be laid out in some form to provide guidelines to a licensed therapist.

In general, in states where massage practitioners are licensed, there will be some division, bureau, or agency of professional regulations, as well as a board specific to massage and bodywork. States also dictate the modalities a massage therapist is legally allowed to practice. Also, it is important for therapists to understand fully how the states where they practice define massage. In most states massage, at a minimum, is defined as a practice that promotes relaxation and well-being.

Massage therapists must act within the scope of practice defined by state licensure laws, acts, regulations, and statutes. These will be specific to massage and pertain to all professions practiced in the state, as well as criminal law. Requirements to obtain and maintain a license vary from state to state. It is up to the massage therapist applying for a license to practice to research the requirements. These are some requirements that may exist and/or vary from state to state:

+ designation: This is the legal title a practitioner may use; it is generally *Licensed Massage Therapist (LMT)*.
+ insurance: Liability insurance may be required by the state before a license is granted.
+ hours of education: The number of hours required varies from 500 to 1,000 hours.
+ license renewal requirements: State renewal can vary from annually up to every four years.
+ continuing education hours: The number of hours between renewal periods varies from zero to twenty-five.
+ accepted exams: These may include one or more of the following: MBLEx, NCBTMB, jurisprudence, and state-based exams.
+ education program: This may include non-accredited, accredited only, and some college credits.
+ additional requirements: These may include courses in CPR, AED, HIV/AIDS, or first aid, as well as physicals or a certificate of health.
+ license to do business: This requirement may apply if you are an owner or operator of a practice.

In addition to states, local municipalities such as counties, cities, and towns may have other laws, rules, and guidelines for the practice of massage.

It is up to the massage therapist to know about legislative changes that may affect the profession. This is when massage therapist organizations, associations, and boards will prove valuable, as they will generally keep track of pending and newly enacted legislation.

Another role that governmental bodies play is reassurance to the public that the services they seek from massage therapists are sanctioned—that therapists have guidelines they must follow and risk repercussions if they do not work within the guidelines.

When a client enters a therapist's place of business, seeing a license to practice displayed shows the client that the therapist has been vetted by the state. The client knows that the therapist is working within professional boundaries.

Professionally, personally, and ethically, a therapist needs to demonstrate **competence** and **accountability**. In order to do this, an ongoing assessment of skills and boundaries needs to be instilled in a therapist's everyday practice.

Competence assessment is honestly practicing skills learned from the school a therapist attended, as well as continuing education. It also means accepting that a weekend workshop, online video, or reading a book is not enough to market and perform techniques and modalities. For example, taking a cranial sacral workshop may give therapists some skills they can incorporate into their practice, but it does not necessarily qualify them to imply they are fully capable of providing this service to the public. The best way to become competent in a modality is not only to take a course, but to understand fully how the modality affects anatomy and physiology, to become familiar with evidence-based studies supporting it, and to have a genuine belief the modality will do no harm.

Self-accountability means behaving with integrity in the absence of external authority. Beyond government oversight, therapists must be careful to remain client-centered and always act in the best interest of the client, keeping scope of practice in mind. They must recognize contraindications, maintain professionalism at all times, and be willing to address their weaknesses. Being accountable may require a therapist to seek out assistance and guidance from mentors and peers and to refer a client to a more qualified massage therapist or another healthcare practitioner, if the client's medical condition requires services that fall outside of the therapist's individual scope of practice.

PRACTICE QUESTIONS

1. Which governmental body has influence on the practice of massage?
    A) state
    B) none
    C) federal
    D) city

    Answers:
    A) **Correct.** Each state determines the legal and professional rules that govern the practice of massage.
    B) Incorrect. While some states do not regulate the practice of massage, most of them do.
    C) Incorrect. The federal government has minimal oversight of the practice of massage.
    D) Incorrect. Most cities adhere to state laws, but some may have additional guidelines and requirements.

2. Which of the following do therapists working within a scope of practice NOT need to do?

A) protect the public

B) be accountable

C) assess their competency

D) be licensed by the state in which they are practicing

Answers:

A) Incorrect. A scope of practice limits practitioners to provide only those services in which they are adequately trained.

B) Incorrect. A scope of practice includes an expectation of accountability by the practitioner.

C) Incorrect. A scope of practice requires honest assessment of skills.

D) Correct. A scope of practice requires therapists to practice within the laws of the state, but only states determine if a license to practice massage is required.

Professional Communication

Visually and verbally, therapists must project an image of professionalism to new and existing clients. How therapists answer the telephone and communicate their businesses on paper and technologically all feed into public impressions of massage therapy and massage therapists.

If a practice uses a cell phone rather than a business landline for communication, it is important to have a designated number or, at least, a designated ringtone so the therapist answers the phone as a businessperson, and not in a casual way. Clients know that massage is a personal, intimate interaction; consequently therapists need to portray themselves as knowledgeable, personable, and genuine. Responding to client calls while driving or sitting in a local bistro where there is background noise and distractions is not appropriate, professional, or reassuring.

When new clients arrive, therapists should greet them, give them the intake form, and be available for questions. (Intake forms, discussed in chapter 3, gather information needed to assess the client and impact the treatment plan.) Also, this is an opportunity to observe the client walking, standing, and sitting. With experience, therapists can learn a lot from visual assessment of a client (observing issues like tight shoulders, a stiff neck, or an irregular gait). Saying to a client, "It seems like you are holding a lot of stress in your upper body" or "I noticed you seem to have some limited range of motion in your neck," shows experience and a client-centered approach. Therapists should ask clients if they need anything before the session begins—for example, a glass of water or to use the restroom.

Once a client completes the intake form, in order to avoid awkward silences, therapists may excuse themselves briefly to look over the medical information provided. Once therapists are in the massage room, they should maintain eye contact as much as possible, and actively listen.

Certain medical data requires gathering additional details. For example, if a client had surgery in the last year, the therapist should determine recovery status. Are there any lingering aches, pains, and areas that should be avoided or might require extra time and attention? A second example would be cancer. Did the client have any lymph nodes removed? Have there been occurrences of lymphedema? Does scar tissue from radiation burns cause the client discomfort and hinder his or her range of motion? Another example would be an autoimmune disease such as MS or rheumatoid arthritis. Is the client having any related flare-ups? How are they being treated?

In general, massage therapists should also become familiar with common medications (including their generic names) and what they do. Knowing the purpose of a medication demonstrates professional knowledge and alerts a therapist to a condition that a client may not have noted on the intake form. For instance, many people take blood-thinning medications. In such cases, the therapist should inform the client that bruising is a potential side effect related to deep massage pressure.

These examples may sound daunting, but it is important to gather the necessary information. It allows the therapist to make a well-informed assessment and recommend the best treatment plan.

At this time, it is necessary to discuss **implied**, **informed**, and **voluntary consent**. When clients schedule an appointment to receive a massage, arrive for the appointment, and complete an intake form, they are basically giving you implied consent to perform a massage. However, a massage cannot proceed until informed consent is obtained. Informed consent is the process by which the massage therapist reviews the information provided, consults face-to-face, asks pertinent and clear questions, discusses plan recommendations, confirms the areas of the body it is okay or not okay to come into contact with, and, based on voluntary consent, receives authorization to proceed with the understanding that the client is within her rights to terminate the massage at any point.

Communication skills when discussing personal, confidential medical information are extremely important. Therapists should be aware of their tone of voice and not overuse medical terminology that may be confusing, come across like they are trying to show off, or sound too clinical. The client is coming for a massage, not a medical exam.

Clients should always feel they are in a safe, nonjudgmental space. The goal should be to maintain a relaxed, conversational tone. Therapists should explain they must ask questions to make the best recommendations for a satisfying massage experience, and avoid hindering any recovery or causing discomfort. In other words, therapists should have a reason for every question. Friendly banter is helpful for establishing rapport, but therapists must be careful to remain professional.

Once therapists have gathered the information they need, they can discuss a recommended treatment plan. Clients need to give informed consent, so they must understand why a therapist cannot perform a specific type of treatment.

Therapists must provide clients with a place to store personal belongings. Personal items left haphazardly around the work space may be accidently disturbed during the massage. Therapists instruct clients to undress to their comfort level, get under the sheet or blanket, and then pull it up to shoulder level. Clients should be comfortable, aware that the therapist will use appropriate draping protocol and that their bodies are only exposed where the therapist is working and with their permission.

Therapists should avoid the terms *prone* and *supine*, and instead inform clients to lie faceup, looking at the ceiling, or facedown, looking at the floor. When stepping out of the massage room, therapists should state they will return shortly and will knock before they reenter.

When entering the massage room, therapists should shut the door immediately, adjust the lighting and music to their preference, and ask clients if they are comfortable. Do they need additional cushioning? Are they warm enough? Therapists can discreetly scan the floor to be sure clients did not leave personal belongings in the work space, asking permission before moving such items to a safer location.

In general, most full-body relaxation massages will begin at the head and neck. This allows easing into the massage before undraping is necessary. The first touch should be light and noninvasive. Some therapists may use this moment to center themselves while allowing the client to adjust to their touch. It is also a good time to remind clients they can give feedback at any point.

When the session is over, therapists communicate they will step out of the room while clients dress; before leaving, therapists should turn up lights enough to allow the client to stand up, dress safely, and begin readjusting to the light. The therapist should be present when the client leaves the room. There is nothing worse than exiting a massage and having no clue which direction to go or what to do next. Therapists should always ask a client how he or she feels and offer water, all the while maintaining a professional distance. Therapists walk clients to the checkout area, cognizant they may still be *out of it*, and inquire if they want to schedule another appointment.

A few key communication techniques valuable for every massage therapist follow.

The therapist's tone should be assertive, not passive or aggressive. Clients receiving a first massage may have heard that deep tissue massage is best, without really knowing what deep tissue massage entails. They approach the massage with a "pain is gain" or "it won't help unless it hurts" perspective. However, the therapist is thinking, "This is the first time this person has received a massage, and I don't want her to wake up sore tomorrow." An assertive response is, "I know that deep tissue seems like a great idea, but, since this is your first massage, I think a better plan is to keep the pressure moderate. I know I can give you a good massage and you will be satisfied. I do believe this is the best approach." An aggressive response is, "I give a lot of massages and I know giving you a deep tissue massage is not the best approach. Do you really want to wake up tomorrow in pain?" A passive response is, "Well, I don't think that is the best way to go, but you are the client so I will do what you think is best."

Therapists should defend their boundaries. When a client calls to schedule an appointment, therapists should inform them of cancellation policies and avoid unreasonably accommodating clients. This sets a bad precedent and gives the impression that it is easy to take advantage of the therapist.

Therapists are not psychologists. The therapist's role is not to solve problems or give advice related to a client's personal life. If a client begins discussing personal problems, the therapist should listen and be compassionate, but not offer solutions or interject personal experiences.

Therapists should be consistent, but willing to adapt. For example, a client has been coming to a therapist regularly. He is always on time and has never missed an appointment. One day he calls to say he is running late but will be there soon. If the therapist's schedule allows her to accommodate the client and give him a full session, she can offer to do so when he arrives, but she should not feel obligated. She can explain she is able to accommodate him today, but not imply she will always accommodate late arrivals.

Communication is a two-way street. Often clients will not want to hurt a therapist's feelings or may be uncomfortable speaking up. It is a good idea to express to clients that they should let the therapist know about any discomfort or if they want more time spent on a particular area. Therapists can phrase this as, "Please communicate and give me feedback at any point during the massage. You will not hurt my feelings if you tell me you are uncomfortable with what I am doing."

Lack of conversation may become an uncomfortable silence for some clients who want to talk. Therapists need to determine their own comfort level here. Therapists who prefer not to have conversation should find ways to deter it without being rude or condescending. They might say, "I really want you to get the most out of this massage, so why don't you try to forget about the world outside. Take some deep breaths and try to focus on the music. This is your time to relax." Other therapists don't mind conversation and may perceive that talking relaxes and makes the client more comfortable during the massage. However, therapists should be cautious. The conversation should primarily be one-sided with the therapist interjecting as little as possible, and remaining on the lookout for transference and countertransference. Conversation that veers into religion, politics, and child-rearing can cross boundaries. Therapists should stay client-centered and professional.

Self-disclosure from a client may reveal information that is not pertinent to the massage. Although this may be an opportunity to build rapport, therapists need to avoid dispensing advice outside their scope of practice and be alert to indications of transference. Also, therapists need to be cognizant of their own self-disclosure. If a client indicates aches and pains as a result of yard work, spring cleaning, or having to manage small children, therapists can express undertanding but should be careful not to lose focus and move away from being client-centered. A therapist needs to stay alert to signs of countertransference. Too much self-disclosure on both sides can become excessive, uncomfortable, and destructive to the therapist-client relationship. The therapist's goal should be to build a strong professional rapport that will keep a client coming back. Being a sounding board for a client's personal issues can be detrimental and inhibit building a strong professional practice. Taking on a client's baggage can lead to burnout and feelings of resentment.

PRACTICE QUESTIONS

1. Which of the following is the best example of implied consent?
- **A)** entering the massage room with the therapist
- **B)** filling out and signing the intake form
- **C)** agreeing to a treatment plan recommended by the therapist
- **D)** disrobing

Answers:
- A) Incorrect. Agreeing to move from the reception area to a massage room is not the best example of implied consent.
- **B) Correct.** Filling out an intake form and signing it is considered implied consent.
- C) Incorrect. A client who agrees to a treatment plan after discussion with a therapist is giving informed consent.
- D) Incorrect. Disrobing before a massage happens after informed consent is given to the therapist.

2. What is NOT a benefit of the massage therapist starting a massage at the head and neck?
- **A)** The therapist has a moment to get centered and focused on the client's massage session.
- **B)** The therapist can work for several minutes before undraping needs to occur.
- **C)** The client can get adjusted to the therapist's touch before undraping occurs.
- **D)** The therapist can do a final check to see if he has any new text messages.

Answers:
- A) Incorrect. Therapists should always take a moment before a massage begins to clear their mind and direct their focus on the client.
- B) Incorrect. The therapist can use this time to move the client into a relaxed and comfortable state of mind.

C) Incorrect. How first touch is perceived by a client is important and can set the tone for the massage.

D) Correct. A therapist should not bring a cell phone into a massage session.

DUAL RELATIONSHIPS

A dual relationship occurs when a therapist-client relationship overlaps with another type of relationship outside of the therapeutic session. Dual relationships may also be referred to as multidimensional relationships. A dual relationship can be one that exists prior to the therapist-client relationship, it can appear after a therapist-client relationship, or it can occur in an unanticipated or accidental way.

Dual relationships can be avoidable, unavoidable, and unexpected.

Types of dual relationships are:

+ family and close friends
+ social
+ communal
+ social media
+ business
+ work-based

The factors that can affect dual relationships and resulting boundary issues are often dependent on whether the relationship existed prior to becoming a massage therapist or after becoming a massage therapist.

A **dual relationship** between a therapist and a family member or close friend can be nebulous. When a massage therapist begins to practice, these relationships can start out as a fun and convenient way to practice new skills. A therapist may be motivated and proud of having the ability to help a family member or friend feel better and relax, which can serve as reassurance that the therapist made a wise decision to enter into the profession. However, if a therapist has a genuine need to generate income through the practice of massage, issues may arise quickly as a result of blurred boundaries and roles. All the boundaries discussed earlier in this chapter are jeopardized in family/friend relationships.

For instance, Marie has been a licensed massage therapist for six months. When she was in school, she often practiced on good friends and family members who were complimentary and supportive, and they would often talk and joke about the usual things. Marie took a job at a massage clinic and is doing well. Her book of business is growing, her skills are developing, and she is looking into continuing education courses to enhance her competence. She is busy most days performing multiple massages. She begins to feel taken advantage of by friends and family members who have been receiving free massages or who have been offering minimal payment for services.

In this scenario, from the outset many boundaries were blurred or crossed because of existing relationships. Marie wants to move away from the expectations that have been placed on her to provide massages on demand. She needs to recognize that this situation is avoidable, start setting limits on her time, and establish rules for family members and friends. She needs to communicate to her family members and friends that her time is more limited, her goal is to earn an income, and when she is not working she wants to actually not work.

A **social dual relationship** occurs between a therapist and acquaintances, friends of friends, friends of family members, and people the therapist knows through affiliations and memberships. A big part of building a practice is relying on referrals. These relationships are avoidable but do not need to be.

One example is John's case. A massage therapist, John has five years of experience. He is well known and respected in his field of practice as a sports massage therapist. John is an avid runner and competes frequently in races. A friend he trains with refers his boss to John. During the intake process, John obtains personal medical information.

The fact that John is now massaging his friend's boss should create no issues as long as John maintains his professional boundaries and adheres to his code of ethics. John must respect the privacy of his new client and must not, under any circumstance, enter into a discussion with his friend about anything learned in the therapist-client relationship he has with his friend's boss.

A **communal dual relationship** occurs when a therapist has an unplanned encounter with a client. This can happen while waiting in a movie line, grocery shopping, attending a church service or PTA meeting, or any other kind of community activity. These are unexpected encounters.

For instance, Barbara has been massaging her client Mr. Williams twice a month for over a year. While attending a local craft fair, Barbara runs into Mr. Williams and greets him congenially. Mr. Williams, caught a bit off guard, appears uncomfortable. They exchange pleasantries and both go their separate ways.

What happened here? Barbara is a thoroughly professional therapist, so why did Mr. Williams appear uncomfortable? As a therapist, it is important to understand that the therapist-client relationship is an intimate encounter. While the therapist does her job every day, respecting boundaries and performing many massages, a client is lying on a table disrobed and in a vulnerable position. Seeing his therapist outside of the therapeutic environment may cause a client discomfort because he knows the therapist is privy to his personal information. Also, even though the therapist practices all appropriate draping protocol and is always cognizant of personal boundaries, a client, in this moment, may only perceive that the therapist has seen him naked and emotionally exposed.

Communal relationships can become tricky if therapists and clients begin to encounter one another frequently. For example, a therapist begins to attend a regular church service a client attends or joins a community group and finds that a client is also a participant in the same group. These types of situations may not be a problem at all. However, the therapist may find that the client stops coming to her or starts to see another therapist where she works. The therapist's role is to maintain her professionalism and respect the client's boundaries. This dual relationship may be too uncomfortable for the client.

Social media dual relationships are relatively new scenarios but can affect client relationships. For example, Maggie is a new therapist who went to massage school right out of high school. She is active on Facebook, checking it every day, posting photos from weekend parties, and expressing personal opinions. A new client, Sue, has seen Maggie for massage a few times. They are close to the same age and find out they have some friends and interests in common. They friend each other on Facebook. A few months later Maggie posts a comment on Facebook: "I'm so ready for my vacation and can't wait to get away from work and stinky feet lol." The next time Sue comes to see Maggie for a massage, she is quick to comment that she hopes her feet don't stink. Maggie is instantly embarrassed and the massage proceeds with tension.

It is important that a massage therapist decides her profession takes precedence. While it may seem harmless to become friendly with someone on social media, negative outcomes can occur. Therapists should focus on their professional practice and maintaining boundaries. Social media can result in blurred or crossed boundaries. The best approach to take is to develop a professional Facebook page or other type of social media profile to which therapists can refer clients with confidence. Therapists can use this site to promote massage, provide links to health-related articles they found useful, communicate about new workshops they attended, and encourage a professional exchange of information. Once therapists begin coming into contact with the public through their work, they should consider enhancing the privacy of their personal Web-based profiles. Social media encounters with clients may occur by invitation or unexpectedly, but they are avoidable.

Business dual relationships occur when massage therapists take on clients they have an existing business relationship with or have hired to provide them with business services. In this example, Tom has set-up a small practice, which is growing. He needs to seek out the services of a Web designer to establish a professional website, but his cash flow is limited. He does some research and finds someone in his local community. He enters into a business arrangement using the barter method and agrees to provide massage services in exchange for website development.

There is absolutely nothing wrong with this type of arrangement. Bartering is a common way of exchanging services and is an accepted form of doing business under federal tax code. However, therapists do need to make sure the services are fair and properly documented. Also, it is always important to check local and state laws to be sure this is an acceptable practice for income-reporting purposes. The only other issues may be related to the services themselves. If either businessperson or entity does not believe the arrangement is working, that party needs to determine how to sever the barter relationship. Maybe the Web designer does not like the therapist's massages, or the therapist feels the Web designer is not reciprocating the same standard of service. In ending this arrangement, the therapist will need to maintain professionalism and decide if he wants to maintain the business relationship on a cash basis or end it completely. Business dual relationships are avoidable.

> According to the IRS, bartering is the trading of one product or service for another, usually without exchange of cash. Barter may take place informally between individuals and businesses or on a third-party basis through a barter-exchange company.

Work-based dual relationships result when a therapist provides massage to a co-therapist, a supervisor, or co-employee. Giving a massage to another therapist is not uncommon. Often these will be done in the form of a trade, meaning "you give me a massage, and I'll give you a massage." Massaging a supervisor can be approached with comfort or discomfort. A therapist may feel she is being graded or that her role as a professional is diminished. This can be especially daunting if the therapist is still new in the field or is intimidated by a supervisor. Massaging a coworker who is not a therapist may occur in any practice or clinic where a therapist works. There may be an arrangement where employees get discounts on massage services as a perk or a therapist may be employed by an organization that provides in-house massage services. A therapist may give someone a massage in the morning, and see that person in the cafeteria at lunch. The key is to stick with one's professional knowledge, ethics, and boundaries. Workplace massages on co-therapists, supervisors, and coworkers are generally unavoidable.

In one example, a coworker comes to a therapist for a massage and discloses to him that she is pregnant but has not told anyone yet. The therapist proceeds with the massage using proper protocol for a pregnant client and is really happy for his coworker. A week or so later, the therapist is on his break and lets it slip that his coworker is pregnant.

The therapist needs to decide quickly the best way to handle this situation. He can certainly ask anyone who heard not to disclose this information, but he cannot be certain they will maintain privacy. The therapist needs to be accountable and communicate with the pregnant coworker that this slip of the tongue happened. The outcome of this disclosure may vary, but being accountable is first and foremost the best approach to take.

PRACTICE QUESTIONS

1. A therapist is grocery shopping one day and runs into a client. What type of dual relationship is this?

    A) communal

    B) social

    C) family and close friends

    D) work-based

Answers:

    A) **Correct.** Accidently running into a client in a grocery store is a communal dual relationship.

    B) Incorrect. A social dual relationship occurs between a therapist and acquaintances, friends of friends, friends of family members, and people the therapist knows through affiliations and memberships.

C)   Incorrect. The client is neither a family member nor a close friend.

D)   Incorrect. A work-based dual relationship is massaging a coworker, supervisor, or owner of the business that employs the therapist.

2.   When a coworker comes to a therapist for a massage and discloses that she takes medication for a mental illness, what should the therapist do?

   A)   Treat this information the same way the therapist would with any other client.

   B)   Let the coworker know she is not alone and the therapist is always available if she wants to talk.

   C)   After the massage, immediately contact the therapist's supervisor and disclose this information for safety and security purposes.

   D)   Tell the coworker about a family member who took the same medication and had really bad side effects.

Answers:

   A)   **Correct.** Clients disclose medical information all the time. Why should this be different?

   B)   Incorrect. This response is inappropriate; the therapist should not assume he or she is now a trusted confidant of the client.

   C)   Incorrect. This action violates numerous codes and standards of conduct and is a stereotypical response to this medical condition.

   D)   Incorrect. This would be a clear violation of boundaries as well as an insensitive thing to say to any client.

ETHICAL RULES IN THE WORKPLACE

Places of employment and professional organizations for massage therapists may have written statements of guiding principles and expectations related to day-to-day responsibilities, procedures, and professional conduct, as well as the repercussions of infractions. These statements may be referred to as codes of conduct or standards of practice. Infractions in the workplace may result in verbal and written warnings or loss of employment. If an organization becomes aware of an infraction committed by a member, it may require a formal review resulting in loss of membership. Infractions that are deemed to be illegal may result in prosecution and loss of license to practice. An employer's code of conduct or standards of practice will generally mimic state law; however, an employer may have stricter guidelines. Codes of conduct and standards of practice generally include some form of the following concepts and terminology:

+   Demonstrate professionalism in treating and communicating with clients, peers, coworkers, and other professionals.

+   Abide by standards of health, hygiene, and safety required by law.

- Clothing should be clean, modest, and professional.
- Obtain voluntary and informed consent before treatment commences.
- Respect and adhere to the client's right to refuse, modify, or terminate treatment.
- Effectively communicate with clients the assessment and treatment plan.
- Use draping protocol that assures clients of both physical and emotional privacy.
- Treat only within one's individual and professional scope of practice.
- When in the best interest of the client, refer to other professionals.
- Seek professional advice when needed.
- Do not malign or falsely accuse coworkers and professional peers.
- Do not malign or speak negatively about other legitimate medical professions or professionals.
- Do not falsely represent oneself regarding education, certifications, and memberships.
- Do not falsely make claims when marketing and communicating with the public.
- Work only within the laws set forth locally, statewide, and federally.
- Do not discriminate.
- Be accountable and accept responsibility for one's actions.
- Report any improper behaviors and practices to authorities both legal and work-based.
- Maintain accurate and truthful records of treatment. Do not modify existing records.
- Do not share or discuss personal or medical information about a client unless required under law or if there is a strong belief the client or others are at risk.
- Keep up-to-date insurance and certifications, and meet continuing education requirements.
- Do not treat under the influence of alcohol or illegal or legal narcotics. In turn, refuse to treat clients who are under the influence or who are physically or verbally abusive.
- Do not meet with clients outside of a scheduled massage.
- Do not enter into a sexual relationship with a client.
- Do not enter into a sexual relationship with a supervisor or a subordinate employee.
- Do not enter into a business relationship with an existing client.
- Client information is the property of the business and may not be used for personal purposes or financial gain.
- Bringing personal media devices into a massage room is not allowed.

PRACTICE QUESTIONS

1. Which may be the repercussion of an employee talking about a "hot" client in the break room of a place of business?

    A) None. It is okay as long as the conversation is with a coworker the therapist is friends with outside of work.

    B) Management informs the therapist he or she will no longer be allowed to massage that client.

    C) The therapist may receive a written warning of termination by his employer.

    D) The coworker will schedule a massage with that client and tell the client the therapist is awesome.

    Answers:

    A) Incorrect. This type of conversation is not acceptable at all in the workplace.

    B) Incorrect. Management will not consider this appropriate and will want to take further action beyond disallowing the therapist to perform massages on this client again.

    C) Correct. The employer will prepare a written explanation of why the behavior was inappropriate and have the therapist sign it.

    D) Incorrect. If the coworker did this, he or she would be in violation as well.

2. Workplace rules will generally cover all of the following but one. Which one?

    A) day-to-day responsibilities

    B) procedures

    C) professional conduct

    D) permitted instances of sexual relations between coworkers outside of business hours

    Answers:

    A) Incorrect. Employers will provide therapists with a written job description and duties.

    B) Incorrect. Employers will provide therapists with a written or video presentation of procedures.

    C) Incorrect. Expectations of professional conduct will be communicated by an employer or prospective employer.

    D) Correct. Many employers discourage sexual relationships between coworkers outside of work, especially between employees of different ranks.

CODE OF ETHICS VIOLATION

As has been discussed, a massage therapist must abide by a code of ethics set forth by the industry, organizations, and government bodies, as well as work-based codes and standards of conduct.

Violations in the workplace can lead to verbal warnings, written warnings, and eventual or automatic termination of employment. In addition, depending on the severity and circumstances of the violation, it can lead to state agency reviews, lawsuits, loss or suspension of license, public backlash and distrust, and increased workplace restrictions. Most established businesses will provide an employee handbook when hired that outlines expectations and the repercussions of violations. Violations can be minor, major, or severe to the point of termination.

Minor violations may be dealt with using verbal or written warnings, depending on the degree of infraction, and may include:

✦ unexplained tardiness

✦ unexplained absences

✦ dress code violations

✦ abuse of workplace resources (i.e., computers, equipment, or supplies)

✦ pilfering

✦ language and behaviors that are offensive to coworkers and clients

In the massage workplace, showing up late to work or not showing up at all can affect clients with scheduled appointments. Further, it can affect staff who now need to reschedule appointments and explain to clients why their therapist is unavailable. Not adhering to a company dress code can create problems with coworkers and supervisors who value the importance clients place on appearance, and who understand the subconscious effect of dress code on boundaries. Other problems may include using company computers without permission or for purposes unrelated to work; intentionally or through improper use, damaging shared equipment such as towel caddies, stools, and massage tables; taking small supplies like massage lotions and towels off the premises to use in a personal practice; and being unconcerned with or unaware of the effect certain language or behavior may have on coworkers who differ on what is considered appropriate behavior and conversation.

Major violations are generally addressed quickly with written warnings or immediate termination. Such violations may include:

✦ aggressive or threatening physical and verbal behavior

✦ brandishing a weapon

✦ theft on a large scale

✦ arriving at work intoxicated or clearly under the influence of a narcotic

✦ verbal or physical sexual harassment of clients or coworkers

Regardless of the type of workplace, these major violations are unacceptable and may result in authorities being notified by the employer or the client. Ultimately, these types of offenses can make their way to agencies, boards, and organizations that have oversight of the profession, potentially resulting in loss or suspension of license. Also, offenses, especially claims of sexual misconduct, can make their way to the media. Reporting by the media can place the business, and employees of the business, under greater public scrutiny; authorities may call into question the business operation and practices.

In addition to workplace violations, code of ethics violations can include providing inaccurate or false information to state agencies, such as:

+ stating that one has taken the required CEUs needed for license renewal when one has not
+ lying about an arrest or a conviction
+ dishonestly claiming to have taken a required updated CPR/AED/first aid course

If a state agency or organization determines a member has committed any of the following acts, massage therapists can face repercussions:

+ false advertising of credentials
+ not operating within the laws of the state in which one practices
+ violation of HIPAA (Health Insurance Portability and Accountability Act) and CDC (Centers for Disease Control and Prevention) rules
+ violation of other codes of conduct that disparage the profession of massage

The practice of massage has come a long way in the United States. A profession that at one time in most states was not regulated and viewed solely as adult entertainment has worked hard to establish its value and validity. States and organizations take codes of ethics and rules of practice seriously and expect practitioners to do the same.

PRACTICE QUESTION

If a massage therapist is late for work and another therapist had to perform her massage, what should she say to management?

A) "Oh well, at least someone else was available to do the massage."

B) "The therapist that did the massage is new and needs the money."

C) "I overslept; it happens. The massage got done, didn't it?"

D) "I am really sorry for the inconvenience. I hope the client was happy with the massage he received."

Answers:

A) Incorrect. This response shows a total lack of respect for the employer.

B) Incorrect. This response is an insult to the employer and the coworker who did the massage.

C) Incorrect. This response displays an absolute lack of professionalism and communication skills.

D) Correct. This response relays regret, acknowledges the impact of the action on others, and shows concern for the client. However, if tardiness becomes repetitive behavior, this regret will be insincere and will most likely impact the therapist's position in the company.

SEXUAL MISCONDUCT

Sexual misconduct is unacceptable behavior that violates the ethics and rules of massage and bodywork organizations and government entities that have the responsibility of overseeing the practice of massage and the conduct of massage therapists. *Proven* claims of sexual misconduct will result in loss of license and professional standing and, in the extreme, in filing of lawsuits, criminal charges, and prosecution.

Sexual misconduct in the massage therapeutic environment can be the result of a massage therapist preying on a client, a client preying on a massage therapist, a mutual undertaking by both the massage therapist and client, or workplace sexual misconduct by a coworker inflicted on another coworker.

If a therapist, without intent or sexual motivation, touches a client inappropriately as the result of a draping mishap or slip of the hand, the therapist should *immediately* respond with a clear and sincere apology, readjust the draping, check in with the client, and establish that the client is comfortable proceeding with the massage. However, *intended* sexual touching of a client by a massage therapist and/or sexually explicit language directed toward a client by a massage therapist is predatory behavior that takes advantage of the power differential between client and therapist and crosses all boundaries. There is no gray area.

A client with the goal of initiating a sexual encounter with a massage therapist may begin by subtly testing boundaries. There are several possible scenarios in this regard. For example, a client might ask leading questions about the therapist's relationship status or interject unsolicited personal information about his or her own relationship status and personal finances. Client comments like "that feels really good" or "your boyfriend or husband is so lucky" can be similarly problematic.

Specific situations test or violate boundaries. One situation might be if a therapist, upon entering a massage room to begin a massage, finds a male client's genitals exposed or a female client's breasts exposed; the client then appears to be embarrassed about misunderstanding the draping instructions. Or a client asks the therapist to focus more on the inner thigh because of a soreness in the groin area that the client did not disclose verbally or in writing in the intake process. Perhaps a client continually tries to readjust the draping. For example, when prone, with the back exposed, the client adjusts the sheet down beyond the lumbar vertebrae.

While the above scenarios may seem obvious or even somewhat comical, they are realistic. A therapist who has greeted a client, assessed, and discussed a treatment plan with the client may have no logical or reasonable sense of impropriety. These scenarios can be nothing more than innocent attempts at conversation, being complimentary, or a genuine misunderstanding of instructions. However, they should be a reminder to the therapist to stay within professional boundaries. Therapists should be polite and professional but also assert themselves in a manner that relays to the client they are not fazed or intimidated. If the client leaves and never returns, there should be no further concern. However, if the client schedules another appointment and the same type of event(s) occur, the therapist needs to address them promptly.

Therapists can communicate to clients they do not, under any circumstance, discuss their personal lives. They can be firm and reiterate the draping policy and imply they will no longer be able to continue massaging the client in the future if the behavior continues. They can seek out support and advice from trusted peers or a supervisor, if they feel they may be in over their head. Also, a supervisor may formally want to note the therapist communicated concerns, and how those concerns have been addressed to date, in the event the client exhibits, or has exhibited, the same behavior with another therapist.

Other situations may not be subtle at all. They can be overt and even criminal. If a client suddenly touches a therapist inappropriately in a way that is clearly not accidental, makes a straightforward request for a sexual service, or begins interjecting sexually explicit language into the conversation, the therapist needs to stop the massage, step away from the table, and inform the client he will not be continuing the massage. The therapist should firmly instruct the client to dress before exiting the room. These are situations where therapists need to have a clear plan of action in place. Therapists may work in their own practice and have no other employees on site or may work for a practice that has a protocol to follow. If a therapist fears for her safety or the safety of coworkers, she should call 911. It is advisable to have a session termination notice available to give clients when they exit the room or at reception. This notice will outline the reason for the termination of massage, instructions regarding payment, and incident review options.

What is considered sexual misconduct may be a mutual desire to embark on a sexual relationship. If a massage relationship with a client has gone from professional to physical, it needs to cease immediately. The therapist is in violation of codes and standards of conduct as well as healthcare workers' professional guidelines.

Sexual misconduct in the workplace between coworkers can be in the form of inappropriate touching, lewd comments directed toward or about a coworker, referring to clients in sexual terms, using sexually explicit language in conversation for humor or intimidation purposes, or viewing pornography in a magazine or on personal technical devices, especially in clear view of coworkers. Sexual misconduct can be overheard or seen by clients waiting for service. Businesses will have clear and written rules regarding sexual misconduct.

PRACTICE QUESTIONS

1. Proven claims of sexual misconduct will most likely NOT result in which of the following?

    A) the state revoking the therapist's license to practice

    B) prosecution

    C) a written warning from the therapist's employer

    D) media and public scrutiny

    Answers:

    A) Incorrect. The therapist will definitely lose his license to practice.

    B) Incorrect. If the claim is proven, the therapist has most likely been prosecuted.

    C) **Correct.** An employer will no longer employ the therapist.

    D) Incorrect. Cases of sexual misconduct, except in certain situations, will be of public record.

2. Which of the following choices may be a *subtle* suggestion of potential sexual misconduct by a client?

    A) A male client pushes the sheet down to just above his genitalia claiming he is too hot.

    B) The therapist enters the room and a female client is fondling her breasts.

    C) A client, while on the table during the massage, asks if the therapist does "happy endings."

    D) A client, while lying face up on the table, keeps extending a hand from under the sheet and touching the therapist's leg.

    Answers:

    A) **Correct.** The client may be overheated, but this behavior should be an indicator to be on guard.

    B) Incorrect. This is not subtle. It is sexual misconduct by the client.

    C) Incorrect. This question contains sexual overtures and is thus not subtle in the least.

    D) Incorrect. While the first time may be an accident, this type of continuous physical contact by a client should indicate to a therapist to end the massage.

THREE: PROFESSIONAL PRACTICE

To work as a professional in massage therapy means more than just getting paid to perform massage. It means being a competent expert in all things related to the health and wellness of a client's muscles and body as a whole. The world of massage therapy holds an unlimited number of possibilities for the therapist who has acquired all the proper certifications and licensures.

Licensing and certifying institutions, as well as employers, establish guidelines to ensure the highest level of professionalism in massage therapy. Through both general and continuing education courses, massage therapists learn how to ensure the best techniques, tools, and equipment are utilized for both their and their clients' benefit.

HIPAA and Confidentiality

Like any professional who deals with clients in close, intimate settings where private details are shared—such as doctors, nurses, and mental health professionals—massage therapists, too, must adhere to guidelines that ensure the client's privacy is respected.

> Do not share information about clients unless for treatment purposes. How would it feel knowing that your doctor was sharing your personal history at a cocktail party? The same goes for massage therapists. Information can be shared with a managing doctor or with other therapists as appropriate. Use discretion.

HIPAA, or the **Health Insurance Portability and Accountability Act**, was enacted in 1996 in order to set a national standard of practices for the electronic exchange, privacy, and security of a client's health information.

A major goal of HIPAA is to ensure that clients' health information is properly protected while allowing the flow of health information needed to provide and promote high-quality health care and to protect the public's health and well-being.

For example, a massage therapist's practice space should be treated as a safe space, where what the client chooses to share in the space stays in the space, unless the client mentions that he intends to harm himself, someone else, or put the therapist at risk.

The Privacy Rule of HIPAA protects all individually identifiable health information, such as the individual's past, present, or future physical or mental health or conditions.

HIPAA rules and regulations are put in place to protect a client's individual case, from his condition to treatment to payment methods.

A good rule of thumb: when in doubt, talk to a fellow medical professional, or reach out to the US Department of Health and Human Services.

PRACTICE QUESTIONS

1. Why is HIPAA used by massage professionals?

A) Massage therapists are doctors.

B) Massage therapists deal with clients' private information.

C) Massage therapists like to talk about clients to their friends.

D) Massage therapists do not know how to follow rules.

Answers:

A) Incorrect. Massage therapists are not doctors; they have a different scope of practice.

B) Correct. Massage therapists deal with clients' private information and, as such, use HIPAA's guidelines to protect their clients.

C) Incorrect. Massage therapists should not discuss their clients with their friends.

D) Incorrect. Massage therapists use HIPAA as a guideline for proper management of clients' private information.

2. What does HIPAA's Privacy Rule protect?

A) a massage therapist's privacy

B) the security of a massage therapist's health information

C) a client's right not to share her information

D) a client's privacy and the security of her health information

Answers:

A) Incorrect. The Privacy Rule does not protect massage therapists.

B) Incorrect. The Privacy Rule does not cover a massage therapist as the provider.

C) Incorrect. The Privacy Rule does not protect a client's unwillingness to share information.

D) Correct. The Privacy Rule protects a client's right to privacy and the security of her health information.

Client Records

Client records are helpful in order to provide the client with the proper care and—state by state—necessary in accordance with the law. The information needed depends on where the client is being treated, whether in a medical clinic or a massage spa setting.

Medical clinics, or offices, offering sports medicine, chiropractic, physical therapy, and the like, will have a different set of records than a massage spa will. At medical offices, not only will the client's main contact information, health history, and reason for visit be taken, but insurance information will also be recorded in the event of treatment issues, or if the treatment is being ordered by a doctor or as the result of an accident and insurance settlement.

The four primary reasons for keeping a client's health record are:

+ to assist the massage therapist in details of the client's history, condition, and treatment provided
+ to assist in continuity of care if other practitioners are called upon to treat the client
+ to provide a record for medical-legal purposes when a client requires a report relating to his treatment
+ to provide a record of events should the client need information for another healthcare provider or an insurance agent

 All client files should be kept for ten years after the final entry of treatment.

Again, under HIPAA rules and regulations, all information the client provides to the massage therapist should be treated as confidential and handled as such.

Each client should receive his own folder with his intake form, contact information, insurance information (should it be relevant), treatment plan, and informed consent. Depending on the therapist and how she stores her clients' information, there may be more or fewer forms included in each client's folder.

In order to protect a client's personal and confidential information, a therapist should take measures to ensure that non-medical, involved persons do not have access to such information. Therapists may take such precautions as keeping files in a locked file cabinet or in a large divided folder system stored in the therapist's office. If files are kept on a computer, precautions should be taken to ensure that the information is kept confidential as well—such as by using a password-protected program.

Client forms should always remain in the office where the client is being treated.

CLIENT INFORMATION & CONSENT FORM

All information provided is for the private use of Ascencia Pharmacy
and will not be shared or distributed

Referred by: _____

Name(please print) _____

Address_____

City, State, Zip _____

Home Phone _____ Work Phone _____

Cell Phone_____ Email _____
(it may be necessary to reach you should a scheduling change occur)

I understand that the massage and bodywork that I receive is provided for the purpose of relaxation, stress reduction and the relief of muscular tension. If I experience any pain or discomfort during the session, I will immediately inform my massage therapist.

I will note on the reverse side any special physical areas of my body to avoid or target. I also understand that Kriya massage is a full body massage during which I have the option to leave on my underclothes or be fully undressed under the massage table linens.

I understand that any illicit or sexually suggestive remarks or advances made by me will result in termination of the session and I remain responsible for payment of the entire scheduled appointment.

My scheduled time slot can only be canceled 24 hours in advance of my appointed session, unless there is a true emergency. If I miss an appoinmtment or fail to cancel within the 24 hour period, I agree to pay the full appointment fee. If necessary, in the future, I may be required to prepay with my credit card number to secure my appointment.

Signature_____ Date _____

Please continue on reverse side

Figure 3.1. Sample Consent Form

PRACTICE QUESTION

How should massage therapists handle clients' private information?

A) make copies and share the records with their neighbors

B) burn or shred records after a client leaves the office

C) store in a secure location, in a client's properly marked file for a period of ten years

D) store in a haphazard, unmarked file cabinet

Answers:

A) Incorrect. Clients' records should not be shared with non-medical professionals.

B) Incorrect. Clients' records should be stored for ten years.

C) **Correct.** Clients' records should be properly marked and stored for ten years.

D) Incorrect. Clients' records should be stored in a properly marked file in a secure location.

INTAKE FORM

One of the best tools at a massage therapist's disposal is the intake form. All new clients should receive and fill out an intake form before the massage treatment begins. The intake form can answer a lot of questions, saving time during the face-to-face intake interview. However, a therapist should still have a conversation with the client about his reason for making an appointment; if he has any injuries, medical conditions, or medications the therapist should know about before beginning treatment; and what he should expect during and after the treatment.

Intake forms cover everything from contact information to health history to the client's reasons for seeking massage therapy.

A typical information-gathering intake form can include, but is not limited to, the following areas:

+ contact information: name, address, phone number, email, and birthday
+ payment information: a credit card to keep on file for ease of payment or in case the client cancels after the allotted grace period
+ insurance information: in the event the therapist, or the office for which she works, takes insurance; ensures clients receive covered care
+ emergency contact information: in the event something happens to the client in the office
+ preexisting health conditions: to help the therapist better treat the client, or to refer out if the client's issue is beyond the massage therapist's scope of practice. Certain issues or diseases may contraindicate receiving massage (see chapter 5 on pathologies and massage benefits).

Ascencia Pharmacy
4894 S. Westbury St.
Akron, OH 33327, 1-800-683-5822
www.AscenciaPharmacy.com
After Hours Emergency: (800) 631-5483

Personal Information

Name _____ Phone (day) _____ (evening) _____
Address _____ City, State, Zip _____
Email (optional) _____ Date of Birth _____ Occupation _____
Emergency Contact _____ Phone _____
Physician _____ Phone _____

Massage Information

How did you hear about us? _____

Have you ever had a professional massage before? ☐ Yes ☐ No

If yes, how often do you recieve massage therapy? _____

If yes, do you have a style or pressure preference? ☐ Yes ☐ No

Specify: ☐ Light pressure ☐ Medium pressure
☐ Deep pressure ☐ Trigger point therapy
☐ Energywork
☐ Other _____

What type of massage are you seeking today?
☐ Relaxation ☐ Deep Tissue/Therapeutic
☐ Senior ☐ Intergrated Bodywork (functional)
☐ Other _____

Are you sensitive to fragrances or perfumes? ☐ Yes ☐ No

Do you have sensitive skin? ☐ Yes ☐ No

Do you wear contacts? ☐ Yes ☐ No

Do you excercise regularly? ☐ Yes ☐ No

If so, what type(s)? _____

What are your common areas of pain or tension?

_____
_____

Circle any specific areas you would like the massage therapist to concentrate on during the session.

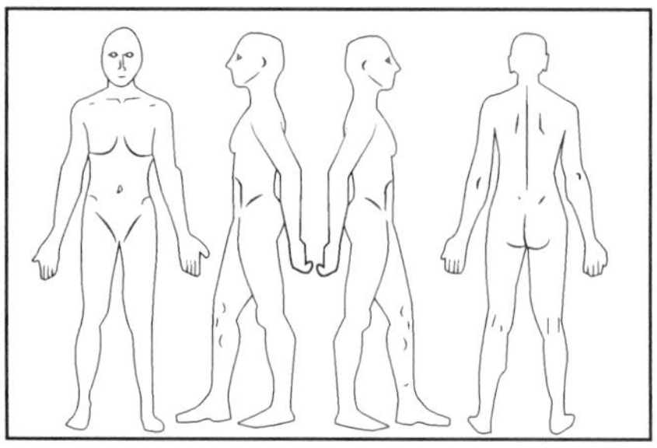

Medical History

Do you suffer from chronic pain or discomfort?
_____

If so, for how long? _____

Do you know what caused it or when the symptoms seem to get worse or better? _____
_____

Do you see a chiropractor? ☐ Yes ☐ No
If so, how often? _____

Are you currently under medical care? ☐ Yes ☐ No

Are you currently taking any prescription medication? If so, for what? _____
_____
_____

Please indicate any conditions that you have had or currently have.

☐ Headaches, migranes   ☐ Varicose veins
☐ Allergies, sensitivity   ☐ Pregnancy
☐ Arthritis, tendonitis   ☐ Blood clots
☐ Cancer, tumors   ☐ Neck/back injuries
☐ TMJ problems   ☐ Diabetes
☐ Abnormal skin condition   ☐ Paralysis
☐ Heart/circulation problems   ☐ Fibromyalgia
☐ Joint replacement/surgery   ☐ Numbness
☐ High/low blood pressure   ☐ Sprains, strains
☐ Major accident   ☐ Recent injuries
☐ Lack of or reduced feeling/sensation _____

Explain any conditions that you have marked above:

_____
_____
_____

Figure 3.2. Sample Intake Form

+ allergies: any known allergies; may call for the avoidance of certain lotions or oils

+ body chart: allows clients to circle their areas of pain or discomfort so therapists know where to focus their energy; helps therapists identify potential causes of clients' physical complaint(s)

+ reason for visit: allows clients to state why they are seeking a massage: pain management, relaxation, pre-/post-sports event, maintenance, new injury, surgery recovery, etc.

+ therapist credentials: a list of a therapist's licenses and certifications to reassure clients of the therapist's education and experience

+ late cancellation period: clear statement of cancellation policy, including the consequences, if any, of arriving late or canceling outside the grace period window

+ possible outcomes: While massage oftentimes is very relaxing, certain treatments use deeper pressure and can cause soreness and/or bruising; an intake form can clearly state these potential adverse outcomes and list ways in which a client can reduce their duration.

Intake forms do not just consolidate information about the client; they also clearly define what is to be expected in the massage treatment. A signed statement like the following can cover a lot of ground:

"I, _____, acknowledge I am receiving this massage for (CIRCLE ONE: pain relief, relaxation, promotion of circulation, other/write in) and I am allowed to terminate the treatment at any time, as is the massage therapist."

Such a statement helps the therapist understand why the client is receiving treatment. Additionally, it clarifies that both parties can terminate the treatment at any time.

A number of basic intake forms can be found online and printed for therapists to use at their practices with their clients.

PRACTICE QUESTIONS

1. Which of the following should NOT be included on a client's intake form?

    A) reason for visit

    B) client's contact information

    C) client's social media information

    D) insurance information

    Answers:

    A) Incorrect. An intake form should include the reason for a client's visit.

    B) Incorrect. An intake form should have the client's contact information.

C) Correct. An intake form does not include a client's private social media information.

D) Incorrect. An intake form should include insurance information, if insurance is accepted.

2. What is the importance of an intake form?

A) to collect a client's information and define what is expected in the massage treatment

B) to collect a client's information to become friends

C) to collect a client's information to share with other professionals

D) to collect a client's information to use his identity

Answers:

A) Correct. An intake form should provide the massage therapist with information to start a professional relationship with the client and should outline the treatment plan.

B) Incorrect. A therapist should not use a client's information to start a friendship with the client.

C) Incorrect. A therapist should treat the client's information as confidential and only share it in accordance with HIPAA; furthermore, the primary purpose of an intake form is to gather information for the massage therapist.

D) Incorrect. It is unlawful to steal someone's identity, and therapists should not abuse their power.

SOAP Notes

SOAP notes are widely used across all medical fields. A SOAP (**S**ubjective **O**bjective **A**ssessment **P**lan) note is a chart primarily used in outcome-based massage. SOAP notes vary in some degree as to how a practitioner fills them out. Not all states require massage therapists to keep SOAP notes for their clients, but it is a good idea to do so anyway, especially if the therapist or the client wants to track the client's progress throughout the course of treatment.

SOAP notes are great reference materials for massage therapists. Not only do they track clients' progress, but in the event a client has not received treatment in a while, the SOAP note serves as a reminder of physical issues and what treatment approach was being applied.

Ideally, SOAP notes should be taken immediately after the therapist finishes a session with the client. In the event of a busy day with back-to-back clients, the therapist can make SOAP notes at the end of the day. Because SOAP notes contain so much information, abbreviations and symbols can be used, but therapists should remain consistent in how they record their notes, potentially keeping a diagram key in the event they share their notes with other massage therapists and/or medical professionals.

When taking SOAP notes, it is important for therapists to keep in mind that they cannot diagnose or prescribe, and should take their notes accordingly. If the therapist feels there is something that a client should do, but it is out of the therapist's scope of practice to recommend, the therapist should refer out to a medical doctor.

> When performing intake with a client, it's good to keep OL' DR. FICARA in mind. Finding out the answers to these questions will allow the therapist to take a full-bodied S of the SOAP note: **O**nset ("When did the pain begin?"), **L**ocation ("Where do you feel pain?"), **D**uration ("How long does the pain last?"), **R**adiating ("Do you feel the pain radiate, and where?"), **F**requency ("How often do you feel the pain?"), **I**ntensity ("On a scale of 0 – 10, how much pain are you in—now, when it flares up, after you____?"), **C**haracteristic ("What does the pain feel like?"—therapists should try not to lead clients here by suggesting words like *burning, aching,* or *numb,* but rather let clients describe the pain themselves), **A**ggravating ("What makes the pain worse?"), **R**elieving ("What makes the pain better?"), **A**ssociated signs and symptoms ("Have you experienced other pain, conditions, or discomfort since the original incident?").

The S stands for the **subjective**, or symptoms the client describes to the therapist. In this section, the therapist notes what the client says, her feelings, and her past and present symptoms. The therapist should also note what improves or worsens the client's condition, and what goals the client has for the massage treatments. If a therapist uses a pain scale, the client's initial number describing the problematic area is recorded here. In this section, it is appropriate for the therapist to note, "Client stated, 'I feel pain when I raise my right arm above my head.'" Additionally, this information can be obtained from the client's intake form.

The O encompasses the **objective**, or what is observed or measured by the massage therapist. The objective section should be the therapist's mirror to the client's subjective information. Findings from palpation during the treatment can be listed here, such as "Client's right upper trapezius and middle deltoid were both hypertonic when palpated." The therapist can also note postural deviations, movement, skin texture and tonicity, lack of symmetry, areas that the client guards against (tensing the muscles), and evidence of injury or scar tissue.

The A can either refer to **application** or **assessment**; regardless, in this section the massage therapist notes what treatment was provided relating back to the client's subjective information. This should include what specific techniques were applied and where, such as "Cross-fiber friction and trigger point treatments were applied to the upper trapezius fibers." The therapist can also note the client's statements after the treatment, including the number used to describe level of pain on the pain scale post-treatment.

The P stands for **plan**, or client homework and future session goals. In this section, the massage therapist notes what stretching and exercise suggestions and recommendations the therapist gave the client. The therapist should also note what techniques should be continued or added in the following treatments. If the therapist and client agreed upon future treatments, the number and frequency of said treatments should be recorded in this section.

Legally, SOAP notes can be shared among medical practitioners and insurance companies. If a client is receiving massage as arranged by an insurance settlement, SOAP notes should definitely be taken in the event the insurance company needs records for the settlement or, worst case, court.

SOAP notes protect not only the massage therapist but also the client. Sometimes, if a therapist works under a medical doctor, the doctor may be the one who records and keeps the client's file, including the SOAP notes. Massage therapists should have a conversation with their head doctor to ensure that SOAP notes are being recorded or, if not, to find out why and possibly take on the task themselves.

PRACTICE QUESTIONS

1. At what point in the SOAP notes should the acronym OL' DR. FICARA be used for gathering information from the client?

A) Subjective

B) Objective

C) Assessment

D) Plan

Answers:

A) **Correct.** Asking a client about his symptoms using OL' DR. FICARA allows the therapist to find out information such as when the symptoms began, their frequency, and other descriptors.

B) Incorrect. The Objective portion is what is observed by the therapist.

C) Incorrect. The Assessment portion describes what type of treatment was provided to the client.

D) Incorrect. The Plan portion notes homework for the client and describes future treatments.

2. Can a massage therapist prescribe to or diagnose a client?

A) no

B) yes

C) sometimes

D) only when the doctor is out of the office

Answers:

A) **Correct.** Therapists are never allowed to prescribe or diagnose, as these actions are beyond their scope of practice.

B) Incorrect. Therapists can never diagnose or prescribe because these were not included in their education.

C) Incorrect. A therapist should never diagnose or prescribe but instead refer a client to a doctor.

D) Incorrect. A therapist cannot diagnose or prescribe and should tell the client to wait for the doctor's input.

3. In which of the following cases are SOAP notes NOT shared?

A) in court when discussing a case involving treatment

B) when talking to a client's doctor about a comprehensive treatment plan

C) at a dinner party

D) when talking to a fellow massage therapist who also sees the client

Answers:

A) Incorrect. SOAP notes can be shared in court cases when applicable.

B) Incorrect. SOAP notes can be shared with a client's doctor to ensure the client receives the best comprehensive care for her condition.

C) **Correct.** SOAP notes should not be shared outside of medical or legal spaces with people unrelated to the client's care or case.

D) Incorrect. SOAP notes can be shared with another massage therapist who also sees the client.

Equipment and Supplies

As massage therapists grow in their education and practice, they will come into contact with an increasing amount of equipment and tools of the trade. As such, therapists should be well-versed in how to keep both themselves and their clients safe when using and storing these tools and equipment. While safety may seem like common sense, what may seem normal, or commonplace, in a therapist's room may be foreign, or unfamiliar, to a client. Being safe means identifying and controlling hazards and risks.

Massage therapists work on their clients on a table; the table itself may be furnished with a heating pad that plugs into the wall. Rooms often contain shelves or cabinets full of extra sheets and supplies, chairs for clients, and stools for therapists. Some therapy rooms may have a **hydrocollator**, a gel-filled pack in a metal tank filled with temperature-controlled water—one of the most common types of heat therapy practiced both in spas and therapeutic settings. If the floor is not carpeted, there may be a rug that could pose a potential tripping hazard.

A **hot towel cabi**, or cabinet that keeps towels warm all day long, can also be used for a variety of treatments. Typically the cabinet has UV-ray lights to kill bacteria, but only clean towels should be used in the hot towel cabi.

Especially if a client is new to the world of massage therapy, or even to the therapist's office, the therapist should clearly instruct the client on how to get on and off the table properly and safely.

A **stationary table** is a heavy, fixed massage table. The stationary table is not easily portable. The legs have a series of holes at different levels; between sessions, therapists can adjust the table height for their comfort and to accommodate clients of varying sizes and shapes. There is typically a storage area under the table for sheets or extra massage-room supplies. The therapist should ensure that all screws are secure and the legs are level and stable.

A **hydraulic table** is the golden goose of massage tables, because it can be adjusted with the press of a button while the client is on the table. Hydraulic tables can be raised and lowered, and some even have adjustable halves so that only the client's upper body is raised. These tables are also stationary. Therapists should make sure they can raise and lower the table before the client gets on, and that the table is plugged in where the client cannot trip on the cord.

While these tools and pieces of equipment make it easier for therapists to do their job more efficiently, they can pose a hazard if they are not placed, or stored, correctly.

PRACTICE QUESTIONS

1. What is one difference between hydraulic and stationary tables?

    A) Hydraulic tables are submerged in water.

    B) Stationary tables can never be moved.

    C) Hydraulic tables can be adjusted while the client is on the table.

    D) Stationary tables can be adjusted while the client is on the table.

    Answers:

    A) Incorrect. Hydraulic tables are not submerged in water.

    B) Incorrect. Stationary tables can be moved when a client is not on them.

    C) Correct. Hydraulic tables can be raised or lowered when a client is on them, with the press of a button.

    D) Incorrect. Stationary tables can only be adjusted when a client is not on them.

2. Which of the following is a safety hazard in a therapy room?

    A) sheets folded and properly stored in a cabinet

    B) rugs or cords that are taped down on the floor

    C) a table warmer cord that runs next to the table

    D a chair that sits in the corner

Answers:

A) Incorrect. Sheets that are folded and put in a cabinet do not pose a hazard to the therapist or client.

B) Incorrect. Rugs or cords that are taped down on the floor reduce the risk of tripping and do not pose a hazard to the therapist or client.

C) Correct. A cord that is not taped down can pose a hazard to the therapist or client.

D) Incorrect. A chair that is not in the walking path of the therapist or client does not pose a hazard.

Proper Setup of Massage Table

In order to provide massage to clients, the therapist must first ensure that the table is properly set up. If the table is portable, the therapist must first remove the table from the storage bag. The table should have latches on the long end. Once the latches and table have been opened, the table's legs should be extended; all four legs must be at an even height and steady. The therapist should put one foot down on the inside of the far table leg and lift the table lengthwise to standing.

Once the table is standing upright on all four legs, the therapist should check the height. The therapist's fingers should gently brush the table when his arms are straightened by his sides. Depending on the size of the client and the type of massage treatment, this measurement can vary. Some therapists like to work high, while some like to work low using a lot of lunging (see "Body Mechanics," below). The height really varies by therapist, so it is important for each therapist to listen to his body and adjust the table height as needed.

Additionally, a client's size can affect the table height. Larger clients lie higher on the table than thin clients do. Before bringing a client into the room, therapists should note any need to adjust the table for the treatment. Once finalizing the height of the table, the therapist must lock its legs into place by securing the screws on the table legs.

After deciding on the table's height, the therapist should adjust the face cradle. The face cradle, when properly adjusted, should put no strain on the back of the client's neck and minimal pressure on the face. The face cradle adjustment can be done before the client arrives—therapists can lie down and check the height, width, and angle themselves—or after the client is already on the table. Some face cradles allow for adjustment, while other face cradles are stationary. Therapists should check in with clients to ensure they are comfortable.

Again, all cords, sheets, and supplies should be properly stored and out of the way for both the therapist's and the client's safety.

Sheets should be discarded into the laundry bin after each client's treatment, and the table should be sanitized either with alcohol-based disinfectant wipes, an alcohol-based disinfectant spray with a paper towel, or a towel that is discarded into the laundry after each use. Clean sheets should be put on the table after it is clean and dry.

PRACTICE QUESTION

Which of the following is NOT a determining factor for adjusting table height?

A) the height of the therapist

B) the weight of the client

C) the height of the client

D) the type of massage treatment

Answers:

A) Incorrect. The height of the therapist is a determining factor for adjusting the table height.

B) Incorrect. The weight of the client is a determining factor for adjusting the table height.

C) **Correct.** The height of the client is not a determining factor for adjusting the table height.

D) Incorrect. Depending on the type of massage treatment, the therapist may prefer variations in table height.

OSHA REGULATIONS

OSHA, or the **Occupational Safety and Health Administration**, has a mission to "save lives, prevent injuries, and protect the health of America's workers." All healthcare professionals, including massage therapists, who may be exposed to bodily fluids or wastes should create or adopt a plan to prevent the exposure or spread of blood-borne pathogenic microorganisms.

Blood-borne pathogens are infectious microorganisms in human blood that can cause disease in humans. Blood-borne pathogens include, but are not limited to, **hepatitis B and C**, **syphilis**, and **human immunodeficiency virus (HIV)**. These diseases live in certain bodily fluids such as blood, wound drainage, semen, and vaginal fluid and can be spread if an infected person's fluids make contact with a wound or other opening on a non-infected person.

The most important things a massage therapist can do are sometimes the simplest, such as keeping a clean space free of litter, broken debris, and the like. Hand washing is the most important practice for preventing the spread of infectious diseases. After every shift, the massage room should be sanitized, especially door handles, light switches, and anything else the therapist or client frequently touches.

To ensure the greatest safety for the therapist and the client, here is a selection of OSHA's basic universal precautions:

+ Treat all individuals as if they are carrying a blood-borne pathogen, and assume that all bodily fluids are infectious and should be treated as such.

+ Wash hands before eating, drinking, smoking, or doing anything else.

- Wear sterile disposable vinyl or latex gloves if either the therapist or the client has an open wound.
- Vaccinations should be up to date for both the therapist and the client.
- Sharp items such as needles, glass, and the like should be treated as if they are infected and disposed of safely.
- Contaminated waste should be double bagged and labeled when disposed.
- Equipment and supplies used should be cleaned and disinfected after each client's treatment to prevent the spreading of infectious diseases.

As seen above, many problems can be avoided with a plan like the one OSHA outlines. Trash bags should be at the ready in the event that sheets become soiled. Vinyl gloves are often preferable as some clients have latex allergies, and should be on-site, ready to use. Ideally, a sink for hand washing should be in or just outside of the room. As always, performing a thorough intake with the client allows the therapist to know if there are any issues or contagions that would prevent the therapist from providing the client with treatment.

Much like other rules and regulations, safety requirements vary by state. If therapists have questions, they should contact their local licensing board for more information.

PRACTICE QUESTIONS

1. Which of the following is NOT part of the OSHA mission?

A) saving lives

B) preventing injuries

C) protesting inequality

D) protecting the health of American workers

Answers:

A) Incorrect. OSHA does work to save lives by promoting safe work environments.

B) Incorrect. OSHA does work to prevent injuries by promoting safe work environments.

C) Correct. OSHA does not protest inequality.

D) Incorrect. OSHA does work to protect the health of American workers through establishing safety guidelines.

2. When should a treatment room be disinfected?

A) at the therapist's discretion

B) before and after each treatment

C) when the boss schedules a cleaning crew

D) weekly

Answers:

A) Incorrect. The therapist should disinfect the treatment room before and after each treatment.

B) **Correct.** The massage room should be disinfected before and after each client.

C) Incorrect. The room should be disinfected before and after each treatment, but a deep clean is a good idea every week or so.

D) Incorrect. The treatment room needs to be disinfected on a regular basis, before and after each treatment.

3. What precautions should a therapist take when working with a client with an open sore or dermatitis?

A) A therapist should use vinyl or latex gloves when working with a client with an open sore or dermatitis.

B) A therapist should put a Band-Aid on a client's open sore.

C) A therapist should refuse to work on a client with dermatitis.

D) A therapists should call in sick if he has a cut on his finger.

Answers:

A) **Correct.** Therapists should use gloves if they, or their client, have an open sore or dermatitis.

B) Incorrect. A therapist should not put a Band-Aid on a client's open sore.

C) Incorrect. A therapist can work on a client with dermatitis but should check with the client to make sure she is comfortable and adjust the treatment to the client's responses.

D) Incorrect. A therapist can still work if he has a cut on his finger, but he should wear gloves.

CLEAN LINENS

All single-service materials, such as towels and linens, must be cleaned after treatment and before they are used with another client. The massage therapist should ensure that towels and linens are washed at 160 degrees Fahrenheit (71 degrees Celsius) or warmer. Sheets, used towels, and clothing worn by the massage therapist should be washed at such a high temperature to kill bacteria and pathogens that may have transferred to the materials. Additionally, detergents are shown to work better in hot water, as the heat assists in killing pathogens.

After towels and sheets are washed they should be folded and stored in a clean cabinet, or stacked on a clean shelf. Bleach can be used to clean white sheets, helping kill pathogens and bacteria. Otherwise, stain-fighting agents can be used to prevent buildup on the sheets from oil and/or clients' makeup (Dawn's original blue dish soap is a good combatant to makeup stains on sheets).

PRACTICE QUESTION

Why is it important to wash sheets at 160 degrees Fahrenheit?

A) Sheets can actually be washed in hot or cold water.

B) Hot water kills pathogens.

C) Sheets should actually be washed in colder water because it is better for the environment.

D) Cold water cleans stains better.

Answers:

A) Incorrect. It is best for sheets and towels to be washed at a high temperature to stop the spread of infections through pathogens.

B) Correct. Hot water kills pathogens that can spread infection or disease.

C) Incorrect. While cold water may be better for the environment, spreading infections through pathogens is not safe for the client or the therapist.

D) Incorrect. Cold water may treat stains better, but hot water kills pathogens that spread infection.

The Therapist

It takes a lot to give a lot, and for that reason it is incredibly important that massage therapists have self-care plans that they use regularly, if not daily. Hour after hour of performing massage, day after day, standing and lifting and moving clients' arms and/or legs, can take a toll on the therapist, mentally and physically. Not only should therapists have healthy exercise and diet routines, but they also benefit from practicing other forms of self-care such as yoga or meditation.

Many massage programs devote time to how therapists can practice self-care as professionals. Simple acts of self-care include, but are not limited to:

+ receiving massage: Not only can massage alleviate a massage therapist's sore muscles, but it can also be educational to play the role of the client.

+ meditation: Carving out time for self-reflection can be beneficial when dealing with other people's energies and emotions; this can come in the form of breath work, journaling, sitting, lying down, and guided meditation, to name a few.

+ diet: Anti-inflammatory foods such as garlic, turmeric, and ginger can be used to keep inflammation from developing in the joints and muscles.

+ exercise: Because massage is such a physically demanding role, therapists should ensure they are able to work by keeping their hearts and bodies strong. Whether that comes in the form of lifting weights, running, or walking, exercise and a healthy heart lead to a healthy therapist.

- self-massage and stretching: Because massage requires a lot of grip strength, forearms, wrists, and hands can develop pain. A regular stretching routine can keep overworked muscles from developing adhesions and knots.
- use of massage tools: A trigger-point massage tool, foam roller, tennis ball, or massage star can all be used for self-care in working out the trickier trigger points that may lie in the upper back or in the gluteal muscles, to name a few.

It is easy to get caught up in the workday and let self-care fall by the wayside, but, as with clients, if therapists let their routines go, their pain can come back and even keep them from being able to perform their jobs. Therapists should practice what they preach to their clients, and set healthy examples for the people they work with on a regular basis.

PRACTICE QUESTION

What is one way of practicing self-care?

A) going to the bar

B) scheduling a busy day with no breaks

C) stretching and exercising regularly

D) crying into a pillow

Answers:

A) Incorrect. Drinking is not a healthy way of practicing self-care.

B) Incorrect. Overscheduling does not promote self-care.

C) **Correct.** Regular stretching and exercise promote a healthy body and mind.

D) Incorrect. While this may feel cathartic, there are better ways to practice self-care more consistently, such as breathing exercises or yoga.

THERAPIST HYGIENE

Due to the nature of massage therapy, therapists are in close contact with their clients. As such, they should keep up with proper hygiene practices: brushing teeth, showering, washing hands, and applying deodorant. First and foremost, a therapist should always look and smell clean.

First impressions mean a lot, especially in the world of massage therapy. Clients want to feel like they are in confident—and clean—hands. Therapists should wear minimal makeup and have short, filed, unpolished and clean nails. (Long nails not only can harbor bacteria, but also potentially scratch and injure a client, and even spread pathogens.)

Additionally, if a therapist chooses to wear a fragrance, it should be light and inoffensive—and oftentimes should just be avoided. Speaking of scents, therapists should avoid eating heavy, fragrant meals (think onions and garlic and loads of spices) before a treatment. Therapists should keep a toothbrush, toothpaste, and mouthwash on-site to use before treatments.

Therapists should always wear clean clothes that are free of scents; their hair should be clean and, if long, pulled away from the face. If a therapist knows he has foot odor and chooses to work barefoot, he should wash his feet before working on clients.

> 🔍 If you can smell it, the client can, too! Do not eat highly fibrous foods before a massage because of their gas-producing effects, or spicy foods if they cause you to sweat. Be mindful if you work in a small room with little air circulation, where the client will be exposed to you and your scents.

It is a good rule of thumb for therapists to think like a client, and ask themselves how they would want their therapist to look and smell. After all, clients consider many factors when choosing a therapist to see on a regular basis. A client may like a therapist's technique, but if the therapist's perfume is too strong, or the therapist appears to be dirty, the client may not come back for another treatment. This would not only hurt the therapist's bank account, but also potentially her credibility.

PRACTICE QUESTION

Which of the following is NOT a proper hygiene practice?

A) washing the hands and forearms in hot, soapy water

B) constantly brushing the therapist's hair behind the ears

C) clean, brushed teeth

D) wearing a lightly scented deodorant

Answers:

A) Incorrect. Hands and forearms should be washed in hot, soapy water.

B) Correct. Therapists should ensure their hair stays pulled back; they should not touch it constantly while working on a client.

C) Incorrect. Having clean, brushed teeth is a good hygiene practice.

D) Incorrect. Wearing a lightly scented deodorant is a good hygiene practice.

BODY MECHANICS

In order to have a long, healthy practice and career in the field of massage therapy, working at the proper table height is high on the list—but it's not the only thing on the list, as will be discussed below.

Working at the proper **table height** allows the therapist to work more efficiently. As discussed above, proper table height can vary depending on both the therapist and the client. Tables can be adjusted either by using pegs and screws on the table's legs, or by using the hydraulic table's button to raise and lower the table.

Commonly, a table should be at the therapist's hips for an average-sized client. (Though it should be noted that some people have longer torsos or longer legs, and a comfortable table height is one that allows the therapist a pain-free experience.) This height allows therapists to lunge into their compressions and strokes without putting excess pressure on their wrists. While hip-height may work for some treatments and clients, it is not necessarily the best height for everyone, and therefore therapists should adjust as necessary, gauging their techniques against their incoming client's size.

More important is how a therapist should be positioned while working. **Stance** should be on relaxed feet and ankles, pointing forward, at shoulder-width. After the feet and ankles are relaxed and pointing forward, the knees, hips, and shoulders should all follow suit—relaxed, with a slight bounce, or give, and pointed forward. Once the therapist feels he has a light, but rooted stance, one foot should be placed in front of the other, with the back foot still on the floor, in a lunge position. The feet are still pointed forward, and the hips and shoulders follow that direction. This is the basis of the massage therapist's stance. The massage therapist can pivot, lunge deeper, and move based on this stance.

> Root In! In a beginning stance, massage therapists should think of their joints like building blocks, relaxed and stacked knees over ankles, hips over knees, and shoulders over hips.

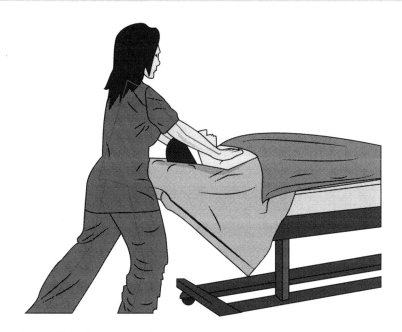

Figure 3.3. Beginning Stance

Relaxed hands and wrists protect the therapist's joints as well as provide a client with a more calming massage. Therapists should not bend their wrists at a 90-degree angle when performing palmar **strokes** or compressions—less than that angle is ideal.

Therapists' arms should not be more than 45 degrees away from the body and, therefore, they should move with longer strokes. Moving the whole body with massage strokes also offers the client a more fluid massage experience. Additionally, therapists should lift with their legs when moving a client, in order to avoid back injury. If possible, a therapist should ask for a client's help in the movement.

Depending on the client, more or less **force** is needed. In order to provide a client with more force, therapists can use their forearms, loose fists, or reinforced fingers. A proper stance will allow therapists to generate their own energy by grounding the back foot. Therapists can think of their core as harnessing the energy they use, the back leg grounding them, and the arms and hands allowing their positive, healing, effortless energy to flow into the client.

Working long shifts can put a lot of pressure on the therapist's body, and it is important to address aches and pains as they come up, adjusting work techniques and tools to ensure that a therapist will have a healthy and long career.

PRACTICE QUESTION

What is the proper starting stance for a practicing massage therapist?

A) toes, knees, and shoulders pointing forward

B) one leg lunged in front of the other, knees and arms straight

C) feet shoulder-width distance apart, toes pointing forward, hips and shoulders relaxed and stacked

D) therapist standing on one foot with the other leg bent at the knee

Answers:

A) Incorrect. The feet should be shoulder-width-distance apart.

B) Incorrect. Starting stance is a relaxed posture with joints stacked strongly on top of one another.

C) **Correct.** Feet are spread slightly apart to make a good, strong base for the rest of the body.

D) Incorrect. Both of the therapist's feet should be on the ground.

Growing and Maintaining a Business

While being their own boss and running a business is a dream for many people, it comes with a lot of responsibilities and challenges, such as following laws and filing taxes, owning insurance, operating a successful office, managing employees, and dealing with difficult clients.

Independent therapists should always research their state's requirements to function as a business. The following are general guidelines.

Operating a business means that everything reflects back on the owner, from the clients' first impressions of the business signage to the moment they step into the office. Clients will observe every detail such as the way the office looks and smells, if the sheets are clean and stored properly, and how the staff works together, among other things.

When massage therapists decide to open their own businesses or practices, it is important they are well-versed in the laws, rules, and regulations of governing bodies to ensure they have long and fruitful careers.

Taxes

Taxes vary on the local and state level, so to ensure there are no surprises at the end of the year, it's a good idea for a massage therapy business owner to work with an accountant. Everything should be accounted for and categorized according to filing laws.

Proper bookkeeping is the best way to ensure a good tax year, without an audit. The IRS will want to know gross income, deductions, and credit details. Proper bookkeeping includes noting everything from how much clients pay or purchase to how much they tip, and notes deductions such as utilities and other business expenses, such as taking the staff out for a meal at the end of a profitable business month.

Liability Insurance

While skilled practicing massage therapists are unlikely to be sued, accidents do happen, so insurance is a therapist's best defense.

There are a number of different insurance types available to massage therapists that cover everything from slips and falls to a product, such as massage lotion, causing an adverse reaction. These accidents could turn into an opportunity for a client to take action in a court of law.

Depending on where a therapist works, it may not be necessary to have extra coverage. Therapists should make sure to ask their employers what kind of liability coverage they have to ensure their careers are not at risk should a lawsuit come to fruition.

+ **General liability insurance** covers trip-and-fall types of cases; if a client comes into an office and has an accident, this type of coverage will protect a therapist's business.
+ **Professional liability insurance** is also known as malpractice insurance. This type of insurance will protect a therapist if a client claims the therapist was not competent in his treatment plan, causing a client injury.
+ **Product liability insurance** offers coverage essential to massage therapists who use lotions or oils during their treatments, in the event that something in the lotion or oil causes injury to the client.

- **Rental premises liability insurance** covers any damage that may occur to a space being rented, such as drywall cracking or a window breaking. This coverage does not take care of contents inside the space.

Different insurance plans will cover damages up to millions of dollars. All plans are different, and as such will have different requirements of the therapist and the practice.

Regardless of the insurance plan and its coverage, massage therapists should read the fine print with a fine-tooth comb, so they do all the right things to ensure that, in the event of a client taking a matter to court, they and their business are protected.

PRACTICE QUESTION

What type of insurance is also known as malpractice insurance?

A) general liability insurance

B) professional liability insurance

C) product liability insurance

D) rental premises liability insurance

Answers:

A) Incorrect. General liability insurance covers slips and falls.

B) **Correct.** Professional liability insurance is also known as malpractice insurance.

C) Incorrect. Product liability insurance covers products used during treatments.

D) Incorrect. Rental premises liability insurance covers any damages that happen to the space.

BUSINESS PLAN

The purpose of a business plan is to assist the massage therapist by clearly outlining realistic goals, from what type of clients the therapist wants to serve to how many, resulting in a specific number of dollars in revenue. Not only is a business plan a good idea for making and reaching goals, but in the event the therapist needs to borrow money, financial lending institutions will evaluate the strength of a business plan to determine if it is worth loaning the therapist money.

Sections to include in a business plan are:
- name: what the business will be called
- place and hours: the location and hours of operation
- mission and objective: outline of the business's goals
- long-term and short-term goals: the financial benchmarks the business will target
- background information: credentials and qualifications of the owner and employees

- ✦ consumer demand and profile: why the business will be a success in the area
- ✦ target clientele: the type of client that is the target market
- ✦ secondary clientele: other types of clients that will be attracted
- ✦ services/products available: what exactly will be bought and sold at the business
- ✦ permits and licenses: which ones are required, and which have already been obtained
- ✦ challenges and risks: factors standing in the way, and how they can be overcome
- ✦ equipment: what type is needed, and what has already been obtained
- ✦ other personnel: others who will be employed at the business
- ✦ marketing plan: the type of marketing to be utilized (advertising, public relations, promotions, mailers, etc.)
- ✦ business policies: how the business will operate on a day-to-day basis; how it will treat its employees and clients (code of ethics, confidentiality practices, fee structure, etc.)

A business plan can be many things; the above is a rough guide to get massage therapists thinking about how they want their businesses to operate. It is a good idea to talk to professionals who already have successful practices, to ensure that everything is covered and to seek out a mentor.

Free business plan guides can be found online, with explanations and tips on how to write a successful business plan.

PRACTICE QUESTION

Which of the following does NOT need to be included in a business plan?

A) business name

B) hours of operation

C) mission

D) role models

Answers:

A)   Incorrect. A name does need to be included in the business plan.

B)   Incorrect. Hours of operation need to be included in the business plan.

C)   Incorrect. Mission should be included in the business plan.

D)   Correct. Role models do not need to be included in the business plan.

HUMAN RESOURCES

One of the great things about being a professional massage therapist, aside from helping people out of pain day after day, is the flexibility in work environments. Massage therapists can choose to go their own way, creating their own business plan and space, or they can choose to work for a spa, office, or clinic. Some places of business offer an employer/employee relationship, while others hire contractors. There are pros and cons, or benefits and negative aspects, to both—it really just depends on the therapist and what she is looking for in her professional career.

Regardless of the place and type of employment, the hiring process can be fairly typical. When applying to a position, therapists should have a resume that states their education, experience, and any other relevant qualifications for the position; a cover letter may also be requested. Once an interview is secured, it is important that therapists are on time, if not early, for the meeting, with a copy of their resume, license, and insurance (if applicable) for the interviewer. Clean, professional-looking clothes may be preferable to a suit—it really depends on the attitude of the workplace. When in doubt, it is okay to ask. Therapists should keep in mind that, if the interview goes well, they will most likely perform a massage, so the interviewer can get a feel for their style and if they will be a good fit.

Being an **employee** can be a good thing. An employer takes care of taxes, scheduling, and all the supplies and services needed for the space outside of performing massage. The downside can be that someone else is in charge of how much a therapist's services are worth. Commissions are standard in the employee world, as are set schedules. W-2 forms are filed, and benefits are sometimes included for those who are considered full-time employees.

Being a **contractor** also can be a good thing. Often schedules are more flexible, and the pay is typically higher—but bear in mind that contractors have to pay their own taxes. Filing a W-9 is standard for an independent contractor and is similar to owning a business. Contractors account for sources of income and take deductions. Therapists may consider saving about 1.5 percent of each paycheck and hiring an accountant to make sure they are prepared at tax season.

FOUR: ANATOMY AND PHYSIOLOGY

The Twelve Human Systems and Their Functions

The **circulatory system**, also known as the cardiovascular system, consists of blood, blood vessels, and the heart. It transports and distributes gases needed for respiration, nutrients, antibodies, waste, hormones, and heat produced by muscles.

The **digestive system** provides the body with the nutrients it needs to survive and function properly. The functions are **ingestion**, **digestion**, **absorption**, and **excretion**. Ingestion is the intake of food, fluid, and medication through the mouth. Digestion refers to the breaking down of food using **mechanical processing** and **chemical digestion**. Mechanical processing includes chewing in the mouth, churning in the stomach, and **peristalsis**, a series of muscular contractions that move digested food through the system. Chemical digestion uses enzymes, stomach acid, bile, and juices to break down proteins, fats, and carbohydrates into nutrients. Absorption occurs after chemical digestion, as the nutrients are pulled through the small intestine lining into blood and lymphatic vessels. Excretion occurs at the completion of the digestive process to rid the body of the remaining indigestible matter.

The **endocrine system** is made up of a group of ductless glands that secrete hormones directly into the bloodstream. At this point, it is especially important to remember that there are two types of glands: **endocrine** and **exocrine**. Exocrine glands have ducts and do not feed directly into the bloodstream. Examples of exocrine glands are sweat, salivary, mammary, sebaceous, and mucous. This section focuses solely on the endocrine glands. The functions of the endocrine system are maintaining homeostasis by regulating organ functions, producing and secreting hormones, helping the body adapt during periods of high stress, sexual development, and the process of reproduction.

The **integumentary system** is the largest organ of the body. It consists of skin and its derivatives: hair, nails, and glands. There are several functions performed by the integumentary system, including **protection**, the first line of defense against bacteria and viruses; **absorption** of ultraviolet (UV) rays from the sun to produce vitamin D; and **secretion** of body waste released through perspiration. **Temperature regulation** occurs to maintain homeostasis through perspiration to release heat and the closing of pores to retain heat.

The **lymphatic system** prevents a buildup of tissue fluid surrounding cells. It has various functions. First, it drains excess interstitial fluid from body tissues to be returned to the venous bloodstream. Second, it transports fats and fat-soluble vitamins from the digestive tract to the blood. Third, the lymphatic system aids the immune system by filtering out pathogens and other impurities. When the blood's circulatory system capillary exchange process occurs, 90 percent of cell waste is gathered from interstitial fluid and diffused back into blood capillaries. The remaining 10 percent enters the lymphatic open-ended capillary vessels. At this point, it is defined as lymph. The lymphatic capillaries evolve into lymphatic vessels; like veins, they contain valves to protect backflow of the lymph. Lymph is moved upward only using skeletal muscle contraction, smooth muscle contraction, and pressure changes in the thoracic region during respiration. Unlike blood circulation, lymphatic circulation is a system with a slow rhythm, low velocity, and low pressure.

The **muscular system** has three types of muscle: **cardiac**, **smooth**, and **skeletal**. The heart is the *only* cardiac muscle in the body. Cardiac muscle cells are striated; each cell has one nucleus, and its sole function is to pump blood involuntarily. In between cardiac muscle cells are membranous junctions that appear as dark bands called **intercalated discs**. Their purpose is to assist in conducting electrical impulses that keep the heart beating. Smooth muscle surrounds hollow internal organs such as the intestines and the uterus. Smooth muscle cells are not striated; each cell has one nucleus, and it functions involuntarily. Its contractions move and push the contents of the organ. Skeletal muscle functions are to produce skeletal movement, maintain posture and body position, support soft tissues, and maintain body temperature. Skeletal muscle is striated; cells have more than one nucleus, and they function voluntarily.

The **nervous system** senses, interprets, and responds to stimuli, cognition, and emotional responses. The nervous system can be divided into two distinct parts: the central nervous system and the peripheral nervous system.

The **reproductive system** produces, stores, nourishes, and transports **gametes**. A gamete in a female is the **ovum** (Latin term for egg; plural: *ova*) and in a male the **spermatozoon** (plural: *spermatozoa*), commonly referred to in the singular and plural as **sperm**.

The **respiratory system's** most important function is to exchange carbon dioxide for oxygen, referred to as the **exchange of gases**. **Olfaction**, the sense of smell, and **speech**, air moving over the vocal cords, are two other functions of the respiratory system. The fourth function, **homeostasis**, maintains oxygen levels in the body by expelling carbon dioxide to regulate tissue and blood pH. The anatomy of the respiratory system is broken down into an upper and lower section. The **upper respiratory system** consists of the **nose**, **nasal cavity**, **sinuses**, **pharynx**, and **larynx**. The structures that make up the anatomy of the **lower respiratory system** are the **trachea, bronchi, alveoli, lungs,** and **respiratory diaphragm.**

The **skeletal system's** functions are to protect internal organs; provide structure, stability, and the attachment sites for muscles, tendons, and ligaments; store minerals and fat; and produce blood cells.

The **immune system** performs the function of defending the body from pathogens (foreign invaders). Pathogens are considered viruses, bacteria, parasites, fungi, and protozoa that enter or attempt to enter the body. Internally, foreign invaders can also be worn out cells that can begin to dysfunction, mutant cells that are abnormal from formation, and cellular debris, which is what remains of broken-down cells.

The **urinary system** eliminates fluid waste, regulates blood pH, regulates blood volume and fluid balance, regulates blood pressure, and maintains homeostasis. There are four basic structures of the urinary system: **kidneys, ureters,** the **urinary bladder,** and the **urethra.**

CIRCULATORY SYSTEM

Blood is considered a liquid connective tissue that is thicker than water. It consists of plasma and blood cells that are transported in the plasma. There are three types of blood cells. **Erythrocytes** are red blood cells that transport oxygen. **Leukocytes** are white blood cells that protect the body from bacteria, viruses, and other pathogens. **Thrombocytes (platelets)** are fragmented cells sent to repair damaged, leaking vessels by clotting the blood, thereby preventing hemorrhaging.

A continuous network of **blood vessels** makes its way through the body. There are two paths of blood circulation: the **pulmonary circuit** circulates blood from the heart to the lungs and back to the heart for the purpose of exchanging carbon dioxide, carried from the veins, for oxygen. (The pulmonary circuit will be discussed in more detail later in this section.) The **systemic circuit** circulates blood from the heart to the body and back to the heart.

The systemic circuit starts with the primary artery, the **aorta**, which receives oxygenated blood from the heart. **Arteries** transport erythrocytes away from the heart. The circuit ends with **veins** carrying blood that now has little to no oxygen back to the heart. One exception to the artery and vein rule of blood transport is a role reversal. The pulmonary artery moves deoxygenated blood from the heart to the lungs and the pulmonary vein moves oxygenated blood from the lungs to the heart. All blood flowing from veins feeds into one of the two *venae cavae* (hollow veins). The **superior vena cava** collects blood from the head, neck, chest, and upper extremities. The **inferior vena cava** collects blood from the pelvic and abdominal region and lower extremities. Artery and vein walls have three layers:

+ tunica intima—innermost
+ tunica media—middle
+ tunica externa—outermost

Because these layers consist partly of connective and smooth tissue, they have elasticity and contractility. This means that the walls can enlarge, referred to as **vasodilation**, and narrow, referred to as **vasoconstriction**. The open, interior channel of the arteries and veins is called the **lumen**. Even though veins have the tunica layers, they are, in comparison to arteries, much thinner, weaker, and easily damaged. When a vein is damaged, the body sends thrombocytes to form a clot.

Among the arteries and veins of the systemic system are **arterioles, capillaries,** and **venules.** Arterioles branch off from main arteries and become smaller and thinner by losing the tunica media and tunica externa layers. Arterioles lead to capillaries, which are thin membranes that move blood slowly while they perform a necessary process called **capillary exchange**. This exchange delivers nutrients and oxygen to tissues and organs while, at the same time, picking up cell waste from interstitial fluid for disposal. From the capillaries small veins called venules start to move blood in the direction of the heart. As the blood starts to move upward, the venules become veins. Veins have the more difficult job of moving blood, because of the decreased pressure and the need to defy gravity as the blood travels back toward the heart. To remedy this hardship, veins are equipped with a valve system known as a **venous pump**. This pump uses endothelium tissue present in the tunica intima to create flaps that open up toward the heart. The opening and closing of the flaps allow blood to move more easily upward and prevent backflow. This flow of blood is further assisted by the contraction of muscles, putting pressure on veins and allowing the blood to propel upward.

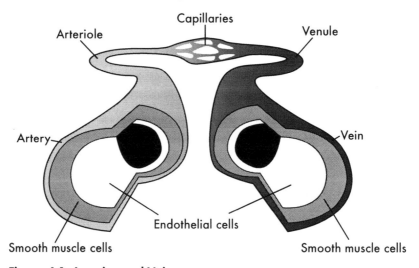

Figure 4.1. Arteries and Veins

The systemic circuit can be further broken down into **venous portal systems** that temporarily redirect blood from the circuit for the purpose of exchange. The **hepatic portal system** routes blood drained from a part of the digestive tract, specifically from the lower esophagus to the upper anal canal. It also collects blood from the pancreas and spleen. This portal dumps the collected blood into the liver, where glucose, fat, and proteins are pulled out for use by the liver before sending the blood back into veins to continue on the circuit. A second portal system is the **hypophyseal** located between the hypothalamus and anterior pituitary for the purpose of hormone exchange. Two unique things about portals are the blood flow is two way, not one way, and the blood carried through them is a mixture of oxygenated and deoxygenated blood.

The **heart** is located in the thoracic cavity behind the sternum, primarily left of midline, resting above the diaphragm. It is commonly considered the size of a clenched fist and is surrounded and protected by the **pericardium**. Also called the pericardial sac, the pericardium has an outer fibrous layer and an inner layer of serous fluid that acts as a lubricant so the pericardium and heart can contract and expand without friction. The walls of the heart consist of three layers:

+ endocardium—innermost
+ myocardium—middle
+ epicardium—outermost

The heart has four hollow chambers named the **left atrium**, the **right atrium**, the **left ventricle**, and the **right ventricle**. The atrium chambers are superior to the ventricle chambers. Blood is delivered through two **atrioventricular (AV) valves** that move blood from the atrium chambers to the ventricular chambers. The AV valves are named the **tricuspid valve**—with three flaps—located between the right atrium and right ventricle,

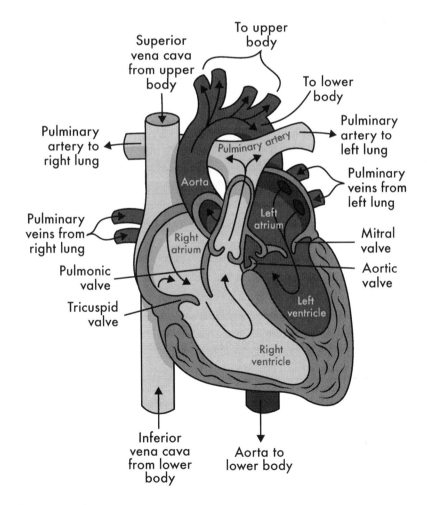

Figure 4.2. The Heart

and the **bicuspid valve**—with two flaps—located between the left atrium and the left ventricle. The bicuspid valve is also referred to as the mitral valve. **Semilunar valves** connect the ventricle chambers to their adjacent arteries. The semilunar valves are named the **pulmonary** semilunar valve, located between the right ventricle and **pulmonary trunk**, and the **aortic** semilunar valve, located between the left ventricle and aorta. The pulmonary trunk extends upward and divides into the right and left pulmonary arteries. Just like the veins, these valves keep the blood moving in one direction as the heart muscle contracts.

As discussed previously in this section, the pulmonary circuit carries blood from the heart to the lungs for gas exchange and then returns it to the heart. The circuit begins with blood carrying carbon dioxide being pumped from the right ventricle through the pulmonary trunk into the right and left pulmonary arteries. The right pulmonary artery routes the blood to pulmonary capillaries in the right lung and the left pulmonary artery routes blood to pulmonary capillaries in the left lung. It is in these capillaries that carbon dioxide is exchanged for oxygen. This newly oxygenated blood flows back to the heart through pulmonary veins that deliver it to the left atrium.

The rhythmic beating of the heart is the result of the **heart conduction system**. Specialized cardiac muscle cells send out signals starting the cardiac cycle. The components of the cardiac conduction system are the **sinoatrial (SA) node** that receives the signal first. It is located in the right atrium and this signal causes the blood flow to be pushed from the right atrium into the right ventricle. It may be referred to as the anatomical pacemaker. The **atrioventricular (AV) node** receives the signal from the SA node. There is a brief delay before the signal moves on to allow the atrium to fully empty. The **atrioventricular bundle**, a bundle of the specialized cardiac muscle cells, also referred to as the bundle of His, breaks into branches that lead to the **purkinje fibers**. These fibers cause impulses to spread throughout the ventricular myocardium, causing the ventricles to contract and force blood into the aorta, the primary artery in the body.

Blood pressure is measured in clinical settings using a **sphygmomanometer**. When the blood is forced from the left ventricle into the aorta, the **systolic** measure (maximum pressure) is obtained. When the ventricle relaxes, the **diastolic** measure (minimum pressure) is obtained. Blood pressure can be affected by blood volume, heart rate, blood viscosity, and vessel elasticity. If areas of the skin become red and warm as a result of increased blood flow, it is referred to as **hyperemia**. A common cause of hyperemia is an inflammatory response. If blood flow to an organ is inadequate or interrupted, it is referred to as **ischemia**. The most common cause of ischemia is a blocked or partially blocked artery. Heart rate can also be measured by taking one's pulse. Each pulse beat reflects the contraction of the ventricles.

✦ ABO is the most common blood-typing system.
✦ The presence or absence of blood antigens defines blood type.
✦ A child's blood type is determined by the parents' blood types.
✦ If a person has only A antigens, that person has type A blood.

- If a person has only B antigens, that person has type B blood.
- If a person has both A and B antigens, that person has type AB blood.
- If a person has neither A nor B antigens, that person has type O blood.
- Type O blood can be donated to anyone regardless of blood type.
- Groups with type O blood are called universal donors.
- Type A blood can be donated to type A and type AB recipients.
- Type B blood can be donated to type B and type AB recipients.
- Type AB blood can only be donated to type AB recipients.
- Groups with type AB blood can be recipients of all blood types.
- Groups with type AB blood are called universal recipients.
- Another blood type classification is Rh+ and Rh−.
- Types Rh+ or Rh− blood can be donated to type Rh+ recipients.
- Type Rh− blood can be donated only to type Rh− recipients.

PRACTICE QUESTIONS

1. What is the name of the cells that transport oxygen through the circulatory system?

    A) leukocytes

    B) thrombocytes

    C) arterioles

    D) erythrocytes

    Answers:

    A) Incorrect. Leukocytes are white blood cells that protect the body from bacteria, viruses, and other pathogens.

    B) Incorrect. Thrombocytes are cells sent to repair damaged vessels by clotting the blood.

    C) Incorrect. Arterioles are vessels that branch off from arteries.

    D) Correct. Erythrocytes are red blood cells that transport oxygen.

2. The tunica intima, tunica media, and tunica externa are layers of what structure(s)?

    A) heart

    B) arteries and veins

    C) capillaries

    D) purkinje fibers

    Answers:

    A) Incorrect. The endocardium, myocardium, and epicardium are the layers of the heart walls.

B) Correct. The tunica intima is the innermost layer, the tunica media is the middle layer, and the tunica externa is the outermost layer of arteries and veins.

C) Incorrect. Capillaries are thin, membranous vessels that move blood slowly.

D) Incorrect. Purkinje fibers cause impulses to spread through the myocardium.

3. What is the name of the fibrous sac that surrounds and protects the heart?

A) aorta

B) pericardium

C) pulmonary trunk

D) venous pump

Answers:

A) Incorrect. The aorta is the primary artery that receives blood from the heart.

B) Correct. The pericardium is also called the pericardial sac.

C) Incorrect. The pulmonary trunk extends upward from the heart and is part of the pulmonary circuit.

D) Incorrect. The venous pump is a valve system in veins.

Digestive System

All the functions of the digestive system occur in the **alimentary canal** that begins at ingestion and ends at excretion. The alimentary canal is also known as the **upper, middle, and lower gastrointestinal (GI) tract**. The upper GI tract performs ingestion, mechanical processing, and chemical digestion. The parts of this section are the **oral cavity, pharynx, esophagus**, and **stomach**. The middle GI tract is the **small intestine**, where the food particles digested in the upper GI tract are transported through intestinal walls for absorption into the blood and lymphatic vessels. The lower GI tract is the **colon**, where the indigestible remainder is transported, stored, and excreted.

Throughout the alimentary canal are important valves called **sphincters**. A sphincter is a circular muscle in the body that contracts to close a passage and relaxes to open the passage. The sphincters associated with the alimentary canal are the **upper esophageal** at the junction of the pharynx and esophagus, the **lower esophageal** at the junction of the esophagus and stomach, the **pyloric** at the junction of the stomach and small intestine, the **sphincter of Oddi** at the junction of the ileum and accessory organ ducts, the **ileocecal** at the junction of the small intestine and the colon, and the **internal anal** and **external anal** sphincters that open and close to control fecal excretion.

The **oral cavity**, better known as the mouth, uses the **teeth** to masticate food by cutting and grinding. The **tongue** is rough to grip food and move masticated food toward the pharynx. **Salivary glands**, considered an accessory organ, secrete saliva used to form a masticated lump called a **bolus**. There are three sets of salivary glands in the mouth. The digestive function of the mouth is a mechanical process and, also, the start of the chemical digestion of starches, fats, and carbohydrates.

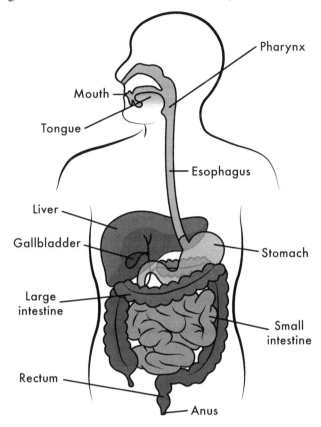

Figure 4.3. The Digestive System

The **pharynx** is the anatomical word for *throat*. It is a muscular tube used by the digestive system to transport the bolus to the esophagus. The respiratory system also uses the pharynx to transport air.

The **esophagus** is a muscular tube that connects the pharynx to the stomach. The upper esophageal sphincter opens to accept the bolus from the pharynx. To prevent regurgitation, the lower esophageal sphincter closes after the bolus has passed to the stomach.

The **stomach** is located on the left side of the abdominal cavity. The bolus is further broken down in the stomach using hydrochloric acid and digestive enzymes. It becomes a semifluid mass called **chyme** that is passed to the small intestine through the pyloric sphincter where it is further digested.

The **small intestine** transports digested food particles through intestinal walls for absorption into the blood and lymphatic vessels. The small intestine is about 10 feet of coiled muscular tubing with an internal surface of ridges and folds. To enhance the absorption process, small fingerlike projections called **villi** line the small intestine. Villi are attached to blood vessels sending the nutrients directly into the bloodstream. When digested food leaves the small intestine, 90 percent of the nutrients have been extracted. The small intestine has three sections. The horseshoe-shaped **duodenum** is the section where enzymes and bile are delivered from the liver, gallbladder, and pancreas. The duodenum controls entry of the enzymes and bile by opening and closing the **sphincter of Oddi**. Second, in the center section, is the **jejunum**, where most of the nutrients are absorbed. The villi are larger, the walls are thicker, and the passage narrower. Third, the final section is the **ileum**. It contains clusters of lacteals (lymph capillaries) to enhance fat absorption. The ileocecal sphincter is where digested materials pass from the ileum to the **colon**.

The colon's primary purpose is to transport, store, and excrete the indigestible material passed from the small intestine. The colon begins with the **cecum**, where digested material is received from the ileum. The cecum moves the digested material into the **large intestine**, which is divided into four colon sections. The **ascending colon** leads upward on the right side to the **transverse colon**; this crosses to the left into the **descending colon**, which leads downward on the left side. The final section is the **sigmoid colon**, which connects the large intestine to the **rectum**, where waste is stored before it is excreted. The stored waste is passed through to the **anal canal**; finally the colon ends at the **anus**, where excretion occurs.

The digestive system also uses **accessory organs** that produce and then deliver fluids that assist with the digestion process:

+ salivary glands—located in the oral cavity
+ liver
+ gallbladder
+ pancreas

The liver is the largest *internal* organ in the body. It is located in the upper-right quadrant of the abdominal cavity and has many important functions in the body. The digestive purpose of the liver is to produce **bile**, an emulsifier that breaks apart large fat globules. Once produced, it is stored in the gallbladder, which is a small organ located inferior and posterior to the liver. The gallbladder sends stored bile to the duodenum section of the large intestine. The pancreas is a glandular organ located behind the stomach that produces an enzymatic juice that breaks down carbohydrates, fats, and proteins. This juice is delivered to the duodenum via ducts. The pancreas also serves a purpose in the endocrine system.

PRACTICE QUESTIONS

1. Where does the alimentary canal begin and end?
   A) It begins at the oral cavity and ends in the large intestine.
   B) It begins in the pharynx and ends at the anus.
   C) It begins at the oral cavity and ends at the anus.
   D) It begins in the stomach and ends at the anus.

Answers:

A) Incorrect. It does begin at the oral cavity; the large intestine is a part of the alimentary canal but not the end.

B) Incorrect. The pharynx is a part of the alimentary canal but not the beginning; it does end at the anus.

C) Correct. The oral cavity is where ingestion begins and the anus is where excretion occurs.

D) Incorrect. The stomach is a part of the alimentary canal but not the beginning; it does end at the anus.

2. What part(s) of the alimentary canal makes up the middle gastrointestinal tract?

   A) small intestine
   B) the stomach
   C) the esophagus and the stomach
   D) small intestine and the colon

Answers:

A) Correct. The small intestine is the only part of the middle gastrointestinal tract.

B) Incorrect. The stomach is part of the upper gastrointestinal tract.

C) Incorrect. The esophagus and the stomach are both part of the upper gastrointestinal tract.

D) Incorrect. The small intestine is correct but the colon is the lower gastrointestinal tract.

3. What is the digestive purpose of the liver?

   A) absorption
   B) peristalsis
   C) form a bolus
   D) produce bile

Answers:

A) Incorrect. Absorption is one of the functions of the digestive system.

B) Incorrect. Peristalsis is a series of muscular contractions that move digested food.

C) Incorrect. A bolus is a masticated lump formed using saliva.

D) Correct. Bile is an emulsifier produced by the liver to break apart large fat globules.

ENDOCRINE SYSTEM

Hormones are commonly known as **chemical messengers**. The four most common types of hormones are **steroids** that alter cell activity, **peptides** that alter cell metabolism, **biogenic amines** that serve as neurotransmitters, and **eicosanoids** that alter smooth muscle contractions.

When hormones are released into the bloodstream, they seek out **target cells**. Each hormone has its own target cell and will bind to receptor molecules on that cell. The way the hormone attaches depends on whether it is **water soluble** or **lipid soluble**. If the hormone binds to receptor molecules *on* the target cell, causing a reaction inside the cell, it is water soluble. If the hormone binds to receptor molecules *inside* the cell's nucleus, controlling the function of the cell, it is lipid soluble.

There are three mechanisms that control the level of hormones secreted into the bloodstream. **Negative feedback** occurs when the amount of a hormone in the bloodstream is communicated back to the endocrine gland that secretes it. If levels are low, the gland will produce more. If levels are high, the gland will cut back on its production of that hormone. **Hormonal control** is when one hormone stimulates or inhibits the release of another hormone. **Neural control** is when secretion of hormones is affected by nerve stimulation. Of the three mechanisms, neural control is the fastest.

There are eight glands of the endocrine system: the **pituitary**, **pineal**, **thyroid**, **parathyroid**, **thymus**, **adrenals**, **pancreas**, and **gonads**.

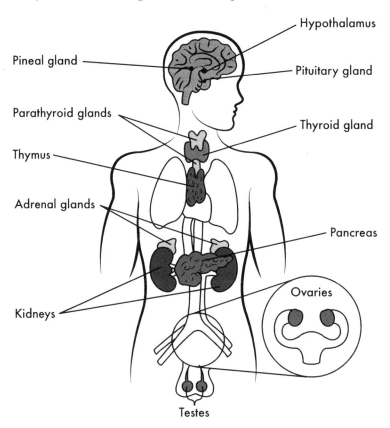

Figure 4.4. The Endocrine System

The pituitary gland is connected to the brain's hypothalamus. It is positioned in a small depression in the sphenoid bone. It has two lobes, the **posterior lobe** and the **anterior lobe**. Seventy-five percent of the pituitary gland is the anterior lobe. The brain's hypothalamus prompts the anterior lobe to release, and inhibit its release of, hormones. The anterior pituitary produces six hormones. The **thyroid-stimulating hormone (TSH)** stimulates the thyroid to produce hormones. The **adrenocorticotropic hormone (ACTH)** stimulates the adrenal cortex, located on the outer portion of the adrenal glands, to produce hormones. **Follicle-stimulating hormone (FSH)** ensures proper functioning of the ovaries and testes. **Luteinizing hormone (LH)** with FSH ensures proper functioning of the ovaries and testes. **Human growth hormone (HGH)** stimulates growth, repair, and reproduction. **Prolactin (PRL)** stimulates milk production in mammary glands. The posterior lobe is not glandular tissue but rather nervous tissue. The hypothalamus produces two hormones that the posterior pituitary stores and releases. They are **oxytocin**, which triggers uterine contractions during childbirth and the release of milk during breastfeeding, and **antidiuretic hormone (ADH)**, which increases water reabsorption in the kidneys.

The pineal gland is pinecone shaped, located behind the brain's thalamus, and active only in low light or darkness. It only produces one hormone, **melatonin**, which helps to regulate the circadian rhythm.

The thyroid gland is located at the base of the neck. It produces three hormones. **Calcitonin (CT)** aids in the absorption of calcium into bone matrix, decreases blood calcium ions, and stimulates osteoblasts. **Triiodothyronine (T3)** regulates growth and development, metabolism, body temperature, and heart rate. **Thyroxine(T4)** performs the same functions as T3 but is not as potent.

The parathyroid gland produces the **parathyroid hormone (PTH)**, which breaks down bone matrix to increase blood calcium ions and stimulates osteoclasts.

The thymus gland is located in the mediastinal region of the thorax and reaches its maximum size in puberty. After puberty, the thymus begins to shrink in size and by adulthood it largely consists of adipose tissue. The thymus gland is also part of the lymphatic system. The thymus produces two hormones, **thymosin** and **thymopoietin**, both of which help train and develop T lymphocytes during fetal development and childhood.

The adrenal glands are located above the kidneys. They have two layers, the **cortex** and **medulla**. The cortex layer produces three hormones. **Cortisol** helps to control how the body uses fats, proteins, and carbohydrates; suppresses inflammatory reactions; and helps to regulate the immune system. **Aldosterone** regulates sodium and potassium levels and helps maintain blood volume and pressure. **Androgen**, a subset of androgenic hormones, is a steroid that is weakly produced by the adrenal cortex and released into the bloodstream. It assists in the development of secondary sex characteristics primarily in males. The medulla layer produces two hormones that respond in high-stress situations that are perceived as dangerous and threatening, commonly referred to as *fight-or-flight* situations. **Epinephrine** stimulates vasoconstriction and increases blood pressure, heart rate, cardiac output, and blood glucose levels. It is also known as adrenaline. **Norepinephrine** maintains the stress response of epinephrine.

The pancreas is located behind the stomach and also has an important role in the digestive system. It is considered a heterocrine gland because it contains both endocrine and exocrine tissue. However, the endocrine cells make up only 1 percent of the pancreas. These cells are found only in small groups named **islets of Langerhans**. There are two endocrine cells, **alpha** and **beta**, each producing a hormone. **Glucagon** is produced by alpha cells and raises blood glucose levels. **Insulin** is produced by beta cells and lowers blood glucose levels.

Gonads produce sex hormones. Female gonads are the ovaries and male gonads are the testes. The gonads produce three hormones. **Progesterone**, a female hormone, is most active during ovulation and pregnancy. **Estrogen**, another female hormone, triggers the development of female secondary sex characteristics such as breasts and pubic hair. **Testosterone**, a male hormone, triggers the development of male secondary sex characteristics such as beard growth and voice deepening.

PRACTICE QUESTIONS

1. Sweat, salivary, mammary, sebaceous, and mucous are what type of glands?

    A) hormonal

    B) exocrine

    C) negative feedback

    D) endocrine

Answers:

    A) Incorrect. There are no hormonal glands.

    B) Correct. Exocrine glands have ducts and do not feed directly into the bloodstream.

    C) Incorrect. Negative feedback is a mechanism that controls hormonal levels.

    D) Incorrect. Endocrine glands are ductless and secrete hormones directly into the bloodstream.

2. Which of the following is NOT a mechanism that controls hormone levels?

    A) hormonal control

    B) Islets of Langerhans

    C) neural control

    D) negative feedback

Answers:

    A) Incorrect. Hormonal control is one of three mechanisms that control hormone levels.

B) **Correct.** Islets of Langerhans are small groups of endocrine cells found in the pancreas.

C) Incorrect. Neural control is one of three mechanisms that control hormone levels.

D) Incorrect. Negative feedback is one of three mechanisms that control hormone levels.

3. The pineal gland produces what hormone?

A) melatonin

B) cortisol

C) calcitonin

D) human growth hormone

Answers:

A) **Correct.** Melatonin helps to regulate the circadian rhythm.

B) Incorrect. Cortisol is produced by the cortex layer of the adrenal glands.

C) Incorrect. Calcitonin is produced by the thyroid gland.

D) Incorrect. Human growth hormone is produce by the anterior pituitary gland.

INTEGUMENTARY SYSTEM

The skin has three separate and distinct layers:

+ epidermis: top layer
+ dermis: middle layer
+ hypodermis: deepest layer

The **epidermis** is made up of mostly avascular **epithelial tissue**. Two primary cell types are in this layer: **keratinocytes**, which produce the protein **keratin** that water-proofs and protects, and **melanocytes**, which produce **melanin**. Melanin provides UV protection and determines skin pigment. The epidermis has five levels. The deepest is the **stratum basale**, also known as the stratum germinativum. The stratum basale is held in place by a **basement membrane**. This membrane is permeable to allow nutrients to be filtered through from the more vascular lower layers. From the stratum basale, cells move upward through the **stratum spinosum**, a bonding and transitional layer nicknamed the prickly layer, to the **stratum granulosum**. In the stratum granulosum, keratinocytes become granulized and begin to die. The next layer up, the **stratum lucidum**, is not present in all people or may only be present in areas such as the hands and feet, where the skin is often thicker. The outermost layer of the epidermis is the **stratum corneum**, which only contains dead cells that flake off continuously.

The dermis is commonly considered the true skin. Capillaries feed blood to this layer that is primarily **collagen** and some adipose tissue. Collagen is a group of structural proteins found not only in the skin, but also in ligaments, blood vessels, and bone. The dermis also contains **elastin fibers**. Elastin is a protein that functions like elastic—meaning, after it is stretched and pulled, it returns to its original shape. Elastin is also found in the arteries and lungs. Collagen and elastin give skin its resiliency and elasticity. The dermis contains two types of glands. **Sudoriferous glands** excrete sweat. Their primary role is to reduce body temperature and remove waste products. The **sebaceous glands** produce sebum, an oily substance that lubricates and waterproofs the skin and hair.

The hypodermis is a subcutaneous tissue layer that separates the dermis from the underlying tissues and organs. Consisting primarily of adipose tissue, it absorbs shock and provides thermal insulation.

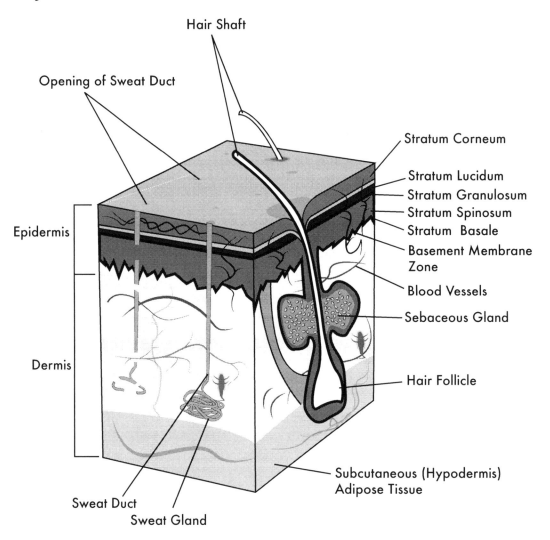

Figure 4.5. The Skin

Hair follicles are small tube-shaped craters contained in the epidermis layer that encloses them. However, the follicle does extend down into the dermis layer where it is nourished. Hair follicles are developed in the womb and, after birth, no new hair follicles are formed. The human body has follicles that number in the millions. The shape of the follicle determines the hair texture (i.e., curly or straight) and is genetically determined. At the base of the hair follicle is a connective tissue structure named the **hair papilla**. It is nipple shaped and is where the **hair bulb** or **root** affixes itself. The hair papilla is vascular and nourishes the bulb. The **hair shaft**, a strand of hair, rises up through the follicle and is considered living. Once it emerges out of the follicle and becomes visible to the eye, it is considered dead. Small muscles called **arrector pili** hold each follicle in place.

Fingernails and toenails grow out of the dermis layer. They have several parts. The **nail plate** is the most visible part of the nail and, comparable to the hair shaft, primarily dead. The **nail bed** refers to the skin underneath the nail plate. The **nail root** is where nail growth begins, comparable to the hair root. The **nail matrix**, a layer of cells, sits underneath the nail root. It is a vascular layer that nourishes the nail root, contains nerves, and populates with keratinocytes. **Nail folds** are where the lateral and proximal edges of the nail meet the skin. The **eponychium**, more commonly known as the cuticle, is in direct contact with the nail matrix and root, providing a waterproof seal. The **lunula**, the only living part that is visible, is the whitish crescent moon shape at the proximal end. Any change or distortion in the shape or coloring of the lunula may be an indication of an underlying health issue. In comparison to toenails, fingernails grow much more rapidly.

The skin contains nerve receptors that are stimulated by the surrounding environment and the perceived activity in that environment. This data is routed to the central nervous system. These receptors are located in different layers. In the epidermis layer, **Merkel's discs** are superficial and respond to sustained pressure and perceive texture, and **free nerve endings** respond to temperature and pain. In the dermis layer, **Meissner's corpuscles** are superficial and highly sensitive to light touch and vibration, and **Ruffini's end organs** respond to continuous touch and pressure. In the hypodermis layer, **Krause's corpuscles** respond to light pressure and vibration, and **Pacinian corpuscles** respond to quick, fleeting touch and vibration (more specific information on vibration and the skin's response is found below in *Joints*, and in chapter 6, *Massage and Its Benefits*).

When the epidermis and dermis of the skin are broken, leaving a wound, there are four phases the skin goes through to heal itself:

1. inflammatory
2. epithelialization
3. proliferative
4. remodeling

The inflammatory phase begins immediately and may last up to twenty-four hours. When the initial trauma occurs, vasoconstriction causes a decrease in blood flow in an attempt to prevent excessive blood loss; this is called **hemostasis**. However, within five to ten minutes, vasodilation occurs as leukocytes, thrombocytes, and other healing aids are rushed into the area. Inflammation is identified as a change in the skin's coloring, usually the result of the increase in blood flow to the injured area, the sensation of heat, the visual appearance of swelling, pain, and possibly some loss of function. Also during the inflammatory phase a scab will begin to form, which is caused by the drying of the clotting agents.

The epithelialization phase is when a temporary protective barrier is formed to keep out bacteria and other pathogens. This barrier is formed by keratinocytes and small proteins called **cytokines**, which regulate the immune responses. In the proliferative phase, the wound begins to fill in with new tissue that forms a lining in the bed of the wound, allowing a scar to form. Also initiated in the phase is a process of **angiogenesis**, the formation of new blood vessels.

The remodeling phase is when the healing process is completed. Scar tissue formed in the proliferative phase changes in appearance from a pinkish red to a pale, whitish patch. These four stages occur, generally, over a ten-day period. The appearance of the scar may take days to years to diminish, depending on the severity of the wound. A **keloid** scar is the result of an overgrowth of scar tissue and can actually be larger than the original wound area. Keloids are raised and may not diminish; they are usually hereditary.

Factors that can slow the healing process are:

+ aging
+ chronic illness
+ suppressed immune system
+ reduced sensation in the skin (i.e., neuropathy)
+ some medications (i.e., steroids, blood thinners)
+ cancer treatments
+ inadequate nutrition
+ stress
+ repeated trauma to the wound site

This discussion of the wound-healing process pertains to **acute** wounds. However, another type of wound is a **chronic** wound. A chronic wound is the result of repeated trauma, continued pressure, ischemia, and illness. Primarily there are three categories of chronic wounds. First, **venous ulcers** usually occur in the lower legs as a result of weakened veins and damaged or ineffective venous flaps or valves. Second, **diabetic ulcers** are most commonly on the feet and usually the result of peripheral neuropathy, arterial disease, and bone malformation. All three of these causes are more common in those with type 1 or type 2 diabetes. Third, **pressure ulcers** are primarily the result of pressure preventing blood flow to an area. These most commonly occur in people who are bedridden and who aren't moved or repositioned on a consistent basis.

Finally, a note on burns. Burns are classified in degrees. A **first-degree** burn is generally considered minor and only affecting the epidermis. Pain and redness result but recede relatively quickly. Some dryness and peeling may occur as the burn heals over a seven-to-ten-day period. A **second-degree** burn affects both the epidermis and the dermis. One or more blisters form and extreme redness and soreness may occur. It can take several weeks to heal and the skin pigment may be altered for months, years, or a lifetime. A skin graft may be required. A **third-degree** burn penetrates all three layers and pain may be diminished or nonexistent as the result of nerve damage. This type of burn results in severe and deep scarring that can affect movement and lead to other health concerns. Surgical intervention may be required at some point. A **fourth-degree** burn may be diagnosed if the damage reaches tendon and bone.

PRACTICE QUESTIONS

1. What is the purpose of melanin in the epidermis?

A) waterproof and protect

B) produce sebum

C) produce collagen

D) provide UV protection and determine skin pigment

Answers:

A) Incorrect. Waterproofing and protection are the purposes of keratin.

B) Incorrect. Sebum is produced by the sebaceous glands.

C) Incorrect. Collagen is a group of structural proteins found throughout the body and makes up most of the dermis layer.

D) Correct. Melanin is produced by melanocytes.

2. Which is the INCORRECT statement related to hair follicles?

A) They are contained in the epidermis.

B) Hair follicles are formed continuously during a lifetime.

C) The human body has hair follicles that number in the millions.

D) Hair follicles are held in place by arrector pili.

Answers:

A) Incorrect. Hair follicles are contained in the epidermis but are nourished by the dermis layer.

B) Correct. Hair follicles are developed in the womb. After birth, no new follicles are developed.

C) Incorrect. The human body does have millions of hair follicles.

D) Incorrect. Arrector pili are small muscles. Each hair follicle is held in place by one of these muscles.

3. What occurs in the proliferative phase of wound healing?

A) Vasodilation of blood vessels occurs.

B) A temporary protective barrier is formed.

C) A scar forms.

D) The healing process is completed.

Answers:

A) Incorrect. Vasodilation occurs in the inflammatory phase so healing aids can be rushed to the wound site.

B) Incorrect. A temporary protective barrier is formed during the epithelialization phase.

C) Correct. In the proliferative phase, the wound begins to fill in with new tissue that forms a lining in the bed of the wound, allowing a scar to form.

D) Incorrect. The healing process is completed in the remodeling phase.

LYMPHATIC SYSTEM

The primary lymphatic structures are **bone marrow** and the **thymus**. These are considered primary because they produce and mature **lymphocytes**, the white blood cells of the lymphatic system. Lymphocytes increase in number in response to infection and can be broken down into two subcategories: **B Lymphocytes**, which stay in the bone marrow and mature, and **T Lymphocytes**, which travel to the thymus and then mature. Bone marrow is located in the hollow cavities of bone. The thymus gland, as already discussed in the *Endocrine System* subsection, is located in the mediastinal region of the thorax. It reaches its maximum size in puberty; it then begins to shrink in size and by adulthood it largely consists of adipose tissue. The thymus gland is also part of the endocrine system. Also present in lymph are **phagocytes**, which are cells that engulf and devour cell pathogens and debris in a process referred to as phagocytosis. **Secondary lymphatic structures**, discussed below, are populated with lymphocytes and phagocytes.

Lymph nodes are bean-shaped structures located along the path of the lymphatic vessels. They collect and filter lymph. Their purpose is to destroy bacteria, viruses, and other foreign substances in the lymph before it is returned to the blood. Lymph flows into the nodes via **afferent lymphatic vessels** to be filtered and cleansed, and **efferent lymphatic vessels** transport the lymph out of the nodes. To allow more time for the lymph-cleansing process, the system has fewer efferent lymphatic vessels. The most superficial nodes are the cervical nodes in the neck, axillary nodes in the armpit, and inguinal nodes in the groin region. Clinically and diagnostically, these nodes are the easiest to palpate.

The **spleen** is the largest lymphatic organ. It is located in the upper left portion of the abdominal cavity beneath the diaphragm and behind the stomach. It is purplish in color. The spleen plays multiple supporting roles in the body. It acts as a blood filter by destroying old and damaged red blood cells but, at the same, salvages from those cells what can reused—for example, iron. Platelets and lymphocytes are stored there. The spleen also helps fight certain kinds of bacteria that cause pneumonia and meningitis. The spleen only has afferent lymphatic vessels.

The **tonsils** are lymph tissue partially encapsulated in mucous membrane. The tonsils are a group of lymph nodules that form a protective ring around the throat. Best known to laypersons are the palatine tonsils located on both sides in the back of the throat. Tonsils are a defense against bacteria and viruses entering through the mouth and nose.

Peyer's patches are nodules found in the mucous membrane of the small intestine. Peyer's patches monitor intestinal bacteria populations and prevent the growth of pathogenic bacteria.

The **vermiform appendix** is located in the lower-right quadrant of the abdomen near where the small and large intestines meet. It is medically questionable whether it serves any modern purpose in human evolution. It *may* assist the digestive system with healing.

Once lymph has been cleansed it returns to the venous bloodstream via **lymphatic trunks** that feed into one of two ducts. The **right lymphatic duct** drains lymph from the right arm, right trunk, and right side of head into the right subclavian vein. The **thoracic duct** is the largest of the two ducts. It drains the majority of the lymph in the body into the left subclavian vein. The **cisterna chyli**, a dilated sac located in the lower abdomen and lumbar region, collects lymph draining from the abdomen and lower body and transports the lymph to the thoracic duct.

PRACTICE QUESTIONS

1. What is NOT a function of the lymphatic system?

A) It drains excess interstitial fluid.

B) It transports fats and fat-soluble vitamins.

C) It transports and distributes gases.

D) It aids the immune system.

Answers:

A) Incorrect. Excess interstitial fluid from body tissues is drained by the lymphatic system.

B) Incorrect. Fat and fat-soluble vitamins from the digestive tract are transported by the lymphatic system.

C) Correct. Transporting and distributing gases is a function of the circulatory and respiratory systems.

D) Incorrect. The immune system relies heavily on the lymphatic system.

2. What are the bean-shaped structures in the lymphatic system?

A) lymph nodes

B) Peyer's patches

C) tonsils

D) lymphatic trunks

Answers:

A) **Correct.** Lymph nodes are located all along the lymphatic vessels.

B) Incorrect. Peyer's patches are nodules found in the small intestine.

C) Incorrect. Tonsils are a group of lymph nodules.

D) Incorrect. Lymphatic trunks feed cleansed lymph into one of two ducts.

3. Which is the largest of all the secondary lymphatic structures?

A) vermiform appendix

B) cisterna chyli

C) thymus

D) spleen

Answers:

A) Incorrect. The vermiform appendix is located in the lower-right quadrant of the abdomen.

B) Incorrect. The cisterna chyli is a dilated sac that collects lymph.

C) Incorrect. The thymus is a primary lymphatic structure.

D) **Correct.** The spleen plays multiple supporting roles in the body.

Muscular System

Muscle is a collection of connective tissues that encase and attach to each other. **Epimysium** surrounds a muscle and contains blood vessels and nerves. Underneath epimysium is **perimysium**, which covers bundles of muscle fibers called **fascicles**. Note that, because muscle cells are long and thin, they can be referred to as muscle fibers. **Endomysium** covers an individual muscle fiber. A single muscle fiber consists of:

+ sarcolemma, a cell membrane
+ sarcoplasm, a muscle cell cytoplasm
+ sarcoplasmic reticulum, a network of muscle cells
+ t-tubules, narrow tubes
+ myofibrils, bundles of protein filaments
+ sarcomeres, bundles of myofibrils in parallel rows

The *t* in t-tubules stands for *transverse*. Viewed microscopically, a sarcolemma will have t-tubules traversing or wrapping around it like rings on a finger. The myofibrils are covered with sarcoplasmic reticulum and can be either *thin* filaments of **actin** or *thick* filaments of **myosin**. Both actin and myosin filaments aid in muscle contraction. Myosin is easily identifiable because it appears as small heads with elongated tails. Actin resembles a twisted double strand of beads covered with two types of protein molecules, **troponin** and **tropomyosin**. These molecules regulate the interaction of actin and myosin during muscle contraction. Sarcomeres, responsible for muscle contraction, have many parts:

+ I Band, thin filaments
+ M Line, thick filaments
+ H Zone, thick filaments
+ A Band, thick filaments with an overlap of thin filaments
+ Z Line, marks the boundary between adjacent sarcomeres
+ zone of overlap, thin and thick filaments overlap each other

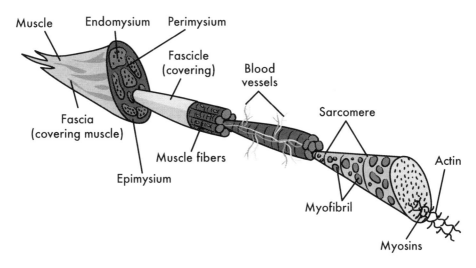

Figure 4.6. Muscle Structure

Each neuron synapse attaches or anchors to a muscle fiber. This meeting of the synapse and muscle fiber is called the **neuromuscular junction**. Contraction of skeletal muscle tissue occurs when actin and myosin filaments slide past each other, causing the sarcomere to shorten. This means that individual filaments do not change length themselves, but overlap each other to shorten the sarcomere. This is called the **sliding filament theory of muscle contraction**. There are multiple steps that occur from inception of the muscle contraction back to a resting state.

At rest, the myosin filaments have **adenosine diphosphate (ADP)** and **phosphate molecules** attached at the end of each myosin head. When ADP and phosphate molecules become energized they form **adenosine triphosphate (ATP)**. When a muscle needs to move, it communicates with the central nervous system, resulting in instructions sent to a neuron; this is defined as an **action potential**. Calcium is released from the sarcoplasmic reticulum. These molecules bind with the troponin molecules, causing tropomyosin molecules to move, revealing myosin attachment sites on the actin myofilaments. The single phosphate attached to the myosin heads gets released as the heads move to connect with the attachment sites on the actin, forming a **cross bridge**. The remaining ADP molecule is brushed off with a **power stroke**, when the myosin heads pull the actin inward. Once the ADP attachment is exhausted, the ATP molecules attach themselves to the myosin heads. These molecules trigger the release of the myosin heads from the actin attachment sites and are broken down into ADP and a single phosphate as the heads move back into a resting position. This is called the **recovery stroke**. If calcium is still present, the cycle will repeat again and the sarcomere will continue to shorten until the calcium ions are transported back into the sarcoplasmic reticulum and the muscle relaxes.

Skeletal muscle will be further discussed in the kinesiology section of this chapter.

PRACTICE QUESTIONS

1. What does endomysium cover?
    A) an individual muscle fiber
    B) bundles of muscle fibers
    C) an entire muscle
    D) fascicles

    Answers:
    A) **Correct.** An individual muscle fiber is surrounded by endomysium.
    B)   Incorrect. Bundles of muscle fibers are surrounded by perimysium.
    C)   Incorrect. A muscle is surrounded by epimysium.
    D)   Incorrect. Fascicles are bundles of muscle fibers.

2. What type of muscle contracts in order to move and push the contents of an organ?
    A) cardiac
    B) neuromuscular
    C) skeletal
    D) smooth

    Answers:
    A)   Incorrect. The cardiac muscle's function is to pump blood.
    B)   Incorrect. There is no muscle type named *neuromuscular*.
    C)   Incorrect. Skeletal muscle produces skeletal movement.
    D) **Correct.** Smooth muscle surrounds hollow internal organs.

3. What wraps around a sarcolemma like a ring on a finger?
    A) I band
    B) t-tubules
    C) zone of overlap
    D) myosin

Answers:

A) Incorrect. I bands are thin filaments on sarcomeres.

B) Correct. The *t* in t-tubules stands for *transverse*.

C) Incorrect. The zone of overlap is where thin and thick filaments overlap each other.

D) Incorrect. Myosin is a type of myofibril.

NERVOUS SYSTEM

The brain and spinal cord are in the central nervous system (CNS). The CNS contains neural tissue, connective tissue, and blood vessels and is protected by **meninges** and **cerebrospinal fluid**. Meninges are connective tissue membranes that have three layers: **pia mater**, **arachnoid**, and **dura mater**. The *pia mater* (in Latin, *tender mother*) is the innermost layer. It adheres to the surface of the brain and spinal cord. The arachnoid is the middle layer and is web-like in appearance. The *dura mater* (in Latin, *tough mother*) is the outermost layer. Cerebrospinal fluid is a clear, colorless liquid that surrounds the brain and spinal cord. It is a lubricant, shock absorber, and helps maintain pressure in the cranium. Portions of the brain are protected by **a blood-brain barrier** that keeps blood and cerebrospinal fluid separated for the purpose of keeping blood-borne pathogens out while at the same time allowing essential molecules needed by the brain to penetrate the barrier.

The peripheral nervous system (PNS) contains cranial and spinal nerves, bundles of axons, connective tissue, and blood vessels. The PNS is further broken down into the:

✦ somatic nervous system (may be referred to as visceral)

✦ autonomic nervous system

The somatic nervous system (SNS) controls voluntary and involuntary skeletal muscle contractions. The autonomic nervous system (ANS) controls subconscious glandular secretions and contractions of the cardiac muscle and smooth muscles. The ANS is further divided into the **sympathetic nervous system** that stimulates—*fight or flight*—and the **parasympathetic nervous system** that relaxes—*rest and digest.*

The nervous system includes all the neural (nerve) tissue found in the body. The two primary cells in the nervous system are **neuron cells**, which send and receive stimuli, and **neuroglia** (glial cells), which support and protect neurons. A typical neuron structure contains a **nucleus** that stores DNA, a **cell body** that houses the nucleus, fingerlike branches named **dendrites** that extend from the cell body, an **axon**, which is a long extension (like a tail) away from cell body that carries electrical signals, and a **synapse**, located on the distal end of the axon. Nerves are bundles of neuron axons. Axons can be **myelinated** or **unmyelinated**. Myelinated axons are fully wrapped to insulate and unmyelinated axons, while they do have insulation, are only partially wrapped. Signals that travel down axons are referred to as **nerve impulse conduction**. Signals conducted down axons that are myelinated are called **saltatory** and are faster. Signals conducted down axons that are unmyelinated are called **continuous** and are slower. Myelinated axons have gaps called **nodes of Ranvier**. The signal of a myelinated axon jumps from node to node, which is why the signal moves faster.

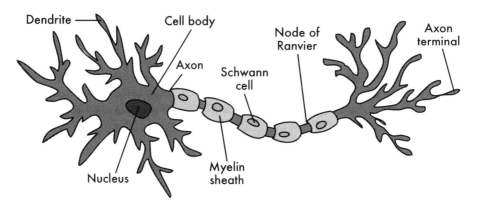

Figure 4.7. Neuron

The nervous system has many **sensory receptors** that detect changes in the external and internal environment of the human body. Sensory receptors are associated with touch, pressure, temperature, and pain. Another category of nervous system receptors is **special senses**. The special senses perceive stimuli from the external environment through smell, taste, vision, and hearing. There are two types of nerves: **afferent** and **efferent**. Afferent nerves receive sensory information and send this information to the brain. The brain processes and coordinates this information and responds with a motor signal to efferent nerves that lead to peripheral muscles and glands in the PNS. This cycle works by sending electrical signals through axons to synapses that emit neurotransmitters into the **synaptic cleft**. The synapse emitting the **neurotransmitter** (to be discussed later in this section) is called **presynaptic** and the synapse receiving or absorbing the neurotransmitter is called **postsynaptic**. The cleft is the space between the pre- and post-synapse.

During nerve transmission and muscle contraction, the **sodium-potassium pump** goes into action. Inside a cell membrane there is a high concentration of potassium ions and a low concentration of sodium ions. This concentration makes the intracellular membrane negatively charged. Outside the cell membrane there is a low concentration of potassium ions and a high concentration of sodium ions. This concentration makes the extracellular area positively charged. This balanced concentration of ions is in a **polarized** or resting state. When a stimulation occurs, extracellular sodium ions are able to permeate the cell membrane, causing the inside charge to change from negative to positive. This concentration of ions inside the cell membrane is now in a **depolarized** state. Meanwhile, the concentration of sodium ions outside the cellular membrane has decreased, causing the extracellular area's charge to change from positive to negative. This is **reverse polarization**. Back inside the membrane ion channels open, allowing potassium ions to flow out, and returning the intracellular and extracellular environments to a resting state. This is **repolarization**.

Neuroglia preserve the physical and biochemical structure of neural tissue and are essential to survival and function of neurons. There are six types of neuroglia: (1) **Astrocytes** maintain the blood-brain barrier. (2) **Ependymal cells** line the spinal canal and ventricles of the brain. (3) **Microglia** destroy pathogens in the central nervous system. (4) **Oligodendrocytes** protect myelin in the central nervous system. (5) **Satellite cells** surround the cell body in the peripheral nervous system. (6) **Schwann cells** insulate neurons in the peripheral nervous system.

The human body has dozens of neurotransmitters in multiple categories that perform various functions. Presented here are key neurotransmitters that work within the nervous system. **Acetylcholine** stimulates muscle contraction. **Dopamine** is related to attention and learning and an imbalance can affect motion. **Endorphins** are pain inhibitors and associated with positive emotions and sensations. **Epinephrine** is a stimulating product of dopamine. **Gamma-aminobutyric acid (GABA)** plays a role in the sodium-potassium pump function. **Glutamate** is a stimulator and is important for memory and learning. **Histamine** stimulates vasodilation. **Norepinephrine** affects attention and consciousness and maintains body temperature. **Serotonin** is a vasoconstrictor and affects emotional state.

On average, the weight of the brain in a human adult is three pounds. It contains approximately one hundred million neurons. Its regions are the **cerebrum**, **cerebellum**, **diencephalon**, and the **brain stem**. The following text breaks out each region into more detail.

The **cerebrum** is the largest region of the brain. It is divided into right and left hemispheres that are connected by the **corpus callosum**. The corpus callosum provides a communication pathway between the two hemispheres. The hemispheres mirror each other having the same four lobes. The **frontal lobe** is related to motor output and cognitive functions such as emotional expression, problem-solving, risk assessment, and language. The **parietal lobe** receives input from skin and muscle. The **temporal lobe** is related to auditory and olfactory input. The **Wernicke's area** of the temporal lobe is important for recognizing speech and interpreting words. The **occipital lobe** receives visual input. The primary visual cortex of the occipital lobe takes input from the retina. The occipital lobe is also important for reading and writing comprehension.

The **cerebellum** is located inferior to the cerebrum's occipital and parietal lobes and, like the cerebrum, has two hemispheres. It regulates motor movements that affect posture, balance, and coordination.

The **diencephalon** is in the center of the brain and houses the **thalamus** and **hypothalamus**. The thalamus makes up 80 percent of the diencephalon. It relays sensory information to and from the cerebral cortex, which covers the outer portion of the cerebrum. The hypothalamus governs the pituitary gland that is connected to it. Another gland housed in the diencephalon is the pineal gland. (Note that the hypothalamus, pituitary gland, and pineal gland are discussed in the endocrine system section.)

The **brain stem** connects the spinal cord to the brain and is divided into the **midbrain** and the **hindbrain**. The midbrain relays auditory and visual information.

The hindbrain contains the cerebellum, **pons**, and **medulla oblongata**. The medulla oblongata controls heart rate, breathing, and blood pressure. The pons coordinates movement and connects the medulla oblongata to the cerebellum.

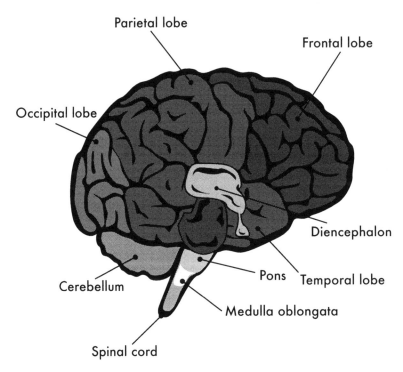

Figure 4.8. The Brain

The **reflex arc** is a neural pathway that controls the reflex response. Normally, when an afferent neuron is stimulated, it routes the information to the brain via an interneuron, also referred to as a relay neuron, in the spinal cord. However, a reflex arc response causes the interneuron to relay an immediate response to a motor neuron, allowing the body to respond more quickly. Thus, while the brain still processes the message delivered, the response is not delayed. For a reflex to occur, stimulation is required, only one or a few neurons are involved, the response is involuntary, and the response occurs the exact same way every time. Types of reflexes are the **withdraw reflex** (i.e., touching something hot), the **innate reflex** people are born with (e.g., sucking), and the **acquired or learned reflex** developed as people grow and develop muscle memory (e.g., a boxing punch or playing an instrument). Reflexes occur in the somatic and autonomic divisions of the PNS. The **somatic reflexes** are related to skeletal muscles. Somatic reflexes are also referred to as myotatic and stretch reflexes. An example of a somatic reflex is when a doctor strikes the patellar tendon with a reflex hammer. **Autonomic reflexes** are related to smooth and cardiac muscles, glands, and adipose tissue. Autonomic reflexes maintain homeostasis. Two examples of an autonomic reflex are the heart beating and pupils' response to dim versus bright light.

Table 4.1. Cranial Nerves

I	olfactory	smell
II	optic	vision
III	oculomotor	movement of eyes and eyelids; regulates pupils and focus
IV	trochlear	eye movements
V	trigeminal	sensory detection in face and head; chewing
VI	abducens	eye movements
VII	facial	expressions, taste, production of saliva
VIII	vestibulocochlear	hearing; balance and equilibrium
IX	glossopharyngeal	taste, swallowing, production of saliva
X	vagus	speech and swallowing
XI	accessory	movement of head and shoulders; speech; swallowing
XII	hypoglossal	tongue movement

PRACTICE QUESTIONS

1. What is the blood-brain barrier?

  A) one of the layers of the meninges

  B) surrounds the cerebrospinal fluid

  C) keeps blood and cerebrospinal fluid separated

  D) another name for the central nervous system

Answers:

  A) Incorrect. The three layers of the meninges are the pia mater, arachnoid, and dura mater.

  B) Incorrect. Meninges protect the brain and spinal cord.

  C) **Correct.** The blood-brain barrier separates blood and cerebrospinal fluid.

  D) Incorrect. The central nervous system consists of the brain and spinal cord.

2. Neurotransmitters are spilled into what aspect of the synapse?

  A) postsynaptic

  B) presynaptic

  C) nodes of Ranvier

  D) synaptic cleft

Answers:

A)   Incorrect. This aspect absorbs neurotransmitters.

B)   Incorrect. This aspect emits neurotransmitters.

C)   Incorrect. Nodes of Ranvier are gaps on myelinated axons.

D)   Correct. The synaptic cleft is located between the pre- and post-synapse.

3.   What is NOT a region of the brain?

A)   cerebrum

B)   cerebellum

C)   neuroglia

D)   diencephalon

Answers:

A)   Incorrect. The cerebrum is the largest region of the brain.

B)   Incorrect. The cerebellum regulates motor movements.

C)   Correct. Neuroglia are cells that support and protect neurons.

D)   Incorrect. The diencephalon houses the thalamus and hypothalamus.

REPRODUCTION

Fertilization is the joining of an ovum and spermatozoon resulting in a **zygote**. Males and females have **gonads**. In the male, the gonad is called a **testis** (plural: *testes*) and in

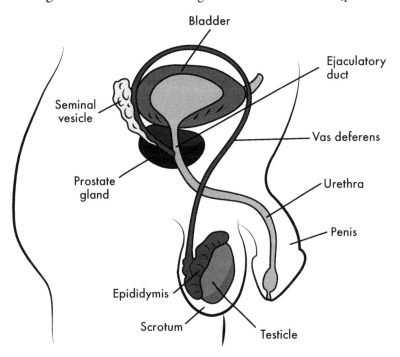

Figure 4.9. The Male Reproductive System

the female, the gonad is called an **ovary**. Males are born with two testes and females are born with two ovaries. Mature male testes are located on the exterior body and each testis is contained in a **scrotal sac**, also referred to as a **scrotum**.

The components of the male reproductive system are the testes, where sperm are produced; a series of ducts and tubes that route the sperm through the system; accessory glands and organs that contribute the fluid referred to as **semen**; and **external genitalia**, consisting of the **penis** and scrotum.

Each testis has an **epididymis** located on its posterior border. The sperm are delivered from the testis to the epididymis where they are stored. Sperm are transported from the epididymis to the **vas deferens** (also referred to as the ductus deferens), a small muscular tube that goes around the rear of the bladder and feeds into an **ejaculatory duct**. Both ejaculatory ducts pass through the **prostate gland** on the way to the urethra and finally the penis, where ejaculation occurs. The urethra serves the dual purpose of receiving both semen and urine.

Sperm and semen are not synonymous. Semen refers only to the fluid itself, not the sperm in it. **Seminal vesicles** contribute 60 percent of fluids. The prostate gland contributes 20 to 30 percent of fluid, and **bulbourethral glands** contribute about 10 percent. Male ejaculate contains 2 to 5 milliliters of fluid containing 20 to 100 million sperm per liter. The role of semen is to protect, nourish, lubricate, and deliver the sperm to the vagina; once there, semen also neutralizes the acidic environment of the vagina.

The components of the female reproductive system include the ovaries, **fallopian tubes** (these may also be referred to as uterine tubes), a **uterus**, and the **vaginal canal**.

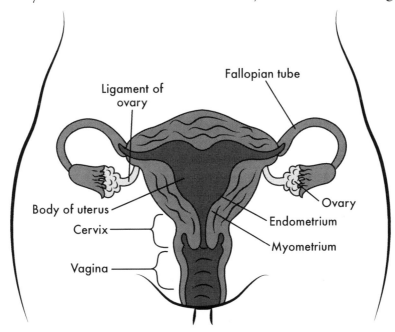

Figure 4.10. The Female Reproductive System

All females are born with immature eggs called **oocytes**. The quantity a female is born with is her lifetime supply. An oocyte matures into an ovum inside a follicle that is located on the outside of the ovary. During each monthly reproductive cycle, a woman's ovaries develop several follicles, each containing a maturing oocyte; however, generally only one is released to travel down the fallopian tube. This is the process of **ovulation**. As a woman ages, the quality and genetic stability of each oocyte begins to degrade. This results in the possibility of pregnancy lessening as she moves into her thirties and forties.

The ovulatory process occurs over a twenty-eight-day period. Days one through thirteen are considered **pre-ovulatory**, day fourteen is generally considered the day of ovulation, and day fifteen through twenty-eight are considered **post-ovulatory**. On the day of ovulation, the egg is released from one of the ovaries' follicles and travels down the fallopian tube. If it becomes fertilized by a sperm, it will move into the uterus to develop. If the egg is not fertilized, it will either disintegrate and get reabsorbed back into the body or be ejected with the menstrual flow.

While many hormones play an important role in reproduction, they are discussed in the endocrine system section. However, for the purpose of this section, it is a good idea to know some of the roles some hormones play in the pre-ovulatory period, during ovulation, and in the event of pregnancy. First, estrogen levels increase when oocytes begin maturing in the follicles to encourage the layer of the uterus, called the **endometrium**, to thicken and become more richly supplied with blood in the event pregnancy does occur. Second, luteinizing hormone levels rise to assist with the maturation of the oocyte into an egg, trigger ovulation, and stimulate the secretion of progesterone. Third, progesterone thickens the endometrium, preparing it for pregnancy and, if a woman becomes pregnant, it inhibits uterine contractions, hinders the development of follicles so no new oocytes are matured, and creates a barrier in the vagina to deter sperm movement.

PRACTICE QUESTIONS

1. What do seminal vesicles contribute?

A) 20 to 30 percent of semen

B) 10 percent of semen

C) They are the sole source of sperm.

D) 60 percent of semen

Answers:

A) Incorrect. Twenty to thirty percent of semen comes from the prostate gland.

B) Incorrect. Ten percent of semen comes from bulbourethral glands.

C) Incorrect. Sperm is produced in the testes.

D) Correct. Most semen is made up of fluid from the seminal vesicles.

2. What is one of the primary roles of estrogen in reproduction?

A) assist with the maturation of oocytes

B) richly supply the endometrium with blood

C) create a barrier in the vagina to deter sperm

D) trigger ovulation

Answers:

A) Incorrect. Luteinizing hormone assists with the maturation of oocytes.

B) **Correct.** Estrogen keeps the endometrium richly supplied with blood in the event of pregnancy.

C) Incorrect. Progesterone creates a barrier to deter sperm movement after pregnancy occurs.

D) Incorrect. Luteinizing hormone triggers ovulation.

RESPIRATORY

The **air conduction pathway** begins when inhaled air is pulled through a **right** and **left nostril** inside the nose. Each nostril leads to a nasal cavity that sits behind and above the nose. The **frontal**, **sphenoidal**, **ethmoidal**, and **maxillary** sinuses are air spaces that open into the nasal cavity, helping to regulate pressure. The nostrils, nasal cavity, and sinuses are lined with mucous membranes that contain blood capillaries, microscopic hairs called **cilia**, and **goblet cells** that produce mucus. As air passes through these areas it is warmed, moistened, and pathogens are filtered out. The pharynx, commonly referred to as the throat, is a muscular tube used by the respiratory system to transport air. The digestive system also uses the pharynx to transport food. Air then passes over the **larynx**, the anatomical word for voice box, which contains the vocal cords that vibrate as air passes, producing sounds and speech.

The **trachea**, commonly referred to as the *windpipe*, is covered by a lid-like piece of cartilage called the **epiglottis**. This lid keeps food and liquid being ingested from entering the trachea. The trachea has a number of *c*-shaped rings called **hyaline cartilage** that keep the trachea from collapsing and blocking air flow. As the trachea extends down into the thoracic cavity, it bifurcates into the right and left **bronchi**. The two bronchi further branch into **bronchioles** that spread throughout each lung. The lungs fill most of the thoracic cavity but weigh less than 1 pound each. The right lung has three lobes and the left lung has two lobes. The left lung is smaller to accommodate the space needed for the heart muscle. At the end of each bronchiole are **alveolar sacs**. Each sac contains two or more alveoli. There are literally millions of alveoli in adult lungs.

The respiratory diaphragm is a dome-shaped muscle that separates the thoracic cavity from the abdominal cavity. The mechanics of breathing involve **pulmonary ventilation** by **inspiration** (inhaling) and **expiration** (exhaling). The movement of air into and out of the lungs is because of a pressure gradient between the lungs and the atmosphere. Inspiration occurs when the pressure within the alveolar sacs falls below the atmospheric pressure, resulting in air entering the lungs. During inspiration, the diaphragm contracts and descends into the abdominal cavity, and the external inter-costal muscles contract to raise the ribs, giving the lungs room to expand. The greatest volume of air that can be pulled into an individual's lungs is called **vital capacity**. Expiration occurs when the pressure in the alveolar spaces exceeds the atmospheric pressure, resulting in air being blown from the lungs. During expiration, the diaphragm relaxes and ascends into the thoracic cavity.

The relationship between the respiratory system and the circulatory system takes place with the exchange of gases. (It may be helpful to review the discussion of the pulmonary circuit in the circulatory system section.) **External respiration** refers to the process in the lungs in which oxygen is transmitted in the alveoli to blood capillaries that lead to the pulmonary vein; in exchange, carbon dioxide from the pulmonary artery is transmitted to the blood capillaries and into the alveoli. The exchange of gases between the blood and body tissues is referred to as **internal respiration**.

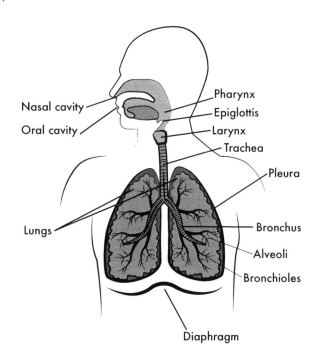

Figure 4.11. The Respiratory System

PRACTICE QUESTIONS

1.   What is commonly referred to as the voice box?

   A)   trachea

   B)   pharynx

   C)   larynx

   D)   frontal sinus

Answers:

A)   Incorrect. The trachea is commonly referred to as the windpipe.

B)   Incorrect. The pharynx is commonly referred to as the throat.

C)   Correct. The larynx contains the vocal cords that vibrate as air passes.

D)   Incorrect. The frontal sinus is one of the air spaces that open into the nasal cavity.

2. What are c-shaped rings?

A) the epiglottis

B) alveolar sacs

C) cilia

D) hyaline cartilage

Answers:

A) Incorrect. The epiglottis is a lid-like piece of cartilage that covers the trachea.

B) Incorrect. Alveolar sacs are located at the end of each bronchiole.

C) Incorrect. Cilia are microscopic hairs in the upper respiratory system.

D) Correct. The trachea has a number of c-shaped rings that keep the trachea from collapsing.

3. Which describes the respiratory diaphragm?

A) During expiration, the diaphragm contracts.

B) During inspiration, the diaphragm relaxes.

C) The diaphragm separates the thoracic cavity from the abdominal cavity.

D) The respiratory diaphragm contains millions of alveoli.

Answers:

A) Incorrect. During expiration, the diaphragm relaxes.

B) Incorrect. During inspiration, the diaphragm contracts.

C) Correct. The diaphragm separates the thoracic cavity from the abdominal cavity.

D) Incorrect. Alveoli are found in the lungs.

SKELETAL

There are five types of connective tissue used to build and maintain bones: **osseous, cartilage, ligaments, periosteum**, and **bone marrow.**

Osseous can be **cancellous (spongy)** or **cortical (compact)**. Spongy tissue is lightweight with a lattice appearance and is highly vascular. Compact tissue is hard and dense. For instance, the scapula's external surface is compact tissue and has cancellous tissue inside. (For more discussion of the scapula, see below.)

Cartilage is found throughout the body. It is firm but flexible. It is avascular, so nutrients need to be diffused into it.

Ligaments are fibrous and elastic. They are bone-to-bone attachments, contain collagen proteins, and are partially avascular. They support and protect joints.

Periosteum is a tough connective tissue membrane that wraps around and protects the bone, except for the articular surfaces of the bone. It contains vessels and nerves and is where osteoblasts (bone-forming cells) are created.

Bone marrow is soft and spongy and lies in the **medullary cavity** of long bones. Marrow is either red or yellow. The red marrow produces red and white blood cells and platelets. The yellow is fat cells. Marrow is highly vascular. From birth until early childhood, most marrow is red. In adults the marrow is about a fifty-fifty mix. The process of producing blood cells is called **hematopoiesis**.

There are 206 bones in the human body. Each bone is put in one of five classifications:

+ long
+ short
+ flat
+ sesamoid
+ irregular

Long bones have a length that greatly exceeds their width. The femur and humerus are two examples of long bones. The shaft of a long bone is called the **diaphysis** and the bulbous ends are the **epiphysis**. In immature long bones, between the diaphysis and the epiphysis is the **epiphyseal (growth) plate**. In mature bones this area diminishes and becomes the visible **epiphysis line**. This area is also referred to as the **metaphysis**. Long bones house bone marrow in the medullary cavity.

Short bones are shaped roughly like a cube and generally are as wide as they are long. These bones provide support and stability with little movement. The carpals of the wrist and the tarsals of the ankle are examples of short bones.

Flat bones serve as muscle attachment sites and protectors of internal organs. Two examples are the scapula and the occipital bone, one of the bones that form the cranium. The scapula is an attachment site for the rotator cuff muscles, and the cranium, of course, protects the brain. In *adult* humans, flat bones produce the largest quantity of red blood cells. Their surface is compact bone with spongy bone in between.

Sesamoid bones are small, roundish bones that are embedded in a tendon to provide greater protection and support. These bones actually grow out of the connective tissue of the tendon. The kneecap (embedded in the quadriceps tendon) is the largest sesamoid bone, and the pisiform in the wrist is embedded in the flexor carpi ulnaris tendon.

Irregular bones are bones that do not meet the requirements of the other classification of bones. The vertebrae, sacrum, and mandible are classified as irregular. These bones serve as anchor points and nerve protectors.

There are two skeletal regions of the human body: **axial** and **appendicular**. The axial region consists of the bones located in the cranium, vertebral column, ribs, and sternum. The appendicular region consists of the bones that make up the **pectoral (shoulder) girdle**, the **pelvic girdle**, and the limbs.

The shoulder girdle structure consists primarily of the **clavicle** and the **scapula**. The clavicle articulates with the manubrium forming the sternoclavicular joint. The scapula articulates with the clavicle forming the acromioclavicular joint and, also, articulates with the humerus, forming the glenohumeral joint.

The pelvic girdle structure consists primarily of the fusion of the ischium, ilium, and pubis bones. These three bones together are known commonly as the hips. Where the hips articulate with the femur is called the acetabulofemoral joint.

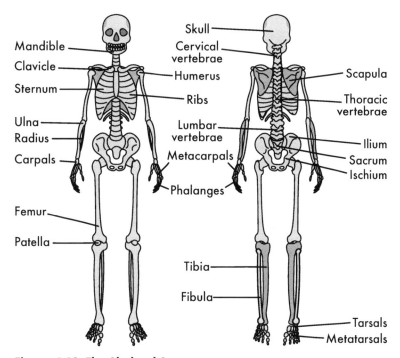

Figure 4.12. The Skeletal System

Bones go through a **remodeling process** throughout their lifetime. This process involves:

+ osteoblasts—form new bone
+ osteoclasts—breakdown bone
+ osteocytes—mature bone cells

Osteoblasts are found in the periosteum and form a bone matrix made up mostly of collagen. This process of building new bone is called **ossification**. Ossification can be:

+ intramembranous—bone forming from membrane
+ intracartilaginous—bone forming from cartilage

Gravitational force, exercise, and injury signal to the body to release the calcitonin hormone. This release signals to osteoclasts to begin breaking down the bone for remodeling. The broken-down bone becomes mineralized and is pulled into the bloodstream. This is called **reabsorption**. An osteocyte results when an osteoblast becomes embedded in the bone matrix. The highest quantity of osteocytes is found in mature adult bones and can last a lifetime. Generally, in the elderly, osteoclasts break down bone faster than the osteoblasts rebuild bone, making the bone more porous. This is called **osteoporosis**. It is important to reiterate that exercise plays a huge role in bone remodeling. When one puts demands on the bones with exercise, the resulting remodeled bone is stronger. This benefits both the bone and the attached muscles, tendons, and ligaments.

All bones have distinguishing features referred to as **bony landmarks**. These landmarks are important because they serve as attachment sites for muscles, tendons, and ligaments. Knowing bony landmarks is beneficial to a massage therapist, as well as to other medical and clinical professionals, because they are often easily palpated. For example, the spine of the scapula is easily palpated. The benefit of knowing this bony landmark is that one can determine where the supraspinatus and the infraspinatus muscles are located on a client or patient. The following is a list of types of bony landmarks with descriptions and examples.

Table 4.2. Bony Landmarks

Type	Description	Example
angle	formed by two diverging lines	The lateral and medial borders of the scapula form the inferior angle.
border	the edge of a bone	The scapula has lateral and medial borders.
condyle	a rounded prominence at the end of a bone to facilitate articulation	The lateral distal end of the femur is a condyle.
crest	prominent elevation	One prominent elevation is the iliac crest.
epicondyle	a condyle above a condyle (like the epidermis is above the dermis)	Tennis elbow, in orthopedic terminology, is lateral epicondylitis.
facet	guides and limits motion; a joint	Vertebrae have multiple facets.
foramen	hole in a bone for nerves or vessels to pass through	One foramen is the obturator foramen of the pelvis.
fossa	shallow depression in bone	The iliac fossa are visible shallow depressions.
groove	shallow indentation	A muscle tendon may lie within a groove to keep it on track, such as the long head of the biceps brachii.
head	rounded end on a bone	The fibular head meets the lateral condyle of the tibia.
line	narrow, less prominent than a crest	the epiphysis line on long bones
meatus	opening or canal	One example of a meatus is the outer to inner ear passage.

Type	Description	Example
notch	indentation	Notches are very visible between clavicles at the base of the neck.
process	outgrowth of bone from a larger body	One example is the xiphoid process.
protuberance	bulge	A protuberance can be felt by placing a thumb on the external occipital bone.
ramus	arm or branch of a bone	The mandibular ramus can be felt from under the ear down to the angle.
ridge	raised margin or border	One example is the temporal ridge, where the temporal and parietal bones meet.
spine	narrow, slender projection	dorsal surface of scapula; supraspinatus (above the spine) fossa and infraspinatus (below the spine) fossa
trochanter	large process found only on femur, *greater trochanter*	The trochanter of the femur articulates at the acetabulofemoral joint.
tubercle	small, rounded nodule or projection	The greater tubercle on humerus is where the teres minor, supraspinatus, and infraspinatus attach.
tuberosity	large, rounded projection	ischial tuberosity, *a pain in the butt*

Skeletal **articulations (joints)** are where two bones come together but are not necessarily movable. There are three classifications of joints:

+ synarthrotic—immovable
+ amphiarthrotic—slightly movable
+ diarthrotic—freely movable

An example of synarthrotic joints are the sutures resulting from the fusing of the frontal, parietal, temporal, and occipital bone. An example of an amphiarthrotic joint is the pubic symphysis where the right and left pubic bones meet.

The diarthrotic joints, also known as the synovial joints, are either:

+ monoaxial—elbow and knee
+ biaxial—wrist
+ triaxial—shoulder or hip

Diarthrotic joints are the most movable but also, as a result, the weakest. In other words, to gain movement, strength must be compromised. There are many structures associated with diarthrotic joints. The **articular capsule** encloses the joint like a sleeve. **Synovial fluid**, a viscous fluid, provides nutrition, lubrication, and shock absorption. The **synovial membrane** secretes synovial fluid. The **joint cavity**, located between the articulating bones, is filled with synovial fluid. A fluid-filled pocket, called **bursae**, contains synovial fluid allowing tendons and ligaments to rub against each other.

Diarthrotic joints allow the following actions to occur:

Table 4.3. Joint Actions

Action	Description	Example
abduction	movement away from the body	while standing erect, moving arms straight out from sides until horizontal
flexion	decreasing the angle of	with arms still horizontal and palms facing the ceiling, bending the elbows
extension	increasing the angle of	returning the elbows to a straight horizontal position
circumduction	a circular movement distally while the joint stays relatively fixed	with arms extended horizontally, rotating from the shoulders to make circles
adduction	movement toward the body	returning arms from extended horizontal position back to sides
supination	lateral rotation of the forearm	extending arms in front of oneself with palms touching and rotating forearms until palms face the ceiling
pronation	medial rotation of the forearm	extending arms in front of oneself with palms touching and rotating forearms until palms face the floor
plantar flexion	extension of the ankle	sitting on the floor with legs extended and extending the ankles until toes point
dorsiflexion	flexing the foot	with toes still pointed, flexing the feet until toes face upward toward the ceiling
inversion	elevation of the medial edge of the foot	with feet in a relaxed, slightly flexed position, turning the feet until the soles face each other
eversion	elevation of the lateral edge of the foot	returning feet back to a relaxed, slightly flexed position, turning the soles outward
rotation	lateral and medial movement	Unlike circumduction, rotation is not a complete circle. Turning the head to look over the left shoulder is a lateral rotation of the head. Returning the head back to face forward is a medial rotation.
elevation	raising a body part	raising the shoulders up toward the ears to elevate the scapula
depression	lowering a body part	dropping the shoulders back down to lower the scapula
protraction	forward movement	moving the jaw until the bottom teeth are in front of the top teeth
retraction	backward movement	moving the jaw until the bottom teeth are behind the top teeth

PRACTICE QUESTIONS

1. Which statement about types of connective tissue is NOT correct?

   A) Osseous tissue is bone that is considered dead.

   B) Cartilage is firm but flexible.

   C) Ligaments are fibrous and elastic.

   D) Bone marrow is soft and spongy and found in the medullary cavity of long bones.

   Answers:

   A) **Correct.** Osseous tissue is highly vascular, not dead.

   B) Incorrect. Cartilage is firm but flexible and found throughout the body.

   C) Incorrect. Ligaments are fibrous and elastic and are a bone-to-bone attachment.

   D) Incorrect. Marrow is soft and spongy and is a mix of red and yellow in adults.

2. What is the benefit of a massage therapist knowing bony landmarks?

   A) They are endangerment sites and should be avoided.

   B) They can be very painful to a client if pressure is put on them.

   C) They can be easily palpated.

   D) They can indicate if a client is developing osteoporosis.

   Answers:

   A) Incorrect. Endangerment sites are related to arteries, veins, and body organs.

   B) Incorrect. Pain related to pressure generally indicates muscle and soft tissue tenderness.

   C) **Correct.** Knowing the location of prominent bony landmarks can help locate muscle sites.

   D) Incorrect. Osteoporosis is a diagnosis made by a physician.

3. What is hematopoiesis?

   A) a blood disease

   B) part of a long bone

   C) the process of producing blood cells

   D) a condition that occurs when bone becomes more porous

   Answers:

   A) Incorrect. Hematopoiesis has nothing to do with diseases of the blood.

   B) Incorrect. There is no long bone part named the hematopoiesis.

   C) **Correct.** Blood cells are produced in the marrow.

   D) Incorrect. That condition is osteoporosis.

Primarily it is the lymphatic system that is most closely associated with the functions of the immune system, but it is not the only system that provides immune response. There are two types of immune responses: **innate** and **adaptive**.

The innate response uses tools and structures in different body systems, such as the integumentary, digestive, and respiratory. It is a rapid response system that occurs within four hours of invasion. It includes the skin, mechanical washing, mucous membranes, hydrochloric acid, cilia, mechanical expulsion, and phagocytes. For example, when the skin is breached, immune cells lying in the dermis of the skin will recognize an invader and route it to the lymphatic system. Mechanical washing occurs when a person chews. Mucous membranes, in the upper digestive tract, trap and destroy pathogens. The stomach contains hydrochloric acid that will destroy pathogens that have made it that far into the digestive process. Cilia, in the upper respiratory system, push and move away pathogens, keeping them from getting into the lungs. Mechanical expulsion occurs in the form of sneezing and coughing. Phagocytes, white blood cells in the blood and lymph, recognize, ingest, and destroy pathogens.

The adaptive response uses the lymphatic system. It is a slow and highly selective response that can take up to ninety-six hours. When a new invader is recognized by a T lymphocyte (T cell), it will communicate instructions to a B lymphocyte (B cell) to begin producing antibodies. This communication occurs when the T cell attaches itself to the B cell. When a B cell receives instructions, it matures into a plasma cell that becomes an *antibody-producing machine* specific to that one invading organism. These become memory cells that will recognize an invader immediately.

There are many influences that may have an effect on the development and maintenance of the immune system and a person's predisposition to an allergic response. Genetic influences begin at conception and prenatal influences may affect fetal immune development. An infection not properly treated *may*, in the near or distant future, negatively impact the immune system. The hygiene hypothesis suggests that birth order plays a role in determining frequency of exposure to pathogens and antigens being developed. For example, a third child may be exposed to more pathogens than a first child is, and thereby develops more antigens early in life. The type or place of occupation may result in overexposure to a pathogen to which a person has a genetic predisposition, and can result in an allergic reaction at some point. This can include anything—for example, latex, rug fibers, or wheat gluten. The geographical habitat where someone is born and raised may affect the development and multitude of antibodies. Examples include growing up in a low-population area versus a high-population area or a desert environment versus a multi-seasonal environment. Finally, the aging process requires careful maintenance to keep a healthy immune system.

The immune system is not necessarily without fault. Microbes can outsmart the immune system and multiply. Worn-out and mutant cells, if not disposed of properly by the immune system, can result in cancer growth. A hyperactive response to a nontoxic substance can result in inflammation, itching, and general discomfort. Finally, **autoimmune diseases**, when immune cells attack themselves, can develop. There are many autoimmune pathologies. This is an active topic of research that is generally theorizing multiple mechanisms that create an autoimmune response.

According to the National Institutes of Health:

> Autoimmune diseases can affect almost any part of the body, including the heart, brain, nerves, muscles, skin, eyes, joints, lungs, kidneys, glands, the digestive tract, and blood vessels.
>
> The classic sign of an autoimmune disease is inflammation, which can cause redness, heat, pain, and swelling. How an autoimmune disease affects you depends on what part of the body is targeted. If the disease affects the joints, as in rheumatoid arthritis, you might have joint pain, stiffness, and loss of function. If it affects the thyroid, as in Graves' disease and thyroiditis, it might cause tiredness, weight gain, and muscle aches. If it attacks the skin, as it does in scleroderma/systemic sclerosis, vitiligo, and systemic lupus erythematosus (SLE), it can cause rashes, blisters, and color changes.
>
> Excerpt from National Institute of Arthritis and Musculoskeletal and Skin Diseases, March 2016, NIH Publication No. 16-7582.
www.niams.nih.gov

PRACTICE QUESTIONS

1. Which of the following is considered an internal foreign invader?

A) viruses

B) fungi

C) cellular debris

D) parasites

Answers:

A) Incorrect. Viruses are considered pathogens that attempt to enter the body.

B) Incorrect. Fungi are considered pathogens that attempt to enter the body.

C) Correct. Cellular debris is what remains of broken-down cells.

D) Incorrect. Parasites are considered pathogens that attempt to enter the body.

CONTINUE

2. How are autoimmune diseases defined?

A) as a genetic influence

B) an allergic reaction

C) a result of the hygiene hypothesis

D) when immune cells attack themselves

Answers:

A) Incorrect. Genetic influences begin at conception.

B) Incorrect. Allergic reactions result from an overexposure to a pathogen.

C) Incorrect. The hygiene hypothesis suggests that birth order affects the development of the immune system.

D) Correct. Immune cells attacking themselves results in an autoimmune disease.

URINARY

The kidneys are a pair of bean-shaped glandular organs. They are positioned in the posterior abdominal cavity against the deep low back muscles. They extend from the lower thoracic rib cage to the third lumbar vertebra. The kidneys filter out waste from blood, route the filtered blood to be reabsorbed, and route the waste to be converted

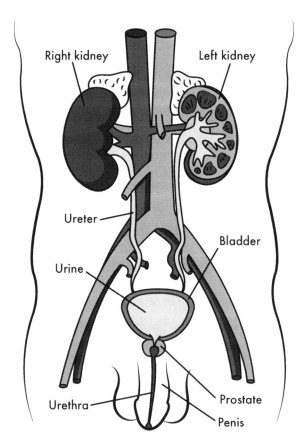

Figure 4.13. The Urinary System

into urine. These functions are performed using millions of structures called **nephrons.** The internal structures of the nephron receive blood through afferent arterioles which passes into clusters of capillaries called **glomeruli** through an absorption process powered by blood pressure. The resulting fluid is called **filtrate.** Ninety-nine percent is reabsorbed into efferent arterioles to continue on in the blood circulatory system. The remaining 1 percent contains toxic waste consisting of organic materials, ions, and by-products of things ingested by the body, such as medications. The removal of waste is important to the maintenance of blood pH. This waste travels through renal tubules and ultimately becomes classified as **urine.**

The **ureters** are tubes that extend from each kidney and transport urine into the urinary bladder. The urinary bladder is located in the pelvis and stores the urine. As the bladder fills, receptors in the bladder walls communicate the urge to urinate. The **urethra** receives the urine from the emptying bladder and **urination** occurs.

PRACTICE QUESTIONS

1. When does urination occur?
   A) when the urethra receives the urine
   B) when urine reaches the bladder
   C) when ureters receive the urine
   D) after the kidneys filter out waste

   Answers:
   A) **Correct.** When the urethra receives urine, urination occurs.
   B.) Incorrect. The bladder empties into the urethra.
   C) Incorrect. The ureters are tubes that route urine from the kidneys to the bladder.
   D) Incorrect. Urine passes through the ureters and bladder before urination occurs.

2. How is the urge to urinate communicated?
   A) when waste is classified as urine
   B) when the ureters transport urine in the urinary bladder
   C) by receptors in the bladder walls
   D) when blood pH is out of balance

   Answers:
   A) Incorrect. Once waste is classified as urine, it needs to reach the bladder before the urge to urinate occurs.
   B) Incorrect. Ureters only transport.

C) Correct. Once the bladder fills, receptors in the bladder wall communicate the urge to urinate.

D) Incorrect. While removal of waste is important to the maintenance of blood pH, it has nothing to do with communicating the urge to urinate.

Energy Body

What has been discussed in this chapter is based on scientific approaches to the study of the human body and its systems. Studies that have been performed in laboratories, through cadaver dissection to identify and name body systems and functions, and evidence-based approaches to assessment, diagnosis, and treatment have resulted in what is defined as **Western** or **allopathic medicine**.

The concept of the energy body has its roots in what is referred to as **Eastern medicine**. Eastern medicine has always been approached as a way of treating not just the physical body, but the emotional and spiritual body as well. It is referred to as a holistic approach to assessment, diagnosis, and treatment. The Eastern medicine approach takes into account the human body inside and out, the visual and vibrational environment that surrounds it, the food we eat, and the air we breathe.

Science, especially in the field of quantum physics, has established that we and the world we live in are, at the core, a field of energy particles and waves. Now being viewed as worthy of scientific study, many types of approaches in Eastern medicine and the use of energy techniques have been incorporated in many hospital, clinical, long-term care, and hospice settings. They are commonly referred to as **complementary and alternative medicine (CAM)**. The rest of this section will focus on the Eastern medicine practices of traditional Chinese medicine and Ayurveda, the energy body, and light touch energy practices.

Traditional Chinese medicine (TCM) is a method of diagnosing and treating illness that is thousands of years old. In TCM the body is assessed in order to keep the body healthy rather than only treated when a sickness develops. There are five beliefs that define TCM. First, it is a philosophy, not a science. Second, there is no division among body, mind, and spirit. Third, illness is viewed as a disharmony in the whole body. Fourth, the goal is to create a balanced body, mind, and spirit. Fifth, it combines treatment of the body's emotions, mind, energy fields, and spirit to promote, maintain, and restore health. TCM uses, as assessment tools, these five steps:

+ looking—observation of demeanor
+ listening
+ smelling
+ asking—lifestyle, daily bodily functions, sensations (*the ten questions*)
+ palpation

TCM believes that elements create a healthy and balanced nourishing cycle. Called the **five elements theory**, the elements of water, wood, fire, earth, and metal need to be in balance. If any element becomes stronger or weaker, an imbalanced nourishing cycle will result. The cycle is described as water nourishes wood, wood fuels fire, fire produces earth, earth contains metal, metal collects water. Each element in the cycle represents a season and an event. Water represents winter, birth, and death. Wood represents spring and growth. Fire represents summer and fulfillment. Earth represents late summer and nurturing. Metal represents autumn and accumulation.

Qi, chi, ki, and prana are terms meaning **energy of the universe or life energy**. (Qi, pronounced, kēē, is the term that will be used in this discussion of TCM.) Qi is in and around everyone, and affects all the senses, tissues, and thoughts. Qi is the source of movement, governs smooth and harmonious transformation, and keeps the body's vital substances and organs in place. Qi comes from three sources: genetics, food, and air. Qi cycles through twelve primary **meridian channels** over a twenty-four-hour period. Meridian channels are defined as organs of physiological function that control the movement of blood, gas, air, and water in the body. Each channel peaks for a two-hour period during the cycle. The twelve meridians, listed below, will be discussed individually in greater detail later in this section.

+ lung
+ large intestine
+ stomach
+ spleen
+ heart
+ small intestine

+ bladder
+ kidney
+ pericardium
+ triple warmer
+ gallbladder
+ liver

To understand the concept of meridians, the theory of **yin/yang** must first be understood. Yin/yang is the belief that the mind, body, spirit, and the entire universe are interconnected and inseparable. The symbol, named *tai-ji*, is a common representation of the yin/yang theory. The curve in the middle represents transformation from one form to another, and the two small circles represent how each contains elements of the other. *Yin* means dark side of the mountain and *yang* means the sun side of the mountain.

In common terminology, these opposite words communicate the balancing aspect of yin/yang:

Table 4.4. Yin and Yang

Yin	Yang
quiet	loud
shady	bright
feminine	masculine
cold	hot
interior	exterior
lethargic	energetic

Meridian organs are either yin or yang with these identifying aspects:

Table 4.5. Aspects of Meridian Organs

Yin Organ Meridians	Yang Organ Meridians
solid	hollow
circulatory	digestive
qi travels from toe to chest or chest to finger	qi travels head to toe or finger to chest
may also be known as *zang*	may also be known as *fu*
lung	large intestine
spleen	stomach
heart	small intestine
kidneys	urinary bladder
pericardium	triple warmer
liver	gallbladder

A few other terms to know are **shen**, a spiritual force or gift from heaven that guides qi. **Jing** is inherited from parents and is defined as essence, a life force, a mover. Qi, shen, and jing are collectively called **the three treasures**.

Ayurveda is a health and treatment system that was derived and developed within India's Vedic culture. *Ayurveda* literally means life (*ayur*) knowledge (*veda*). It is a holistic approach to maintaining health and healing. The core beliefs in the Ayurvedic approach are that most illness begins during the digestive process and that negative emotions have a huge impact on health and well-being. In the Ayurvedic system, there are eight steps involved in a good health regimen. These steps are referred to as the **eight pillars**: first, a healthy daily routine; second, adapting seasonally; third, a healthy and positive mental and emotional environment; fourth, responding promptly to the body's functional needs (i.e., urination and evacuation); fifth, a balance of liquids and solids ingested into the body; sixth, eating on a schedule; seventh, adequate sleep; eighth, creating a healthy environment and avoiding caustic ones.

In the Ayurvedic system, a patient's **dosha**, or force, plays a primary role in assessment and treatment. There are three doshas and all individuals have aspects of all three; however, one dosha is always dominant. A practitioner of Ayurveda will use assessment tools to define a patient's dosha. Much like TCM, the assessment involves the practitioner's interpretation of what he or she sees, hears, and smells, and the questions the practitioner asks, especially related to diet and bodily functions. Once a patient's primary dosha is determined, the practitioner will treat with the goal of returning the person to a balanced state. Elements are also used in Ayurveda; however, they differ from those in TCM. They define how the dosha is formed. The elements are air, ether, fire, water, and earth. The following table lists each dosha with descriptors.

Table 4.6. The Doshas

Dosha Name	vata	pitta	kapha
Interpretation	wind	fire	earth
Formation	air and ether	fire and water	water and earth
Governs	movement	transformation	structure
Physique	tall and lean	medium build	short and stout
Related Systems and Functions	nervous system, circulation, digestion	metabolism, endocrine system, digestion	structure, bodily fluids
Eliminated Via	defecation	sweat	urine
In Balance	lively, creative, enthusiastic, energetic, changeable	disciplined, goal-oriented, warm, friendly, good leader	easygoing, supportive, stable, nurturing
Out of Balance	anxious, insomnia, dry skin, constipation, difficulty focusing	compulsive, irritable, indigestion, inflammation	sluggish, weight gain, sinus congestion

An Ayurvedic treatment plan will primarily involve dietary changes. However, multiple other techniques and methods may be incorporated, such as the use of herbs, massage techniques and strokes using dosha-related oils, meditation, and chakra balancing.

Chakras are considered energy channels in the body that function separately and together to maintain balance. This practice began in India. While different societies may have their own versions of chakra-balancing techniques, this discussion will focus on the basic seven chakras of the Indian tradition. Chakras relate to areas that run along the midline and are associated with organs, systems, and anatomical locations of the human body. The intention of this practice is to maintain healthy energy fields and return imbalanced energy fields to a harmony that aligns one mentally, physically, and spiritually. Each chakra is associated with a color that is formed by vibrational frequencies and wavelengths. Gemstones may also be incorporated as they are believed to carry vibrations that will assist with the balancing process. The following table lists and defines each chakra and its focus in the balancing process.

CONTINUE

Table 4.7. The Chakras

Chakra	Name	Location	Organs, Systems, and/or Regions	Color	Emotion
7th	crown	above the head	pineal gland, hair, central nervous system	violet	compassion, oneness
6th	third eye or brow	forehead	pituitary gland, hypothalamus, eyes, autonomic nervous system	indigo	visualization, intuition
5th	throat	notch between clavicles	thyroid, parathyroid, ears, neck, atlas, sinuses, upper respiratory system	blue	communication, creativity, self-expression
4th	heart	sternum between the breasts or nipples	thymus gland, lungs, heart, lymphatic and immune system	green	harmony, love, kindness, affection, compassion
3rd	solar plexus	between the xiphoid process and belly button	stomach, liver, small intestine	yellow	mental and spiritual energy, self-esteem, control
2nd	sacral	between the belly button and pubic symphysis	spleen, ovaries, uterus, adrenal glands, kidney, urinary tract	orange	sexuality, intimacy, passion
1st	root or base	the open area between the upper and mid-thighs	sex organs, perineum, coccyx, lower extremities	red	basic bodily needs, ground, stable, secure

Acupressure is a technique that is rooted in TCM. It is like acupuncture but, instead of needles, it relies on the fingers, palms, elbows, and feet to apply pressure to acupressure points. The goal is to release muscular tension, promote circulation, and free stagnant qi to restore health and balance.

Shiatsu originated in Japan in the early 1900s. The term *shiatsu*, translated to English, literally means finger (*shi*) pressure (*atsu*). Shiatsu is similar to TCM acupressure in several ways: the application of pressure to defined points on the body; sessions that include assessment, diagnosis, and treatment; and its reliance on the body's own power to heal. However, it differs from acupressure in that it only uses thumbs, palms, and fingers. Shiatsu points are called **tsubo (vital) points**, not acupressure points. The tsubo points are based more on anatomic locations and structures. Shiatsu also incorporates techniques defined with terms like shaking, hooking, plucking, patting, and brushing. The theory of shiatsu incorporates the belief that when the palm presses against the tsubo point, negative ions in the palm react with the positive calcium ions in the bloodstream. This exchange causes an increase in the calcium component in the bloodstream, in turn decreasing the potassium component that interferes with blood flow. The result is an increase in blood flow. (See chapter 6 for more information about shiatsu and other forms of massage.)

Using the hands to promote healing by correcting disturbances in energy fields in and around the body has roots not only in Eastern medicine but also in holistic nursing and osteopathy. Referred to as light touch therapies, energy healing is done with the intent to correct disturbances in the energy fields within and surrounding the body. Following is a list of some forms of light touch therapies:

- healing touch
- Jin Shin
- Jorei
- polarity therapy
- quantum touch
- Reiki
- therapeutic touch

PRACTICE QUESTIONS

1. The three treasures are related to which Eastern medicine practice?

    A) Ayurveda

    B) yin/yang

    C) shiatsu

    D) traditional Chinese medicine

    Answers:

    A) Incorrect. Ayurveda has no relationship to the three treasures.

    B) Incorrect. Yin/Yang is a belief that all things are interconnected and inseparable.

    C) Incorrect. Shiatsu is a treatment developed in Japan.

    D) Correct. Qi, shen, and jing are called the three treasures in traditional Chinese medicine.

2. Which term is NOT associated with Ayurveda?

    A) eight pillars

    B) life knowledge

    C) dosha

    D) acupressure points

    Answers:

    A) Incorrect. In Ayurveda, the eight pillars refer to eight steps related to a good health regime.

B) Incorrect. Ayurveda means life knowledge.

C) Incorrect. In Ayurveda, doshas play a part in assessment and treatment.

D) Correct. Acupressure points are related to traditional Chinese medicine practices.

3. Crown, sacral, and third eye are related to what Eastern medicine practice?

A) healing touch

B) chakra balancing

C) polarity therapy

D) acupressure

Answers:

A) Incorrect. Healing touch is a light touch therapy.

B) Correct. There are seven chakras that are considered energy channels.

C) Incorrect. Polarity therapy is a light touch therapy.

D) Incorrect. Acupressure is a practice that applies pressure to acupressure points.

The Meridians

This discussion of each meridian channel will begin with a description of each meridian channel's path from origin to termination. There are many different ways to describe and learn the path of each meridian channel.

 To remember the meridians, starting with the lung meridian channel, note the patterns and relationships between meridian channels:

circulation, digestion, digestion, circulation, circulation, digestion, digestion, circulation...

also,

yin, yang, yang, yin, yin, yang, yang, yin...

also,

3:00 a.m. – 5:00 a.m., 5:00 a.m. – 7:00 a.m., 7:00 a.m. – 9:00 a.m...

Table 4.8 is a summary of meridian channels ordered by peak time. In-depth explanations of the meridian channels follow in this section.

Table 4.8. Meridian Channels

Meridian Channel	Abbrev-iation	Circulation or Digestion	Yin or Yang	Peak Time	Element	Number of Points
lung	LU	circulation	yin	3:00 a.m. – 5:00 a.m.	metal	11
large intestine	LI	digestion	yang	5:00 a.m. – 7:00 a.m.	metal	20
stomach	ST	digestion	yang	7:00 a.m. – 9:00 a.m.	earth	45
spleen	SP	circulation	yin	9:00 a.m. – 11:00 a.m.	earth	21
heart	H	circulation	yin	11:00 a.m. – 1:00 p.m.	fire	9
small intestine	SI	digestion	yang	1:00 p.m. – 3:00 p.m.	fire	19
bladder	BL	digestion	yang	3:00 p.m. – 5:00 p.m.	water	67
kidney	KI	circulation	yin	5:00 p.m. – 7:00 p.m.	water	27
pericardium	P	circulation	yin	7:00 p.m. – 9:00 p.m.	fire	9
triple warmer	TW	digestion	yang	9:00 p.m. – 11:00 p.m.	fire	23
gallbladder	GB	digestion	yang	11:00 p.m. – 1:00 a.m.	wood	44
liver	LI	circulation	yin	1:00 a.m. – 3:00 a.m.	wood	14

LUNG

The lung meridian channel originates on the anterior upper portion of the pectoralis major, above the nipple and beneath the clavicle. It moves slightly upward and then lateral across the shoulder joint, descends down the anterior lateral side of the arm, and terminates on the lateral side of the thumb.

The lung channel governs qi and houses the corporeal soul. It is paired with the large intestine channel. It controls respiration, the balance of bodily fluids, and influences urine production. It is commonly used to treat respiratory-related conditions, cold and hot sensations, and skin issues.

The abbreviation for the lung channel is LU; it is a yin organ of circulation, peaking from 3:00 a.m. to 5:00 a.m.; its element is metal; and it has eleven acupressure points.

Large Intestine

The large intestine meridian channel originates from the tip of the index finger (between the thumb and third digit) on the dorsal side of the hand. It ascends the posterior lateral arm, crossing the shoulder joint up the anterior lateral of the neck, crossing the jawline, and moving medially, crossing underneath the nose and terminating on the other side of midline.

The large intestine channel rules elimination and is paired with the lung channel. It is commonly used to treat toothaches, nosebleeds, excessive thirst, shoulder and arm pain, and intestinal disorders.

The abbreviation for the large intestine channel is LI; it is a yang organ of digestion, peaking from 5:00 a.m. to 7:00 a.m.; its element is metal, and it has twenty acupressure points.

Stomach

The stomach meridian channel originates on the center of the orbital ridge beneath the eye. It descends toward the jawline before forming a lateral hook that ascends to the brow, moving medially before it descends along the outside of the nose. It then crosses the jawline down the anterior neck, meeting the clavicle and moving slightly laterally to continue down, crossing the nipple, moving back toward the midline, and descending the torso to the inguinal crease. The channel then moves slightly laterally and descends the anterior leg, terminating on the medial side of the second toe.

The stomach channel digests, absorbs, and transports. It is paired with the spleen channel; it is commonly used to treat stomachaches, mouth sores, nausea, edema, and sore throat.

The abbreviation for the stomach channel is ST; it is a yang organ of digestion, peaking from 7:00 a.m. to 9:00 a.m.; its element is earth; and it has forty-five acupressure points.

Spleen

The spleen meridian channel originates on the medial side of the big toe, ascends to the medial side of the patella, continues up the medial thigh, moving slightly laterally, and continues ascending to the axillary area before descending sharply and laterally a few inches to termination.

The spleen channel is the primary qi-producing organ and houses thoughts. It is paired with the stomach channel; it is commonly used to treat breast and abdominal pain, menstrual disorders, anorexia, and bleeding disorders.

The abbreviation for the spleen channel is SP; it is a yin organ of circulation, peaking from 9:00 a.m. to 11:00 a.m.; its element is earth; and it has twenty-one acupressure points.

Heart

The heart meridian channel originates in the axillary, travels down the medial arm across the wrist and palm, and terminates on the radial side of the little finger.

The heart channel governs the mind and spirit. It is paired with the small intestine. It is commonly used to treat palpitations, coma, vertigo, insomnia, excessive dreaming, cyanosis, anxiety, and depression.

The abbreviation for the heart channel is H; it is a yin organ of circulation, peaking from 11:00 a.m. to 1:00 p.m.; its element is fire; and it has nine acupressure points.

Small Intestine

The small intestine meridian channel originates on the ulnar side of the tip of the little fingernail, travels up the ulnar side of the hand to the wrist, ascends up the posterior arm, moves laterally to the scapula and, zigzagging upward, ascends the side of the neck, terminating in front of the ear at the temporomandibular joint.

The small intestine channel separates pure food, liquids, and thoughts from impure ones. It is paired with the heart; it is used to treat forgetfulness, sore throat, shoulder pain, hearing problems, and digestive issues.

The abbreviation for the small intestine channel is SI; it is a yang organ of digestion, peaking from 1:00 p.m. to 3:00 p.m.; its element is fire; and it has nineteen acupressure points.

Bladder

The bladder meridian channel originates on the inner corner of the eye, ascends straight up to the hairline, and veers slightly laterally before continuing over the top of the head, descending straight down along the lateral side of the spinal column, crossing the gluteal and continuing to descend the posterior leg to the heel. There, it turns to continue along the lateral side of the foot, terminating on the lateral side of the tip of the small toe.

The bladder channel is the longest channel of the twelve meridians. It transforms qi and stores and eliminates fluid waste. It is paired with the kidney channel. It is used to treat spinal nerve problems, headaches, sinus issues, hair loss, urinary disorders, calf cramps, and foot problems.

The abbreviation for the bladder channel is BL; it is a yang organ of digestion, peaking from 3:00 p.m. to 5:00 p.m.; its element is water; and it has sixty-seven acupressure points.

Kidney

The kidney meridian channel originates on the bottom of the foot between the second and third metatarsals, travels across the arch moving toward the medial edge of the foot to the ankle bone, which it circles counterclockwise, and then continues ascending up the medial side of the lower leg to the popliteal crease. It then moves up the thigh, crossing diagonally from medial to the anterior thigh, continuing up the midline, passing the outside of the belly button to the xiphoid process, and moving slightly laterally as it continues to ascend the pectoralis, terminating at the clavicle.

The kidney channel is considered the root of life and stores essence. It is paired with the bladder channel, and is used to treat back pain, sexual dysfunction, urinary disorders, edema in the lower extremities, ringing in the ears, vertigo, and osteoporosis.

The abbreviation for the kidney channel is KI; it is a yin organ of circulation, peaking from 5:00 p.m. to 7:00 p.m.; its element is water; and it has twenty-seven acupressure points.

Heart Governor or Pericardium

The heart governor (or pericardium) meridian channel originates on the chest above the nipple, arches over the axillary region down the anterior arm, crosses the wrist and palm, and terminates at the tip of the middle finger.

The heart governor channel is considered the protector of the heart. It governs the blood and, with the heart, governs the mind. It is paired with the San Jiao/triple warmer channel. It is used to treat heat stroke, angina, seizures, nausea and vomiting, psychological disorders, fevers, dry mouth, and tongue sores.

The abbreviation for the heart governor channel is P; it is a yin organ of circulation, peaking from 7:00 p.m. to 9:00 p.m.; its element is fire; and it has nine acupressure points.

Triple Warmer

The triple warmer (San Jiao) meridian channel originates on the dorsal side of the ring finger (between the third and fifth finger), ascends posteriorly until it reaches the base of the ear, circles around the back of the ear until it meets the tip of the zygomatic bone in the front of the earlobe, and moves diagonally to the outer corner of the eye, where it terminates.

The triple warmer channel is obviously not a physical organ. Its primary function is to circulate source qi (liquid energy) to all organs. There is an upper, middle, and lower warmer. It is paired with the pericardium channel. It is used to treat irritability, mood swings, fevers, chills, sore throat, earaches, blurred vision, Bell's palsy, and pain and stiffness in the neck, shoulder, and arms.

The abbreviation for the triple warmer channel is TW; it is a yang organ of digestion, peaking from 9:00 p.m. to 11:00 p.m.; its element is fire; and it has twenty-three acupressure points.

Gallbladder

The gallbladder meridian channel originates at the outer corner of the eye, moves diagonally down and around the base of the earlobe to meet the occipital edge. It then ascends, tracing a big arc to the brow, sharply returns tracing a broader arc back around to the occipital edge, and descends down the side of the neck to the shoulder. The channel then begins arcing around the shoulder joint by moving medially across the anterior around to the side of the upper rib cage, down and around the bottom of the rib cage toward the midline, and descending diagonally to the lateral side of the abdomen until just above the top of the hip (ASIS). It begins arcing by moving medially across the anterior around to the greater trochanter, descends the lateral side of the leg, crossing the ankle, and terminates on the dorsal of the foot between the fourth and fifth metatarsal.

The gallbladder channel ensures the smooth flow of qi and governs decision-making. It is paired with the liver channel, and it is used to treat headaches, migraines, eye problems, neck tension, asthma, shingles, groin pain, and arthritic hips.

The abbreviation for the gallbladder channel is GB; it is a yang organ of digestion, peaking from 11:00 p.m. to 1:00 a.m.; its element is wood; and it has forty-four acupressure points.

LIVER

The liver meridian channel originates on the dorsal side of the big toe at the bed of the nail, moves across the dorsal of the foot toward the ankle, ascends the medial side of the leg to the crease of the groin, ascends laterally to the waistline, and moves diagonally toward the midline until meeting the lowest rib, terminating a few finger widths below the nipple.

The liver channel is often considered the second heart. It assures the flow of emotions, qi, and blood. It controls immune responses and ligaments, tendons, and muscles. It is paired with the gallbladder channel and is used to treat liver and digestive problems, genital and reproductive issues, candida, skin problems, thigh and knee pain, and fingernail and toenail issues.

The abbreviation for the liver channel is LI; it is a yin organ of circulation, peaking from 1:00 a.m. to 3:00 a.m.; its element is wood; and it has fourteen acupressure points.

PRACTICE QUESTIONS

1. Which meridian channel has the most number of acupressure points?

A) kidney

B) heart

C) bladder

D) gallbladder

Answers:

A) Incorrect. The kidney has twenty-seven acupressure points.

B) Incorrect. The heart has nine acupressure points.

C) Correct. The bladder has sixty-seven acupressure points.

D) Incorrect. The gallbladder has forty-four acupressure points.

2. Which meridian channel peaks from 3:00 a.m. to 5:00 a.m.?

   A) lung
   B) liver
   C) heart
   D) kidney

   Answers:

   A) Correct. The lung meridian is the first in the twenty-four-hour cycle.
   B) Incorrect. The liver meridian peaks from 1:00 a.m. to 3:00 a.m.
   C) Incorrect. The heart meridian peaks from 11:00 a.m. to 1:00 p.m.
   D) Incorrect. The kidney meridian peaks from 5:00 p.m. to 7:00 p.m.

3. Which meridian is NOT associated with the fire element?

   A) heart
   B) pericardium
   C) kidney
   D) small intestine

   Answers:

   A) Incorrect. The heart is associated with fire, yin, and circulation.
   B) Incorrect. The pericardium is associated with fire, yin, and circulation.
   C) Correct. The kidney is associated with water, yin, and circulation.
   D) Incorrect. The small intestine is associated with fire, yang, and digestion.

Kinesiology

Kinesiology is the scientific study of the movement of the human body. It is used in clinical settings to determine structural, chemical, and brain dysfunction. Based on evaluation, treatment is determined.

Muscles originate from an attachment site, usually a bony landmark, which *does not move* during muscle contraction. The origin may begin as a tendon that transforms into a skeletal muscle. Some muscles have more than one origin, such as the biceps brachii and triceps brachii. The insertion point is generally another bony landmark that *does move* during contraction. The origin is generally proximal and insertion distal. Ligaments, aponeurosis, fascia, and membrane may also be part of the origin and insertion of muscle.

There are classifications of muscle fibers that define the shape and degree of capabilities of the muscle. **Circular muscles**, like sphincters, surround an opening. **Fusiform** muscles, like the biceps brachii, are shaped like a spindle, have a quick response time and a wide range of motion, but are not very powerful muscles. **Parallel** muscles, like the rectus abdominis, have great endurance but are not as strong as other muscle fiber classifications. **Convergent** muscles are triangular in shape, like the pectoralis major. They are broadest at origin and converge to a single tendon insertion site. They provide maximum force of contraction. **Pennate** muscles appear feathery and have a central tendon. They are very powerful and stabilizing muscles with minimal flexibility. Pennate muscles can be **unipennate**, meaning the fibers feather out from only one side of the tendon, such as the extensor digitorum longus. **Bipennate** fibers feather out from both sides of the tendon, such as the rectus femoris. **Multipennate**, such as the deltoid, have multiple pennate that branch out from the central tendon.

Proprioceptors are sensory receptors that communicate speed, angles, and balance to the central nervous system. They coordinate movement by detecting the body's position in space and movement through space. Proprioceptors can be found in the inner ear, synovial joints, skeletal framework, tendons, and muscles. They are important in the development of muscle memory and hand-eye coordination. **Muscle spindles** and **Golgi tendon organs** are two types.

Muscle spindles are proprioceptors that sense muscle stretching. They are very sensitive to changes in muscle length. Muscle spindles respond to these changes by routing a signal via the reflex arc. The reflex arc is a communication directly to the spinal column, not the brain. This is a mechanism that keeps the muscle from injury as a result of overstretching. The result of a reflex arc is the muscle contracting and, thus, discontinuing the stretch. For example, the sensation of reaching an *endpoint* when stretching for exercise or warm-up is due to the muscle spindles relaying information through the reflex arc. (A more detailed discussion of reflexes and the reflex arc is available in the nervous system section.)

Golgi tendon organs sense muscle tension when the muscle is contracted. They protect muscle from overexertion. If they detect that the tension exerted will cause excessive damage to the muscle, they will inhibit the action. For example, a weight lifter attempting to lift too much weight can suddenly drop the weight.

In kinesiology, **range of motion (ROM)** is defined as **active**, **passive**, and **resistive**. Anytime a joint is engaged in activities of daily living, such as showering, dressing, getting in and out of a vehicle, and exercising, active ROM is engaged. Passive ROM is when a person moves someone else's joints without that person having any active involvement in the movement. Resistive ROM is a technique in which a force is applied to create resistance, resulting in increased strength, flexibility, and improved ROM.

MUSCLES

The **rotator cuff** attaches to the humerus with the corresponding muscle's tendon. This group of muscles provides stability while allowing the shoulder to rotate. The rotator cuff consists of four muscles that originate at the scapula:

+ teres minor
+ infraspinatus
+ supraspinatus
+ subscapularis

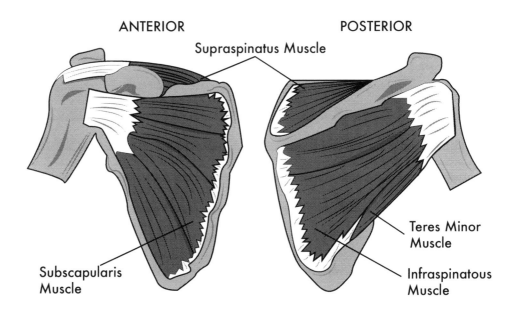

Figure 4.14. Rotator Cuff

Injury to the rotator cuff usually involves a tear in the tendon of the muscle.

The **hand and forearm extensor group** consists of five muscles:

+ extensor carpi radialis brevis
+ extensor carpi radialis longus
+ extensor carpi ulnaris
+ extensor digitorum
+ extensor indicis

The primary actions of these muscles are to extend, abduct, and adduct the wrist; to assist with elbow flexion; and to assist with finger extension. The first four muscles originate at the lateral distal end of the humerus. The extensor indicis originates from the distal end of the ulna. All five insert into metacarpals and phalanges.

The **hand and forearm flexor group** consists of five muscles:

+ palmaris longus
+ flexor carpi radialis
+ flexor carpi ulnaris

+ flexor digitorum superficialis
+ flexor digitorum profundus

The primary actions of these muscles are to flex, abduct, and adduct the wrist; to assist with elbow flexion; and finger flexion. The first four muscles originate at the medial distal end of the humerus. The flexor carpi ulnaris has two heads: one is the humeral head and the second is the ulnar head. The ulnar head originates on the proximal end of the ulna. The flexor digitorum profundus originates at the proximal end of the ulna. All five insert into metacarpals and phalanges.

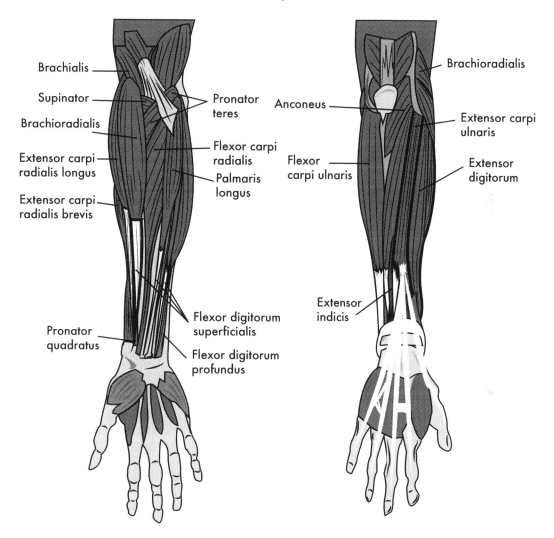

Figure 4.15. Hand and Forearm Muscles

The **abdominal group** consists of four muscles:
+ external oblique
+ internal oblique
+ rectus abdominis
+ transverse abdominis

The primary actions of these muscles are to flex and rotate the vertebral column and compress the abdominal contents. In general, these muscles originate from mid-to-low ribs, pubic and iliac crest, and the thoracolumbar fascia and insert into mid-to-low ribs and the abdominal aponeurosis to linea alba.

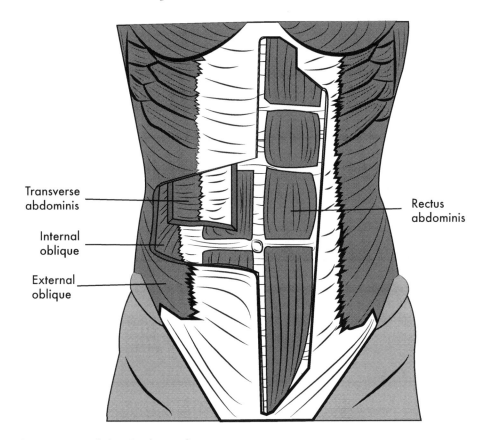

Figure 4.16. Abdominal Muscles

The **erector spinae group** consists of three columns of muscles. Each column has three distinct muscles:

+ iliocostalis cervisis, thoracis, lumborum
+ longissimus cervisis, thoracis, capitis
+ spinalis cervisis, thoracis, capitis

These columns of muscles run parallel to the entire vertebral column, giving it a vast amount of flexion and extension capabilities.

There are four muscles that have the sole function of assisting with inhalation and exhalation:

+ external intercostals
+ internal intercostals
+ serratus posterior superior
+ serratus posterior inferior

The intercostals function by drawing the ribs superiorly for inhalation and drawing the ribs inferiorly for exhalation. The intercostals originate and insert in between the ribs. The serratus posterior superior elevates the ribs during inhalation and the serratus posterior inferior depresses the ribs during exhalation. Both the superior and inferior serratus posterior muscles originate on spinous processes and insert on rib surfaces.

Following are five muscles that are involved in moving the mandible. These muscles *may* have some involvement in temporomandibular joint (TMJ) syndrome:

- ✦ masseter—elevate
- ✦ temporalis—elevate and retract
- ✦ lateral pterygoid—laterally deviate and protract
- ✦ medial pterygoid—laterally deviate, elevate, and protract
- ✦ platysma—depression

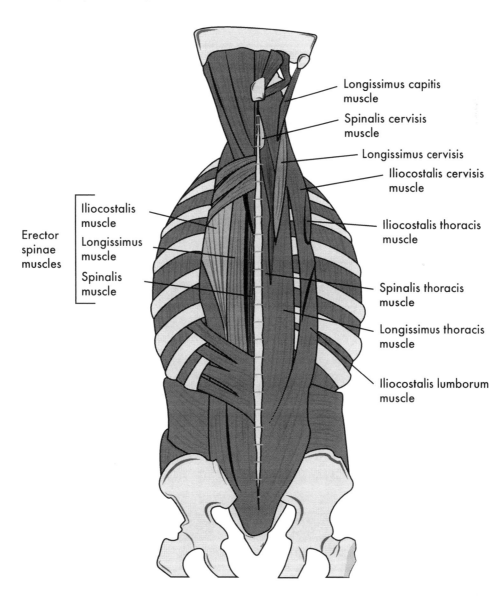

Figure 4.17. Erector Spinae Muscles

Key muscles that are involved in lateral neck flexion, head rotation, and elevation of the ribs to assist with inhalation are the:

+ anterior scalene
+ middle scalene
+ posterior scalene
+ sternocleidomastoid (SCM)

Table 4.9 is a detailed list of muscles broken down by region and muscle groups. It provides muscle name, action, origin, and point of insertion.

Table 4.9. Shoulder and Upper Arm Muscles

Name	Action	Origin	Insertion
biceps brachii	flex the elbow and shoulder supinate the forearm	*short head*: coracoid process of scapula *long head*: supra-glenoid tubercle of scapula	tuberosity of the radius and aponeurosis of the biceps brachii
coracobrachialis	flex and adduct the shoulder	coracoid process of the scapula	medial surface of mid-humeral shaft
deltoid	*all fibers*: abduct the shoulder *anterior fibers*: flex, medially rotate, and horizontally adduct the shoulder *posterior fibers*: extend, laterally rotate, and horizontally abduct the shoulder	lateral one-third of clavicle, acromion, and spine of scapula	deltoid tuberosity
latissimus dorsi	extend, adduct, and medially rotate the shoulder	spinous processes of last six thoracic vertebrae, last three or four ribs, thoracolumbar aponeurosis and posterior iliac crest	crest of the lesser tubercle of the humerus

Name	Action	Origin	Insertion
levator scapula	*unilaterally*: elevate and downwardly rotate the scapula; laterally flex the head and neck; rotate the head and neck to the same side *bilaterally*: extend the head and neck	transverse processes of first through fourth cervical vertebrae	upper region of medial border and superior angle of scapula
pectoralis major	*all fibers*: adduct and medially rotate the shoulder; assist in elevating the thorax during forced inhalation *upper fibers*: flex and horizontally adduct the shoulder *lower fibers*: extend the shoulder	medial half of clavicle, sternum, and cartilage of first through sixth ribs	crest of greater tubercle of humerus
pectoralis minor	depress, abduct, and anteriorly tilt the scapula assist in forced inhalation	third, fourth, and fifth ribs	coracoid process of the scapula
rhomboid major	adduct, elevate, and downwardly rotate the scapula	spinous process of T2 to T5	medial border of the scapula between the spine of the scapula and inferior angle
rhomboid minor	adduct, elevate, and downwardly rotate the scapula	spinous processes of C7 and T1	upper portion of medial border of the scapula, across from spine of the scapula
serratus anterior	abduct and depress the scapula hold the medial border of the scapula against the rib cage	surfaces of upper eight or nine ribs	anterior surface of medial border of the scapula

Table 4.9. Shoulder and Upper Arm Muscles (continued)

Name	Action	Origin	Insertion
subclavius	draw clavicle inferiorly and anteriorly elevate first rib during inhalation stabilize the sternoclavicular joint	first rib	inferior, lateral aspect of the clavicle
teres major	extend, adduct, and medially rotate the shoulder	lateral side of inferior angle and lower half of lateral border of scapula	crest of the lesser tubercle of the humerus
trapezius	*upper fibers*: bilaterally extend the head and neck and unilaterally flex the head and neck to the same side; rotate the head and neck to the opposite side; elevate and upwardly rotate the scapula *middle fibers*: adduct and stabilize the scapula *lower fibers*: depress and upwardly rotate the scapula	external occipital protuberance, medial portion of superior nuchal line of the occiput, ligamentum nuchae and spinous processes of C7 through T12	lateral one-third of clavicle, acromion and spine of the scapula
triceps brachii	*all heads*: extend the elbow *long head*: extend and adduct the shoulder	*long head*: infraglenoid tubercle of the scapula *lateral head*: posterior surface of proximal half of the humerus *medial head*: posterior surface of distal half of the humerus	olecranon process of the ulna

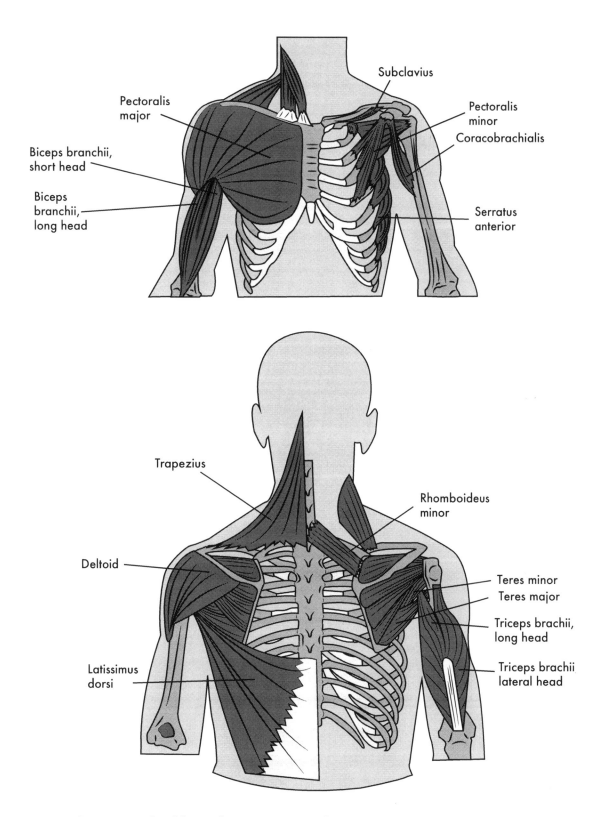

Figure 4.18. Shoulder and Upper Arm Muscles

Table 4.10. Forearm Muscles

Name	Action	Origin	Insertion
anconeus	extend the elbow	lateral epicondyle of the humerus	olecranon process and lateral edge of ulnar shaft
brachialis	flex the elbow	distal half of anterior surface of humerus	tuberosity and coronoid process of ulna
brachioradialis	flex the elbow	lateral supracondylar ridge of humerus	styloid process of radius
pronator quadratus	pronate the forearm	medial, anterior surface of distal ulna	lateral, anterior surface of distal radius
pronator teres	pronate the forearm and assist in flexion of the elbow	medial epicondyle of the humerus, and flexor tendon and coronoid process of ulna	middle of lateral surface of the radius
supinator	supinate the forearm	supinator crest of the ulna	radius

Table 4.11. Pelvis and Thigh

Name	Action	Origin	Insertion
iliacus	flex, laterally rotate, and adduct the hip	iliac fossa	lesser trochanter
psoas major	flex, laterally rotate, and adduct the hip	transverse processes of lumbar vertebrae	lesser trochanter
psoas minor	tilts pelvis posteriorly	transverse process of L1	superior ramus of pubis
quadratus lumborum	laterally tilt the pelvis and laterally flex and extend the vertebral column	posterior iliac crest	last rib and transverse processes of L1 – L4
sartorius	flex, laterally rotate, and abduct the hip / flex and medially rotate the knee	anterior superior iliac spine (ASIS)	proximal, medial shaft of the tibia
tensor fasciae latae	flex, medially rotate, and abduct the hip	iliac crest	iliotibial tract

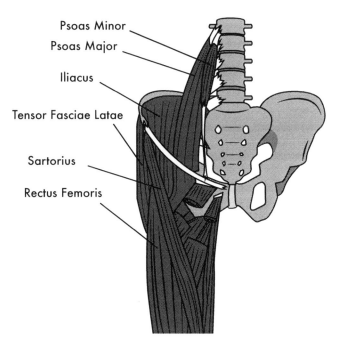

Psoas Minor
Psoas Major
Iliacus
Tensor Fasciae Latae
Sartorius
Rectus Femoris

Figure 4.19. Pelvis and Thigh Muscles

Table 4.12. Lower Leg and Foot

Name	Action	Origin	Insertion
gastrocnemius	flex the knee and plantar flexion of the ankle	posterior surface and condyles of the femur	calcaneus
peroneus brevis	evert the foot and plantar flexion of the ankle	distal lateral fibula	tuberosity of fifth metatarsal
peroneus longus	evert the foot and plantar flexion of the ankle	proximal lateral fibula	first metatarsal and medial cuneiform
plantaris	flexion of the ankle and knee	lateral condyle of the femur	calcaneus
popliteus	flex and medially rotate the knee	lateral epicondyle of the femur	proximal posterior tibia
soleus	plantar flexion of the ankle	posterior surface of tibia, proximal posterior of fibula	calcaneus
tibialis anterior	invert and dorsiflex the ankle	proximal lateral surface of tibia	medial cuneiform and base of the first metatarsal
tibialis posterior	invert and plantar flex the ankle	proximal posterior shaft of the tibia and proximal fibula	navicular, cuneiforms, cuboid and second through fourth metatarsals

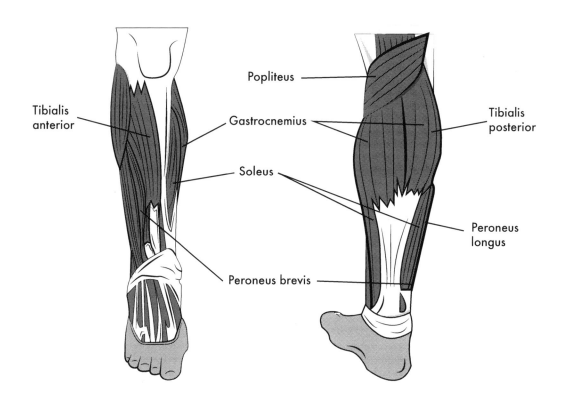

Figure 4.20. Lower Leg and Foot Muscles

Table 4.13. Pelvis and Thigh Adductor Group

Name	Action	Origin	Insertion
adductor brevis	adduct and medially rotate the hip and assist with hip flexion	inferior ramus of pubis	pectineal line of ramus and linea aspera of femur
adductor longus	adduct and medially rotate the hip and assist with hip flexion	pubic tubercle	linea aspera of femur
adductor magnus	adduct and medially rotate the hip and assist with hip flexion posterior fibers extend the hip	inferior ramus of the pubis, ramus of ischium and ischial tuberosity	linea aspera of femur and adductor tubercle
gracilis	adduct and medially rotate the hip knee flexion and medial rotation of flexed knee	inferior ramus of pubis and ramus of ischium	proximal medial shaft of tibia
pectineus	adduct and medially rotate the hip and assist with hip flexion	superior ramus of pubis	pectineal line of femur

Table 4.14. Pelvis and Thigh Gluteals

Name	Action	Origin	Insertion
gluteus maximus	extend, laterally rotate, and abduct the hip lower fibers adduct the hip	coccyx, edge of sacrum, posterior iliac crest, sacrotuberous and sacroiliac ligaments	gluteal tuberosity and iliotibial tract
gluteus medius	*all fibers*: abduct the hip *anterior fibers*: flex and medially rotate the hip *posterior fibers*: extend and laterally rotate the hip	gluteal surface of the ilium	greater trochanter
gluteus minimus	abduct, medially rotate, and flex the hip	gluteal surface of the ilium	greater trochanter

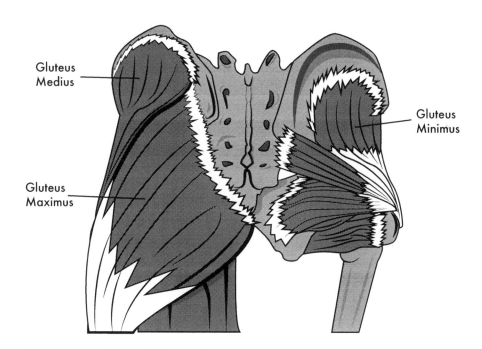

Figure 4.21. Pelvis and Thigh Gluteal Muscles

Table 4.15. Pelvis and Thigh Hamstrings

Name	Action	Origin	Insertion
biceps femoris	flex the knee and laterally rotate the flexed knee extend and laterally rotate the hip tilt the pelvis posteriorly	*long head*: ischial tuberosity *short head*: linea aspera of femur	head of fibula
semimembranosus	flex the knee and medially rotate the flexed knee extend and medially rotate the hip tilt the pelvis posteriorly	ischial tuberosity	medial condyle of tibia
semitendinosus	flex the knee and medially rotate the flexed knee extend and medially rotate the hip tilt the pelvis posteriorly	ischial tuberosity	proximal, medial shaft of the tibia

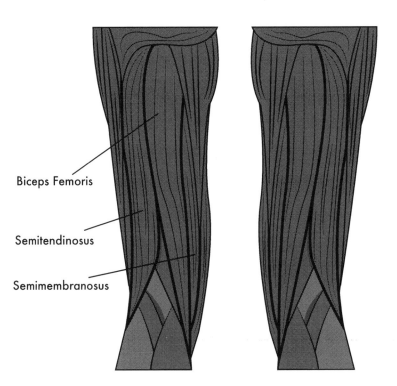

Figure 4.22. Pelvis and Thigh Hamstrings

Table 4.16. Pelvis and Thigh Lateral Rotators of the Hip

Name	Action	Origin	Insertion
gemellus inferior	laterally rotate the hip	ischial tuberosity	greater trochanter
gemellus superior	laterally rotate the hip	ischial spine	greater trochanter
obturator externus	laterally rotate the hip	rami of pubis	trochanteric fossa of femur
obturator internus	laterally rotate the hip	obturator membrane and obturator foramen	greater trochanter
piriformis	laterally rotate the hip and abduct the hip when flexed	surface of sacrum	greater trochanter
quadratus femoris	laterally rotate the hip	lateral border of ischial tuberosity	intertrochanteric crest

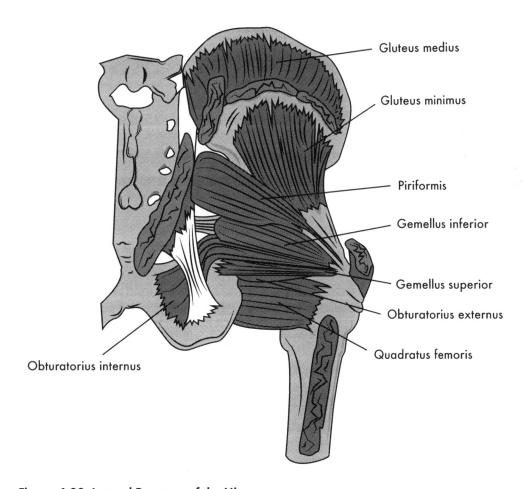

Figure 4.23. Lateral Rotators of the Hip

Table 4.17. Pelvis and Thigh Quadriceps Femoris Group

Name	Action	Origin	Insertion
rectus femoris	extend the knee and flex the hip	anterior inferior iliac spine (AIIS)	tibial tuberosity
vastus intermedius	extend the knee	anterior and lateral shaft of the femur	tibial tuberosity
vastus lateralis	extend the knee	lateral linea aspera and gluteal tuberosity	tibial tuberosity
vastus medialis	extend the knee	medial linea aspera	tibial tuberosity

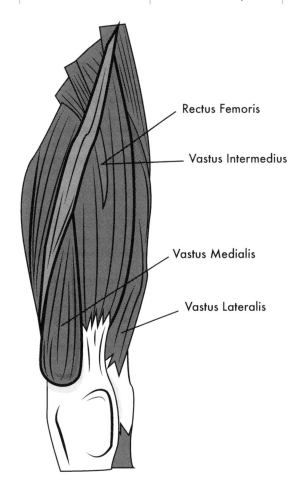

Figure 4.24. Quadriceps Femoris Group

There are two types of muscular contractions: **isometric** and **isotonic**. Isometric is when tension rises but the length of the muscle remains the same. The movement is static. The muscle contraction does not result in a change of the muscle's length. Think of it as a force being applied against resistance. For example, putting a hand on the side of the head above the ear, and then pressing the head against the hand without moving the hand will cause muscles to contract but not shorten. Isotonic is an active voluntary movement. There are two types of isotonic contractions: **concentric** and **eccentric**. A concentric contraction, for example, is what occurs when someone lifts a hand weight. The muscle will tighten and shorten and force the elbow joint to engage. An eccentric contraction occurs, for example, when someone lowers the weight back down with deliberate control, moving against gravity and the weight itself. The thing that isometric and isotonic have in common is that a force or physical stress needs to be applied.

Muscle contractions require a large amount of energy. **Aerobic metabolism** provides most of the adenosine triphosphate (ATP) needed for contraction. Aerobic metabolism means a person is breathing, taking in oxygen. **Anaerobic metabolism** relies on anaerobic glycolysis, which is the conversion of glucose to lactate. Track and field sprinters may not breathe when they perform, so they will produce ATP using glycolysis conversion. The body can also rely on a reserve of **creatine phosphate (CP)** to convert adenosine diphosphate (ADP) to ATP during anaerobic metabolism. The CP reserve can rapidly respond when needed. The liver and kidneys, the primary producers of CP, route it through the bloodstream. The body is about 1 percent CP; most of that is in skeletal muscles.

A **muscle cramp** is an involuntary contraction. If a muscle exceeds a threshold, a cramp will protect the muscle from further damage. When there is not enough energy to release the muscle from contraction, a cramp may result. Muscle imbalances that pull the body out of alignment and mineral deficiencies can be further causes. A **muscle spasm** is also an involuntary contraction but is neurological in nature. Severe and repeated spasms should be addressed by a physician.

Skeletal muscle injury usually results from direct trauma, such as lacerations, strains, and contusions. The primary concern is that scarring may hinder the muscle from ever regaining full strength and mobility. Scar tissue is always inferior to the pre-injured muscle fibers, and it will remain more susceptible to being reinjured. A skeletal muscle injury heals over three phases: **inflammatory**, **repair**, and **remodeling**.

The inflammatory phase lasts one to three days. During this time, muscle fibers rupture and die, a hematoma (bruise) forms, and inflammatory cells, leukocytes, monocytes, and macrophages invade the injury site.

The repair phase lasts three to four weeks. During this time, damaged muscle fibers start repairing, and a connective tissue scar forms. The scar will give the healing muscle strength to withstand contractions and give fibroblasts—collagen-producing cells—an anchoring site to do their job. However, it is important to note that if the injury is extreme in size and damage, the scar that naturally forms may actually hinder the repair process by interfering with muscle fiber regeneration. Also, if nerve damage occurred when the muscle was injured, it may affect the repair phase, too. Both of these factors may contribute to an incomplete functional recovery during the remodeling phase.

The remodeling phase occurs over a three-to-six-month period. In this phase, the newly formed muscle fibers mature and the scar tissue reorganizes to align with existing muscle fibers.

Therapeutic approaches to skeletal muscle injury may include:

+ RICE
+ NSAIDs
+ early mobilization
+ progressive exercise
+ surgery

In the inflammatory phase, rest, ice, compression, and elevation—commonly referred to as RICE—are applied. Ice should be applied intermittently for fifteen to twenty minutes, with thirty-to-sixty-minute intervals in between.

Non-Steroidal Anti Inflammatory Drugs (NSAIDs) may be administered. However, there is dispute over this practice or frequency of this practice, as some in the medical community believe these drugs may interfere with the natural healing process.

Early mobilization is thought to promote the regeneration of muscle fibers, resulting in the muscle more rapidly regaining its strength. However, early mobilization may result in the scar rupturing. Standard practice is to wait at least three to seven days to give the scar time to strengthen. After this period of time, mobilization, as long as it is pain free, is beneficial. Going too long without mobilization may result in atrophy of healthy muscle and delayed or retarded recovery of muscle strength.

Exercise after a skeletal muscle injury should begin gradually with isometric exercise, progressing to isotonic exercise, progressing to exercise that involves more speed and mobility.

In the event of severe injury, surgery may be an option. The factors considered are whether the injury was excessive and affected a large area, whether a complete strain or tear of the muscle occurred, if the damage to the belly of the muscle exceeds 50 percent, and if constant pain continues over a four-to-six-week period.

Proprioceptors

Proprioceptive neuromuscular facilitation (PNF) treatment was developed in the mid-1900s by neurophysiologist Herman Kabat, MD, PhD, and physical therapists, Margaret Knott and Dorothy Voss. The original intent was to focus on patients with paralysis, but it evolved into a therapeutic tool used to address ROM limitation in all types of patients and athletes. A primary tenet of PNF is to improve communication between the muscles and the nervous system. PNF is based on movement defined as **spiral-diagonal**. This is the theory that muscles spiral around bones from origin to insertion and, when contracted, the muscle movement *spirals* around the bone. The diagonal aspect is that movement occurs through multiple planes, not straight lines. PNF stretching is usually passive or active-assisted stretching (both discussed in "Range of Motion" later in this section). It also utilizes isometric and isotonic muscular contractions. The two types of facilitated PNF stretches are **PNF hold-relax** and **PNF contract-relax**. Both are intended, with repetition, to increase ROM.

PNF hold-relax is used if ROM is limited or weakness and pain are excessive. This is an isometric technique. An example is if a patient, lying flat, extends his leg as far as possible. Once there, the therapist creates resistance by pushing against the limb, attempting to increase the stretch. The patient pushes against the resistance and holds for several seconds before both patient and therapist relax the hold.

PNF contract-relax is used if there is limited ROM. This technique is both isometric and isotonic. For example, the patient lies flat; the therapist passively lifts and moves the limb to its extension limit, then instructs the patient to attempt to return the limb to its starting point while the therapist resists. However, the therapist allows the patient to rotate the limb at the joint. This is held for several seconds before both patient and therapist relax the hold.

MUSCLE FIBERS

Energy production and its use depend on the muscle activity being performed. A fatigued muscle will no longer contract once energy sources are exhausted, and the muscle builds up lactic acid. A recovery period is required and will begin immediately after the activity ends. At this point, the body may be in oxygen debt and vast amounts of oxygen need to be consumed. For example, after an all-out sprint or intensive workout, the body will consume a large amount of oxygen to begin the recovery process.

There are three kinds of skeletal muscle fibers related to muscle energy use. The type of fiber determines how fast the muscle uses stored energy (ATP). **Slow twitch fibers** are found in red meat. They have a lot of mitochondria (cell respiration) and myoglobin (red protein). They break down ATP slowly and are not easily fatigued. **Fast twitch A fibers** are a combination of red and white fibers and may appear pink or pale when viewed. They have mitochondria and myoglobin, but not as much as slow twitch fibers, and they produce a lot of ATP, which is quickly broken down. Fast twitch A fibers may be referred to as intermediate fibers. **Fast twitch B fibers** are white in appearance, have the least number of mitochondria and myoglobin of the three, and fatigue rapidly. Human beings have a mix of fiber types but the quantity and percentage are usually determined genetically.

JOINTS

In the skeletal system section, the types of skeletal articulations (joints) were discussed. In kinesiology, the primary joint of discussion is the diarthrotic joint, also referred to as the synovial joint. It is the most movable joint, but also the weakest. This joint provides structure, stability, and attachment sites. The key components of a musculoskeletal diarthrotic joint are:

+ aponeuroses
+ articular capsule
+ articular cartilage
+ bone

+ bursae
+ cartilage
+ fascia
+ joint cavity

+ ligaments
+ synovial fluid
+ synovial membrane
+ tendons

The joints of the body also have kinesthetic joint receptors that are stimulated by the surrounding environment and the perceived activity in that environment. Pacinian corpuscles (found in joint capsules) respond to quick and fleeting touch and vibration. Ruffini's end organs, also found in joint capsules, respond to continuous touch and pressure. Free nerve endings are found in joint connective tissue, and respond to temperature and pain. (These three receptors are also discussed in the system section of this chapter.)

The skeletal system and the muscular system work together to produce joint movement. This is done using the concept of **levers**. Levers work using a **fulcrum**, **applied force**, and **resistance**. A lever can be first, second, or third class.

A **first-class lever** has the fulcrum in the middle and applied force and load are on each end. An example of a first-class lever is head nodding. The atlas is the fulcrum, the force is the muscles used in nodding (i.e., trapezius), and the load is the head.

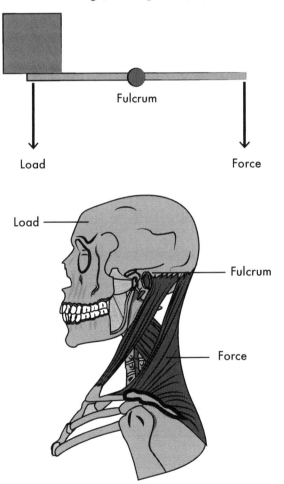

Figure 4.25. First-Class Lever

A **second-class lever** has the load in the middle and the fulcrum and applied force on each end. An example of a second-class lever is elevating the body onto the toes. The toes are the fulcrum, the force is the muscles involved in elevating the body (i.e., gastrocnemius), and the load is body weight.

A **third-class lever** has the applied force in the middle and the fulcrum and load on each end. An example of a third-class lever is flexing the elbow while holding a weight. The elbow joint is the fulcrum, the force is the muscles involved in the flexion (i.e., biceps brachii), and the load is the weight.

When joint movement occurs, different muscles play different roles.

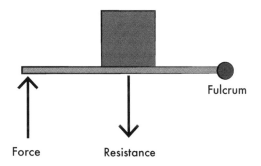

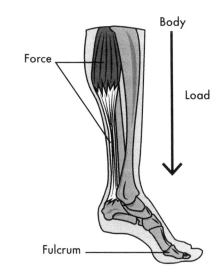

Figure 4.26. Second-Class Lever

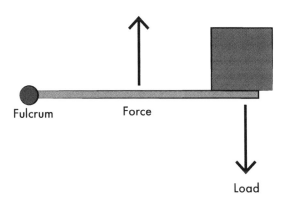

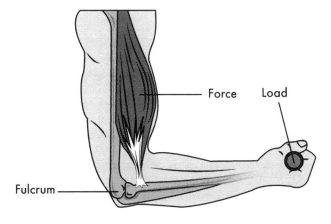

Figure 4.27. Third-Class Lever

The three main roles are:

+ prime mover
+ synergist
+ antagonist

The prime mover is the main muscle used in the movement and it contracts the most. The synergist can be one or more muscles that assist with the movement and/or stabilize the joint. The number of synergists involved varies, depending on the type and force of movement. The antagonist muscle opposes the movement. For example, when flexing the elbow, the prime mover is the biceps brachii, the synergists are the pectoralis major and deltoid, and the antagonist is the triceps brachii. Other muscles may be identified as **fixators** that keep the prime mover stabilized while performing its action.

Joint degeneration may occur as the result of aging, overuse, inadequate blood supply, an injury that did not adequately repair, and disease. Osteoarthritis, rheumatoid arthritis, TMJ, bursitis, and fibromyalgia are some of the other conditions that can affect the joints, resulting in pain, stiffness, and limited ROM. Massage can provide relief by increasing blood flow to the area, contributing to functional improvement, maintaining and improving flexibility using gentle ROM techniques, and relaxing tight muscles around the joint.

RANGE OF MOTION

Active ROM occurs whenever a joint is used in carrying out daily activities; limitations to active ROM can have an adverse effect on a person's ability to perform daily tasks and functions. Also, athletes may use active ROM techniques to enhance and improve physical performance. Active ROM may be done with assistance.

Passive ROM is when a person moves someone else's joints without that person having any active involvement in the movement. In the event of a joint being affected by injury or illness, passive ROM techniques may be used to encourage blood flow to the joint and the anatomy surrounding the joint, and to increase or maintain the flexibility of the joint. Examples are someone who is bedridden or in recovery from a surgical procedure, and joint injuries that require prescribed clinical treatment. Also, like active ROM, passive ROM techniques may be used by athletes.

Resistive ROM is a technique in which a force is applied to create resistance, resulting in increased strength, flexibility, and improved ROM. This technique is also used clinically to determine weaknesses in ROM and the extent of injury to a joint and the anatomy surrounding it.

PRACTICE QUESTIONS

1. Which of the following terms does NOT define range of motion?

A) passive

B) active

C) isotonic

D) resistive

Answers:

A) Incorrect. Range of motion is defined as passive.

B) Incorrect. Range of motion is defined as active.

C) Correct. Isotonic is a type of muscular contraction.

D) Incorrect. Range of motion is defined as resistive.

2. Which is an example of a circular muscle?

   A) rectus femoris

   B) pectoralis major

   C) deltoid

   D) sphincter

   Answers:

   A) Incorrect. The rectus femoris is classified as a bipennate muscle.

   B) Incorrect. The pectoralis major is classified as a convergent muscle.

   C) Incorrect. The deltoid is classified as a multipennate muscle.

   D) Correct. Sphincters are classified as circular muscles.

3. Together what do the teres minor, infraspinatus, supraspinatus, and subscapularis define?

   A) erector spinae

   B) rotator cuff

   C) abdominals

   D) coracobrachialis

   Answers:

   A) Incorrect. The erector spinae group are muscles related to flexion and extension of the spine.

   B) Correct. The rotator cuff provides stability during shoulder rotation.

   C) Incorrect. The abdominal muscles primarily flex and rotate the spine and compress abdominal contents.

   D) Incorrect. The coracobrachialis is a single muscle involved in flexion and adduction of the shoulder.

4. When a skeletal muscle injury occurs, what therapeutic approach is most favored during the inflammatory phase?

   A) surgery

   B) early mobilization

   C) RICE

   D) non-steroidal anti-inflammatory drugs

   Answers:

   A) Incorrect. Unless the injury is considered extremely severe, surgery would not be performed in this phase.

   B) Incorrect. Standard practice is to wait three to seven days to give the scar time to strengthen.

C) **Correct.** RICE (rest, ice, compression, elevation) is most favored during the inflammatory phase.

D) Incorrect. NSAIDs can be used, but may interfere with the natural healing process.

5. The skeletal and muscular systems work together to produce joint movement using the concept of what?

A) levers

B) applied force

C) synergy

D) proprioceptive neuromuscular facilitation

Answers:

A) **Correct.** The concept of levers in explaining joint movement considers applied force, load, and fulcrum.

B) Incorrect. Applied force is one of three parts of the lever concept.

C) Incorrect. Synergy relates to muscles that assist with movement and joint stability.

D) Incorrect. PNF is a treatment developed in the mid-1900s.

FIVE: PATHOLOGY AND CONTRAINDICATION

All massage therapists must be familiar with conditions resulting from illness, disease, and injury. First, a therapist may need to empathetically refuse massage to clients who suffer from certain conditions that would cause massage to be harmful. Therapists must also always keep in mind their scope of practice and are obligated to refuse massage to clients who have conditions that they are not qualified to treat. In addition, a therapist may need to avoid massaging an area on a client's body if massage would exacerbate a site-specific condition. Massage might irritate, inflame, or spread a contagious pathogen to other areas of the client's body, or even to the therapist. Furthermore, a therapist may need to adapt a massage routine, pressure, and positioning for the benefit and safety of the client. Finally, a therapist may need to obtain medical clearance from a doctor before proceeding with a massage, based on a client's disease or condition.

Pathology

Of Greek origin, the word **pathology** literally means the study of disease. Pathologists study how a disease progresses. A pathologist determines the cause, development, effect on cells, and the consequences that result from the progression of disease.

Practicing massage therapists may encounter many common diseases or conditions and should have a basic knowledge of them.

Acquired Immunodeficiency Syndrome (AIDS) is the result of the human immunodeficiency virus (HIV). If HIV is not detected and treated, T-cells—an essential part of the immune system—are continually targeted and destroyed, leading to an immune system breakdown. As AIDS progresses, it allows the human body to more easily develop diseases and/or conditions such as pneumonia and cancer.

Alzheimer's disease is a degenerative disorder that causes the brain to shrink and neural tissue to die. Mostly found in the elderly, it presents as memory loss, deterioration of language and cognitive skills, disorientation, and ultimately the inability to care for oneself.

An **aneurysm** is an outward bulge in a vein, artery, or even the heart itself when the vessel wall weakens, usually due to hypertension. Considered a silent killer, a cerebral aneurysm generally goes undiagnosed. An aneurysm that ruptures causes hemorrhaging with a high risk of fatality.

Angina pectoralis is a pain in the chest resulting from **myocardial ischemia**, or insufficient flow of blood to the heart. This pain may radiate into the left arm and be perceived as a heart attack. This condition may be chronic or acute.

Ankylosing spondylitis is a type of arthritis that primarily affects the spine; however it can appear where tendons and ligaments attach, such as the ribs and Achilles tendon. It usually begins with pain and stiffness in the sacroiliac joint, bone fusion, and ligament and tendon pain and inflammation. It is progressive and may have a genetic link. Its consequences are loss of flexibility and range of motion.

Arteriosclerosis is a hardening of arteries and a reduction in arterial elasticity. This condition can lead to **atherosclerosis**, a buildup of plaque in the arteries and thickening of the arterial wall. The plaque can cause blood clots; additionally, this condition negatively affects the functioning of the circulatory system and leads to high blood pressure, or **hypertension**.

Asthma occurs when the smooth muscle that makes up the bronchial tubes spasms and constricts in response to an allergen, stress, or inflammation. Excessive mucus production can result. An asthma attack causes coughing, wheezing, and difficulty breathing.

Bronchitis occurs when the bronchial tubes are inflamed and mucus production increases. **Acute bronchitis** is a side effect of an infection such as influenza. **Chronic bronchitis** is a progressive disorder following years of exposure to damaging irritants.

Individuals with **celiac disease** suffer from intestinal inflammation, damage, and destruction of intestinal villi upon consumption of gluten. This damage also interferes with the digestion of nutrients. There is debate over whether it is an autoimmune disease or an allergic reaction to gluten. It is believed to have a genetic link. Celiac disease may cause gas, bloating, and diarrhea as well as other symptoms including irritability and depression. It can be mild to severe.

Cellulitis is a bacterial skin infection affecting both the lymphatic and circulatory system. It usually presents on the face and lower legs as a defined area that becomes red, swollen, and tender.

Cerebral palsy results from injury to the brain during fetal development, birth, and infancy.

Cirrhosis is the result of long term dysfunction of and damage to liver cells. It can be caused by fatty deposits both related and unrelated to alcohol abuse and hepatitis B and C.

Chronic obstructive pulmonary disease (COPD) refers to a collection of chronic lung conditions such as asthma, emphysema, and bronchitis.

Crohn's disease is an autoimmune disorder in which the immune system attacks healthy cells in the gastrointestinal tract, causing inflammation.

Cystic fibrosis is a genetic disorder. It causes the production of thick mucus affecting the intake of air in the respiratory tract and the absorption of nutrients in the digestive tract. Overall it can affect respiration, exocrine glands, reproduction, and skin. The death of someone with cystic fibrosis will most likely be the result of a respiratory system collapse or infection.

Deep vein thrombosis (DVT) is an inflammation of a deep vein caused by a blood clot, most frequently in the popliteal, femoral, and iliac veins.

Diabetes mellitus is a condition classified as **type 1** and **type 2**. Type 1 occurs when the pancreas does not produce enough of the insulin hormone which regulates the uptake of glucose, a type of sugar that results when carbohydrates are digested. Type 2 occurs when the insulin the body does produce is unable to break down glucose. Improperly treated and managed diabetes can result in **diabetic neuropathy**, which is a form of nerve damage that progresses from the feet upwards and may ultimately affect the fingers, hands, and arms.

An **embolism** is a blood clot or gas bubble that moves throughout the circulatory system potentially lodging in the heart, lungs, or brain inhibiting or blocking blood flow.

Emphysema occurs when the alveoli in the lungs are severely damaged or destroyed over a long period of exposure to an irritant that affects the ability of the lungs to exchange gases.

Fibromyalgia syndrome is a chronic pain disorder accompanied by moderate to severe fatigue, sleep disorders, problems with cognitive functioning, irritable bowel syndrome, headaches and migraines, anxiety and depression, and environmental sensitivities. Traditional diagnosis relies on symptoms lasting for at least three consecutive months and tenderness in eleven of eighteen designated tender points.

Gastroesophageal reflux disease (GERD) is when the lower esophageal sphincter at the junction of the esophagus and stomach becomes weak or malfunctions thus allowing stomach acids to backsplash into the esophagus.

Grave's disease is an autoimmune disorder that causes an overproduction of thyroid-producing hormones.

A **heart murmur** is a malfunction or disorder of a heart valve that causes blood to flow backwards and may pool. Increases blood clotting risk. A heart murmur may be present at birth or it may develop at some point in the life. It is possible to surgically repair.

Hepatitis literally means *inflamed liver* usually resulting from a viral infection that affects liver functioning. The most common types of hepatitis are A, B, and C. A is typically caused by contaminated food and water, B is the result of contact with an infected person's body fluids, and C is the result of blood to blood contact.

The **human immunodeficiency virus (HIV)** enters the body by way of blood, semen, vaginal secretions, and breast milk. With detection and treatment, a person can survive indefinitely with HIV. If not detected and treated, t-cells continually are targeted and destroyed leading to an immune system breakdown diagnosed as AIDS.

Hyperthyroidism is an overproduction of thyroid-producing hormones most commonly caused by Grave's disease. **Hypothyroidism** is the underproduction of thyroid-producing hormones.

Lupus is an autoimmune disease that can affect any connective tissue in the body when autoantibodies are created by the immune system and attack connective tissue. Inflammation, pain, and damage can result. It is considered chronic if symptoms last for at least weeks into stretches of years. Anyone can develop lupus but is most common in women of color.

Caused by the **Epstein-Barr virus** which is in the herpes family, **mononucleosis (mono)** is transferred saliva-to-saliva; hence, the reference to it as the *kissing disease*. Fever, fatigue, sore throat, and swollen glands are signs and symptoms of mono. It may last for several weeks and can be minor to debilitating. Possibly related to the Epstein-Barr virus is **chronic fatigue syndrome (CFS)**. CFS is still not fully understood. It appears to affect multiple body systems including the immune, endocrine, and nervous. Like mononucleosis it may be minor to debilitating and last for long periods. Aside from fever, fatigue, sore throat, and swollen glands it also seems to affect short term memory and concentration, as well as induce insomnia.

Multiple sclerosis (MS) targets the central nervous system. While it is related to immune function, not everyone in the healthcare field considers it an autoimmune disease. Myelin sheaths and nerve fibers are attacked and scar tissue forms, affecting nerve function. Studies have determined that MS occurs more frequently in individuals who grew up furthest from the equator, suggesting that vitamin D absorption may be a factor. Childhood exposure to certain bacteria and viruses may also contribute to the development of MS. The effects of the disease can vary. Some individuals rarely have flare-ups, while others experience only brief respite between them. MS may progress rapidly and can become permanently debilitating.

In **muscular dystrophy (MD)**, gene mutations interfere with proteins needed to develop muscle. The result is muscle weakness and atrophy. Many people diagnosed with MD end up wheelchair bound and have difficulty breathing and swallowing. MD may be diagnosed in early childhood, adolescence, or early adulthood.

Osteoporosis generally appears in the elderly. Osteoclasts break down bone faster than the osteoblasts rebuild bone, and the bone becomes more porous and brittle as a result.

Parkinson's disease is a degenerative brain disorder in which production of the neurotransmitter, dopamine, decreases over time. Dopamine affects the ability to regulate movements and emotions. Early stages involve tremors, inability to coordinate movement, and rigidity.

The suffix *–plegia* means *paralysis*. **Paraplegia** is paralysis of the lower abdomen and legs with partial or full use of the arms and hands; **quadriplegia** is paralysis from the neck down. Quadriplegics have the ability to eat, breathe, talk, and move their heads as the cranial nerves are not affected. Paraplegia and quadriplegia are the result of concussion, contusion, compression, laceration and/or transection of spinal nerves. **Hemiplegia** is when one side of the body becomes paralyzed as the result of a stroke.

Raynaud's syndrome occurs when arterial vessels spasm causing vasodilation and inhibiting the flow of blood to fingers and toes. Raynaud's syndrome can be primary or secondary. Secondary is considered more serious as it is generally a symptom of an underlying condition.

Rheumatoid arthritis (RA) is an autoimmune condition that occurs when the synovial fluid in a joint is attacked by the immune system. Left untreated, it will result in further damage to the cartilage and surrounding bone. Aside from pain and inflammation, joints can become unstable, immobile, and deformed. The hands, feet, elbows, wrists, and ankles are most affected.

A **transient ischemic attack (TIA)** occurs when a small blood clot blocks the flow of blood to the brain for a brief period before it breaks up or dissolves. Sometimes referred to as a *mini-stroke*, it is actually a warning sign of a potential future massive stroke.

Ulcerative colitis is an inflammatory bowel disease that affects the large intestine and rectum sections of the colon. It may be considered an autoimmune disorder, but ulcerative colitis is a chronic condition.

Vertigo describes a sensation of spinning and feeling off balance. It is generally believed to be caused by an inner ear disorder such as a buildup of fluid, pressure, or calcium particles; an infection; or injury to the head or neck. Treatment depends on the cause.

Whiplash occurs when tendon, muscles, and ligaments in and around the neck are sprained or strained by a violent thrusting forward motion of the head. Most commonly caused by a car accident, whiplash may cause significant pain, headaches, dizziness, vertigo, and limit range of motion.

PRACTICE QUESTIONS

1. Which of the following is an autoimmune disorder that attacks connective tissue in the body?

    A) multiple sclerosis (MS)

    B) lupus

    C) rheumatoid arthritis

    D) Crohn's disease

Answers:

A) Incorrect. MS targets the central nervous system.

B) **Correct.** Lupus can affect any connective tissue in the body.

C) Incorrect. Rheumatoid arthritis occurs when the synovial fluid in a joint is attacked by the immune system.

D) Incorrect. Crohn's disease affects the gastrointestinal tract.

2. Which of the following is a degenerative disorder that causes the brain to shrink and neural tissue to die?

A) Parkinson's disease

B) transient ischemic attack (TIA)

C) Raynaud's syndrome

D) Alzheimer's disease

Answers:

A) Incorrect. Parkinson's disease is a neurological degenerative brain disorder in which production of the neurotransmitter dopamine decreases over time.

B) Incorrect. A TIA occurs when a small blood clot briefly blocks the flow of blood to the brain before breaking up or dissolving.

C) Incorrect. Raynaud's syndrome occurs when arterial vessels spasm causing vasodilation and inhibiting the flow of blood to fingers and toes.

D) **Correct.** Alzheimer's disease is mostly found in the elderly and presents as memory loss, deterioration of language and cognitive skills, disorientation, and ultimately in the inability care for oneself.

3. Which one of the following is NOT associated with the respiratory system?

A) −plegia

B) emphysema

C) cystic fibrosis

D) asthma

Answers:

A) **Correct.** The suffix −plegia means paralysis.

B) Incorrect. Emphysema affects the ability of the lungs to exchange gases because of damaged or destroyed alveoli.

C) Incorrect. Cystic fibrosis causes the production of thick mucus, hindering the intake of air in the respiratory tract and the absorption of nutrients in the digestive tract.

D) Incorrect. Asthma occurs when the smooth muscle of the bronchial tubes spasms and constricts in response to an allergen, stress, or inflammation, hindering breathing and resulting in excessive mucus production.

4. Which of the following is the result of long term dysfunction of, and damage to, liver cells?

A) cirrhosis

B) celiac disease

C) cellulitis

D) Grave's disease

Answers:

A) **Correct.** Cirrhosis can be caused by fatty deposits related or unrelated to alcohol abuse, and by hepatitis B and C.

B) Incorrect. Celiac disease is indicated by intestinal inflammation, damage, and destruction of intestinal villi upon consumption of gluten. This damage also interferes with the digestion of nutrients.

C) Incorrect. Cellulitis is a bacterial skin infection that can affect both the lymphatic and circulatory systems.

D) Incorrect. Grave's disease is an autoimmune disorder that causes thyroid-producing hormones to be overproduced.

SITE-SPECIFIC PATHOLOGIES

Acne is a bacterial infection of the sebaceous glands most commonly found on the face, neck, and upper back. While it presents at any age, acne is most common in adolescence due to high levels of testosterone that cause excess production of sebum.

Adhesive capsulitis is most commonly referred to as *frozen shoulder*. It occurs in the synovial joint capsule at the glenohumeral joint and is preceded by a condition that causes inflammation. As it progresses, the joint capsule begins to adhere to bone, ultimately limiting range of motion (ROM) in the shoulder.

A **Baker's cyst** may also be referred to as a **popliteal cyst** because it appears behind the knee. It is a fluid-filled bulge that can cause tightness and pain especially during full flexion or extension. It may be caused by cartilage damage or arthritis. The pain can extend into the calf.

Bell's palsy is a condition caused by the impairment, inflammation, or damage to the facial nerve, known as the seventh cranial nerve, resulting in facial muscle weakness or paralysis. The primary triggers are the herpes simplex virus and Lyme disease. Its onset is usually sudden but short term.

Burns are classified in degrees. A **first-degree** burn is generally considered minor and only affects the epidermis. Pain and redness results but recedes relatively quickly. Some dryness and peeling may occur as it heals over a seven- to ten-day period. A **second-degree** burn affects both the epidermis and the dermis. One or more blisters form, and extreme redness and soreness may occur. A **third-degree** burn penetrates all three layers and pain may be diminished or nonexistent as the result of nerve damage. This type of burn results in severe and deep scarring that can affect movement and lead to other health concerns. Surgical intervention may be required.

The body has numerous bursae—connective tissue sacs filled with synovial fluid. **Bursitis** is an inflammation of these sacs, which are intended to protect tendons. The most common inflamed bursae are located in the knee, shoulder, and elbow.

Carpal tunnel syndrome is caused by compression of the median nerve by the transverse carpal ligament. It results in a loss of function and sensation in the hand. It can be caused by repetitive stress. Treatment may be the use of a splint or brace and physical therapy or in extreme cases, surgery. Pregnant women may develop carpal tunnel syndrome as a result of hormones released during pregnancy which will usually subside within weeks or months after birth.

Contact dermatitis refers to an inflammation of the skin that results after contact with an allergen or overexposure to a chemical, cleaning product, or lotion ingredient. A reaction may develop within minutes, hours, or days after exposure. Hypersensitivity may even develop over a period of years to a previously innocuous substance. Contact dermatitis is extremely itchy; scratching can cause the inflammation to spread and weep. It is not contagious.

A **decubitus ulcer** may be referred to as a **pressure ulcer** or **bedsore**. It is primarily the result of pressure preventing blood flow to an area. These most commonly occur in people who are bedridden and not moved or repositioned on a consistent basis.

Dislocation is when the articulating bones that form a joint separate. This can result in damage and inflammation to the muscles, tendons, vessels, nerves, and bursae that are associated with the joint itself. The cause is usually the result of trauma, degeneration, or disease.

Eczema is a skin condition like contact dermatitis, but it is believed to be caused by a dysfunctional immune response to irritants and stress. Eczema is believed to have some genetic origin and can appear at any point in life. The most common indication of an eczema outbreak is red, flaky, dry patches on the skin, yellowish oily patches on the skin, and small, fluid-filled blisters. It is not contagious.

Edema is a general term referring to the accumulation of interstitial fluid in the lymphatic and circulatory capillaries. Causes are generally an inflammatory response from an injury or trauma, infection, illness, and inadequate functioning of the heart, lymphatic system, kidneys, and/or liver. **Pitting edema** occurs when a finger pressed into the location of the edema leaves an indentation that remains after several seconds, indicating a potentially dangerous condition in the body that should be promptly addressed by a physician. **Lymphedema** may occur when the lymph nodes are removed or damaged as the result of surgery and cancer treatments. It usually affects a singular limb or part of a limb.

Ganglion cysts are small connective tissue pouches filled with fluid that form around joints. They are normally not dangerous or painful. However, depending on their size and location, they can interfere with joint function. They may be surgically removed, but this is not recommended unless they adversely affect functioning.

A **goiter** is an enlargement of the thyroid gland.

Gout is a form of arthritis that becomes inflamed. It results from an excess amount of uric acid that is a byproduct of digested proteins, referred to as **hyperuricemia**. Excess uric acid forms into sharp crystals that cause pain, irritation, and inflammation in the lower legs and feet. While the kidneys generally dispose of uric acid, age can affect this function. Gout affects mostly males over the age of seventy-five.

A **hernia** is a protrusion of an organ or other internal body material through the membrane that encases it. A **herniated disk** is due to trauma, weak spinal ligaments, or degenerative disk disease caused by aging and lifestyle, or rupture. These can cause disk material to protrude beyond the vertebrae, causing pain and inflammation.

Herpes simplex is a virus that can cause blisters around the mouth, lips, genitals, thighs, and buttocks. It can be transmitted orally (type 1) or sexually (type 2) through secretions. Oral herpes is generally contracted in childhood. It can lie dormant for many years. Herpes sores around the mouth may be referred to as **fever blisters** or **cold sores**. Herpes is highly communicable. Herpes is most transferrable through contact with blisters that are erupting and oozing.

Hives are an inflammatory skin reaction to an allergen or stress. They appear as small, red, slightly raised areas. They are relatively harmless and usually last for short periods of time. They may be itchy and are usually treated with over-the-counter anti-histamines.

Impetigo is a highly contagious infection caused by the staphylococcus and streptococcus bacteria. It appears as a rash with small, fluid-filled blisters. When the blister fluid seeps, it causes a crusty appearance. Initially impetigo begins around the mouth and nose but can spread to other parts of the body. It is most prevalent in children.

Lipoma is a benign fatty tumor encased in connective tissue. They are quite common and usually appear in adulthood. They can be found throughout the body but many are superficial and easily palpated. They are normally not removed except for cosmetic purposes or if they hinder function.

A **migraine headache** may be the result of genetics, environmental factors, and chemical imbalances in the body. It is generally caused by a dilation of cranial blood vessels. Migraines can be severe and may hinder an individual's ability to carry on daily functions and routines.

A **mole** is formed by an excessive amount of melanin. Moles initially appear as small, symmetrical, flat, brownish marks and may become elevated and rough in appearance. Moles are benign but should be monitored for changes in overall appearance as they can develop into a malignant form of skin cancer. Use the ABCDE method to assess:

+ **A**symmetry—potentially malignant moles become asymmetrical.
+ **B**order—uneven edges appear scalloped or notched.

- ✦ Color—color change from brownish to blackish.
- ✦ Diameter—increase in diameter beyond a quarter inch.
- ✦ Elevated—changes from flat to elevated.

> 🔍 Always alert a client if he or she has a mole with the above characteristics. Some clients may already be aware and are under the care of a dermatologist. Clients that are unaware will appreciate your notification. Also, approach this conversation calmly and professionally. Waiting until a massage is completed and the client is dressed is a good time to raise your concern, not during the massage.

Osteoarthritis results when the hyaline cartilage between articulating bone wears away. Friction between the now-unprotected bones causes pain and inflammation. Osteoarthritis is also known as *wear-and-tear* arthritis.

Phlebitis is inflammation of a vein usually caused by trauma or damage to blood vessel walls, inhibited venous flow, and abnormal blood coagulation factors.

The skin condition **psoriasis** results from rapid replication of epithelial cells. Itchy, pink, and red scaly patches appear on the skin. Its cause is not fully understood, but a genetic link is believed. Psoriasis can be chronic or acute. It also is linked to **psoriatic arthritis**—joint inflammation. It is not contagious.

Sciatica is pain resulting from irritation or impingement of the sciatic nerve. The sciatic nerve originates from the spinal cord and travels down the leg. It is the largest nerve in the body. The nerve runs under the piriformis muscle or, in some cases, through it. Pain is usually in the low back and may radiate down the leg.

The term *shin splints* describes pain resulting from microscopic tears and inflammation of the fascia and periosteum of the tibia, and primarily the anterior and posterior tibialis muscles. Causes include athletic overtraining; changes in a training routine at the beginning of a new exercise program; walking, running, or dancing on hard surfaces for long periods; inadequate footwear and ankle support; and general overuse.

Shingles is a viral infection of the nervous system. Anyone exposed to chickenpox as a child is at risk of developing shingles in adulthood, with the statistical probability progressively increasing after the age of fifty. Furthermore, adults of any age who have a compromised immune system are at risk. Shingles starts with pain followed by the appearance of a red rash that may appear as a strip or band. It is most common on the torso but may also occur around the forehead and eyes. The blisters will erupt and scab over. The blistering is an extremely painful condition that can last for several weeks, but the associated pain may continue for months. Clinically it can be referred to as **varicella zoster virus** and **herpes zoster**.

Skeletal fractures may appear as hairline or stress fractures, partial breaks, or the complete break of a skeletal bone. A **simple fracture** is contained under the skin; a **compound fracture** breaks through the skin, making it more susceptible to infection. Fractures can result from injury or trauma. Due to osteoporosis, the elderly are more susceptible to fractures. Fractured bones may be secured in a cast or splint, could require surgical intervention, and may eventually need physical therapy.

There are three primary classifications of **skin cancer. Basal cell carcinoma (BCC)** is the least serious and most common of the three. Slow growing, it results when unprotected skin is overexposed to the sun. It is an abnormal growth of basal cells in the deepest layer of the epidermis. It rarely metastasizes and presents as a shiny pink or red patch, or as an ulcerated sore. **Squamous cell carcinoma (SCC)** is a more aggressive form of skin cancer that arises from squamous cells in the epidermis. It presents as a scaly red patch, an open sore, and elevated growth that crusts and bleeds. Sores may appear in the mouth and throat as well as on the surface of the skin. Like BCC, SCC is usually due to sun exposure. However, in the mouth and throat SCC may be the result of smoking or chewing tobacco. Finally, **malignant melanoma** is the most lethal type of skin cancer and is caused by mutated melanocytes that form a tumor.

Spinal deviations refer to curvature of the spine. There are three types. **Kyphosis** is an overdeveloped thoracic curve that may result from a muscular imbalance, osteoporosis, or ankylosing spondylitis. In layperson terminology, it can be referred to as *humpback*. **Lordosis** is an overexaggerated lumbar curve due to muscle imbalance, muscle weakness, and the vulnerability of the spine to stress and pressure placed on it by the rest of the body. In layperson terminology, it can be referred to as **swayback**. Finally, **scoliosis** is a curvature of the spine most frequently to the right; it commonly develops during female adolescence. Scoliosis causes muscle pain, tension, and nerve impingement and irritation. Extreme curvature may restrict in the rib cage, affecting the lung and heart functions. Surgical intervention is used only in the most severe cases.

Discussed elsewhere in this book, a **sprain** is an injury to a ligament and may affect associated muscle. A **strain** is an injury to a tendon; it can also affect associated muscle. There are three grades of sprains and strains. **Grade one** has no tearing and little to no inflammation, accompanied by some pain. **Grade two** is a partial tearing accompanied by bruising and inflammation. **Grade three** is a complete rupture that will usually require surgical intervention and physical therapy.

Temporomandibular joint syndrome (TMJ) is caused by trauma to the joint or muscles around the joint, clenching and grinding of the teeth, and stress. Pain may be significant when opening and closing the mouth, and a clicking noise may be heard.

Tendonitis is inflammation resulting from injury to, or overuse of, the junction where tendon meets bone or muscle. The patellar, medial epicondyle, and lateral epicondyle tendons are most commonly affected. **Medial epicondylitis**, commonly known as *tennis elbow*, is related to the overuse or damage to the wrist extensors. **Lateral epicondylitis**, commonly known as *golfer's elbow*, is related to the overuse or damage to the wrist flexors.

Thrombophlebitis is an inflammation of a vein caused by a blood clot in superficial veins. It most frequently occurs in the calves, thighs, and pelvic region.

Tinea is a lesion caused by a fungal infection and is generically referred to as **ringworm**. It presents as a red, circular, itchy patch and can spread on the body and to other people. Tinea most commonly appears on the back of the neck, the scalp, the feet, and the groin. On the feet, it is also known as **athlete's foot**, and in the groin area it is commonly referred to as **jock itch**.

Trigeminal neuralgia is extreme nerve pain marked by sensations of burning and electrical impulses in the lower face and jaw. The cause is believed to be impairment, inflammation, or damage to the trigeminal nerve, known as the fifth cranial nerve. It can cause tics and spasms lasting for varying durations of time.

A **varicose vein** is a superficial vein that becomes twisted and swollen because of damaged or weakened vessel valves. The upward flow of blood is hindered, and pooling results.

A **wart** is a small tumor that arises from the epidermis and is viral in nature. Warts may disappear on their own or be treated by a health care provider. They are usually not problematic unless irritated or damaged by an abrasive, in which case they may become tender, painful, and possibly spread.

PRACTICE QUESTIONS

1. Which of the following is commonly referred to as *frozen shoulder*?

A) bursitis

B) dislocation

C) trigeminal neuralgia

D) adhesive capsulitis

Answers:

A) Incorrect. The body has multiple bursae, or connective tissue sacs filled with synovial fluid. Bursitis is an inflammation of these sacs.

B) Incorrect. A dislocation occurs when the articulating bones that form a joint separate.

C) Incorrect. Trigeminal neuralgia is extreme nerve pain marked by sensations of burning and electrical impulses in the lower face and jaw.

D) Correct. Adhesive capsulitis occurs in the synovial joint capsule at the glenohumeral joint and is preceded by a condition that causes inflammation. As it progresses, the joint capsule begins to adhere to bone, ultimately limiting range of motion in the shoulder.

2. Which of the following is the medical term for *ringworm*?

A) impetigo

B) phlebitis

C) tinea

D) varicose vein

Answers:

A) Incorrect. Impetigo is a highly contagious infection caused by staphylococcus and streptococcus bacteria.

B) Incorrect. Phlebitis is the inflammation of a vein usually caused by a trauma or damage to blood vessel walls, inhibited venous flow, and abnormal blood coagulation factors.

C) Correct. Tinea is a lesion caused by a fungal infection and is generically referred to as ringworm.

D) Incorrect. A varicose vein is a superficial vein that has become twisted and swollen.

3. Which of the following is also called a popliteal cyst?

A) Baker's cyst

B) ganglion cyst

C) lipoma

D) wart

Answers:

A) Correct. A Baker's cyst is also known as a popliteal cyst because it appears behind the knee.

B) Incorrect. A ganglion cyst is a small connective tissue pouch filled with fluid that forms around the joints.

C) Incorrect. A lipoma is a benign fatty tumor encased in connective tissue.

D) Incorrect. A wart is a small tumor that arises from the epidermis and is viral in nature.

4. Which of the following is NOT related to the spine?

A) kyphosis

B) lordosis

C) gout

D) scoliosis

Answers:

A) Incorrect. Kyphosis is an overdeveloped thoracic curve that may result from a muscular imbalance, osteoporosis, or ankylosing spondylitis.

B) Incorrect. Lordosis is an overexaggerated lumbar curve resulting from muscle imbalance, muscle weakness, and the vulnerability of the spine to stress and pressure placed on it by the rest of the body.

C) Correct. Gout is a form of arthritis that is the result of excess uric acid and causes inflammation in the lower legs and feet.

D) Incorrect. Scoliosis is a curvature of the spine (most frequently to the right).

Contraindication

A **contraindication** is a condition preventing the performance of a massage. Some conditions are contraindicated for some types of massage but not for others. For example, a client who has hypertension, a history of heart disease or stroke, a diagnosed aneurysm, deep vein thrombosis, embolism, atherosclerosis, or arteriosclerosis might not be a candidate for Swedish massage. However, the provider may perform energy healing or a type of light touch therapy such as cranial sacral work.

It is important to fully assess a client's condition and obtain informed consent. Pitted edema, lymphedema, a contagious airborne illness, and acute conditions are considered **total** or **absolute contraindications**. A person who is under medical care or treatment for an illness or disease is not necessarily precluded from receiving a massage, but he or she still exhibits a **medical contraindication**, which means permission from the client's physician should be obtained in writing. Three examples of medical contraindications follow.

If a client is under treatment for *cancer*, she or he may still be able to receive a massage. It depends on the current phase of treatment. Practitioners must always obtain a doctor's permission in writing with recommendations for treatment and precautions.

If an HIV client's condition has progressed to *AIDS*, but the client is not confined to a care facility, the practitioner may perform massage with a doctor's permission. Of utmost importance is recognizing that the client's immune system is compromised, so therapists must be especially alert to germs or bacteria. The focus should be relaxation, comfort, and light pressure. Lighting should be at a level where skin is clearly visible. The therapist's nails should be cut short to avoid accidently tearing or damaging the client's skin, and the therapist should wear gloves if necessary. Finally, the therapist's clothes should be clean and freshly laundered. Some states do require specialized training for massage therapists before they work with clients who are living with AIDS.

If a client has recently had *surgery*, the risk of blood clot formation is higher up to four to six weeks after the procedure, depending on the type and length of the surgery performed. The client should have medical clearance and recommendations. In addition, the therapist should be aware of any medication the client may have been prescribed post-surgery; an anticoagulant is an indicator of increased risk.

SITE-SPECIFIC CONTRAINDICATIONS

A site-specific pathology is also a **site-specific contraindication** or a **local contraindication**. This does not imply that massage is an absolute contraindication or that a particular type of massage cannot be performed at all; it does mean, however, that the area in question should be avoided for the safety, comfort, and well-being of the client. A therapist must not spread or aggravate an existing condition.

SPECIAL CIRCUMSTANCES

When providing massage to a client who is affected by a condition, illness, or disease that is detrimental to his or her health and well-being, it is important to ensure that whatever is done during treatment will not exacerbate that condition. A therapist must follow all hygienic precautions, work under the direction of a physician or medical specialist when necessary, and be sure to position the client in a way that will not aggravate an existing condition. Some clients or, often in these cases, patients, may need to stay in bed; a therapist will need to adapt the massage to the situation. Some examples of special circumstances follow.

+ working in a long-term care facility, a rehabilitation center, or hospice
+ treating a client in the home under the care of a physician or hospice nurse
+ treating a client who has an illness that affects mental and cognitive skills and who may require the presence of an adult caregiver
+ elevating the head and upper body of a client with vertigo or GERD during massage
+ adapting massage to meet the needs of a wheelchair-bound client, allowing him or her to remain in the chair
+ treating clients with diabetes, who are less sensitive to pressure and temperature as a result of this condition
+ offering additional cushioning and adaptive positioning to a client with a spinal column condition

It is not the role of the massage therapist to provide assistance dressing or undressing. A caregiver needs to assist before and after treatment.

Therapists must always work within their scope of practice when it comes to contraindications, whether absolute, medical, or local. A massage therapist's level of training and years of experience will factor in to different situations. Therapists should never hesitate to ask for additional information and follow their instincts when it comes to determining capability and comfort performing massage based on legitimate medical concerns. Do not hesitate to refer a client to a more experienced therapist as needed.

MEDICATIONS

Knowledge of medications is important for a massage therapist, as they are an indicator of a client's overall condition. Also, knowing the effects of the medication on the body enables the therapist to adapt treatment as necessary. In this section, many commonly prescribed medications are listed by brand name; their pharmaceutical name, route of administration, and purpose are described.

Advair Diskus® (fluticasone propionate) is a corticosteroid inhaler used to treat COPD.

Amoxil® (amoxicillin) is an oral antibiotic used to treat bacterial infections of the ear and skin, as well as strep throat, pneumonia, and urinary tract infections.

Crestor® (rosuvastatin) is an oral drug that lowers cholesterol and slows the buildup of arterial plaque.

Coumadin® (warfarin) is an oral medication that treats existing blood clots (i.e. DVT, pulmonary embolism) and prevents new clots from forming. New clots may form as the result of atrial fibrillation, heart valve replacement, a history of heart attack, and recent hip and knee surgeries.

Deltasone® or **Sterapred®** (prednisone) is corticosteroid oral medication used to treat inflammation and suppress the immune system. Conditions treated include allergic disorders, arthritis, blood disorders, breathing disorders, cancer, eye problems, immune system disorders, lupus, psoriasis, eye problems, and ulcerative colitis.

Eliquis® (apixaban) is an oral medication that reduces the risk of stroke and blood clots in people diagnosed with atrial fibrillation, as well as those who have had recent hip and knee replacements.

Glucophage® (metformin) is an oral medication used to treat type 2 diabetes.

Januvia® (sitagliptin) is an oral medication for type 2 diabetes.

Lantus® or **Solostar®** (insulin glargine) is an injection pen that treats type 2 diabetes.

Lipitor® (atorvastatin) is an oral medication used to treat high cholesterol and to lower the risk of stroke, heart attack, or other heart complications in people with type 2 diabetes, coronary heart disease, or other risk factors.

Lyrica® (pregabalin) is an oral medication that treats diabetic nerve pain, fibromyalgia, spinal cord nerve pain resulting from injury, and persistent nerve pain resulting from having shingles. It is also used as an accompaniment to epileptic drugs.

Neurontin® (gabapentin) is an anti-epileptic medication used to treat seizures and nerve pain resulting from shingles.

Nexium® (esomeprazole) is an oral medication used to treat gastroesophageal reflux disease (GERD) and other gastrointestinal disorders by blocking the production of stomach acid. This drug is taken over a four-to six-week period.

Niravam® or **Xanax®** (alprazolam) is an oral medication used to treat anxiety and panic disorders.

Norco®, **Vicodin®**, or **Xodol®** (hydrocodone/acetaminophen combination) is an oral medication that is a combination of an opioid narcotic and analgesic drug used to treat pain.

Norvasc® (amlodipine) is an oral medication that dilates blood vessels. It is used to treat pectoral angina and conditions related to cardiovascular disease and conditions, such as hypertension.

Prinivil® or **Zestril®** (lisinopril) is an oral medication that treats hypertension and congestive heart failure.

Spiriva HandiHaler® (tiotropium) is an inhaler used to treat COPD flare-ups. Its purpose is to block the neurotransmitter acetylcholine in the brain.

Synthroid® (levothyroxine) is an oral, synthetic hormone replacement drug used to treat hypothyroidism.

Ventolin HFA® (albuterol) is an inhaler used for bronchodilation. It is primarily prescribed to treat asthma and allergies.

Vyvanse® (lisdexamfetamine) is an oral medication used to treat attention deficit hyperactivity disorder (ADHD) in adults and children, as well as binge eating disorder. It is a schedule 2 controlled substance, meaning it can be habit forming.

PRACTICE QUESTIONS

1. Synthroid® is used to treat what condition?

A) anxiety and panic disorders

B) hypothyroidism

C) seizures and nerve pain

D) gastroesophageal reflux disease

Answers:

A) Incorrect. Niravam® and Xanax®, also referred to as alprazolam, are used to treat anxiety and panic disorders.

B) Correct. Synthroid® is an oral, synthetic hormone replacement drug used to treat hypothyroidism. It is also referred to as levothyroxine.

C) Incorrect. Neurontin®, also referred to as gabapentin, is an antiepileptic medication used to treat seizures as well as shingles-based nerve pain.

D) Incorrect. Nexium®, also referred to as esomeprazole, is used to treat GERD and other gastrointestinal disorders.

2. Which is NOT a reason a massage therapist should be familiar with diseases and conditions that could potentially harm a client?

A) A therapist needs to know when massage is contraindicated.

B) A therapist can avoid spreading a contagious condition further.

C) A therapist can recommend over-the-counter products and homeopathic remedies.

D) A therapist can determine when a doctor's clearance is required.

Answers:

A) Incorrect. It is indeed important to recognize contraindications for massage.

B) Incorrect. A massage therapist must avoid spreading a contagion on the client's body and to him- or herself.

C) **Correct.** Suggesting medications or homeopathic remedies is outside of a massage therapist's scope of practice.

D) Incorrect. It is important to understand when additional permission to perform massage is needed.

SIX: MASSAGE AND ITS BENEFITS

The Benefits of Touch

There are many different types of massage, from Reiki, where massage therapists use no, or light, touch to move around energy or *qi*, to Ashiatsu massage, which primarily requires massage therapists to use their feet as their hands, standing on clients to provide deep-pressure treatment.

The benefits of massage are far-reaching, regardless of whether the client is healthy or unwell (as long as there are no known contraindications that would keep someone from receiving a massage). On a physiological scale, research has shown that massage improves the body's functioning, from increasing blood circulation to decreasing stress and tension, both within the massaged areas and the body as a whole.

Massage therapists should always converse with their clients, prior to the start of the massage, about the clients' goals for the massage, which may include therapeutic healing and/or relaxation so as to achieve peace of mind, a better night's sleep, and more.

> **?** If a first-time client is experiencing headaches and is also nervous about getting a massage, how should her therapist communicate the steps pre-massage, during massage, and post-massage? Role playing, or coming up with hypothetical game plans for a variety of patients and/or client concerns, can help prepare therapists for their first day on the job.

A common benefit of massage is helping the body to achieve and maintain **homeostasis**, or the ability of the body to regulate equilibrium or balance across all systems. On a daily basis, the human body regulates itself due to stress, activity, and temperature, among other factors. (For example, when people run in hot summer weather, their bodies produce sweat to cool them down.)

Both external and internal factors can disrupt the body's homeostasis. If a person has poor posture in his upper back—maybe from driving, or spending a lot of time at the computer—his shoulders can slump forward, which can cause compression in the chest, affecting the lungs and his ability to breathe deeply and fully, causing the body's functioning to spiral downward in trying to make up for the lack of oxygen all the way down to the cellular level. This is where massage can positively affect a client in hitting a sort of reset button in terms of posture, which will positively affect the rest of the body and its ability to maintain homeostasis.

Physically, when a client has misalignment either due to poor posture, illness, or degenerative disease, certain muscles work harder than they need to while opposite, or antagonist, muscles are unable to do their jobs. Specifically, in the shoulder girdle, it is the job of the powerful pectoral muscles to rotate internally and flex the glenohumeral joint. The problem arises when the upper back muscle group tries to do its job of externally rotating and extending the glenohumeral joint. The upper back muscles try to fire against the pectorals, but they are like kids playing tug-of-war against adult bodybuilders—they lose the game and become exhausted in the process.

This exhaustion can translate into pain in the upper back muscles, specifically in the upper- and midtrapezius and rhomboid muscles, or the space in between the shoulder blades at the base of the neck. This posture is otherwise referred to as **upper crossed syndrome** and translates into tight pectorals, neck flexors (sternocleidomastoids), upper trapezius and levator scapula, and inhibited rhomboids and serratus anterior.

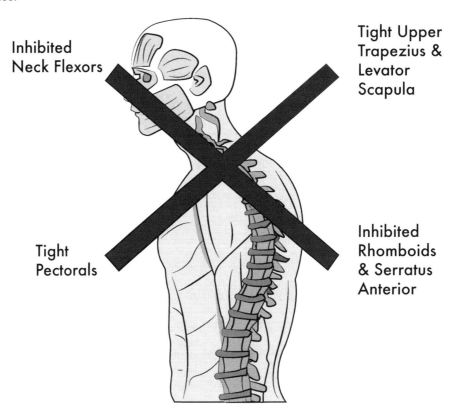

Inhibited Neck Flexors

Tight Upper Trapezius & Levator Scapula

Tight Pectorals

Inhibited Rhomboids & Serratus Anterior

Figure 6.1. Upper Crossed Syndrome

These so-called *power plays* take place all over the body, not just in the upper back and shoulders. A strong knowledge of anatomy and kinesiology benefits massage therapists. By asking clients about their daily activities and areas of pain, and thinking about how the muscles move to achieve clients' tasks, they will know where to spend their time and energy during a massage. This applied knowledge will allow massage therapists to address and, over time, resolve their clients' pain.

It is important for therapists to remind their clients that, while it may feel like their pain came about overnight, it did not, and it won't go away overnight, either. It is important for therapists to help clients see the value of continued, frequent massages—how they help clients in their day-to-day lives, allowing them to perform their activities pain free. If possible, it is best to have the client book a series of massages relating to a treatment plan discussed with the therapist, in order to help the client better manage his or her pain, and ultimately achieve a pain-free lifestyle.

Generally, it is recommended that healthy clients receive massages every four to six weeks for maintenance purposes. If a client has a specific issue, whether an acute or chronic injury or condition, the therapist will need to assess the client and his or her progress, possibly starting with massage one or more times a week, and then gradually spacing the treatments further apart as the client begins to make larger strides in his progress.

ACHIEVING A PAIN-FREE LIFESTYLE

It is known that massage can decrease stress, anxiety, and muscle tightness from daily activities and life in general, but how does the body achieve this level of well-being?

Medium-to-firm-pressure massage stimulates the client's **parasympathetic nervous system**, or the "rest-and-digest" system. The parasympathetic nervous system slows down heart rate and reduces the stress hormone cortisol. It also increases bladder, intestinal, and digestive functions like saliva output.

When the parasympathetic nervous system is in charge, the body works more efficiently in a resting phase. The body is calm and body systems perform their jobs in a timely fashion—like the heart pumping blood throughout the body or the lungs drawing in oxygen. A person in the parasympathetic phase will generally feel at ease.

> Take note of clients' verbal and nonverbal communication before and after a massage. How do they report feeling before the massage? Are they stressed, irritated, or uncomfortable? How are they standing or moving? What about after the massage? Depending on the treatment, are they sleepy or smiling? Do they report no longer experiencing pain, and are they feeling relaxed? This is a case of massage in action.

Light-pressure touch can encourage the client's **sympathetic nervous system**, or the *fight-or-flight* system. The sympathetic nervous system increases heart rate and cortisol levels and decreases urination and digestion. Incredibly deep pressure work, like trigger point release, or working too deep too fast, can also send the client into sympathetic mode and limit the body's ability to heal itself.

The sympathetic nervous system can be activated in moments of stress. When prompt people run late, they may feel their sympathetic nervous systems begin firing, putting them into panic mode. Breath can become shallow and short, and their heart rates can increase.

Table 6.1. The Parasympathetic and Sympathetic Nervous Systems

Effects of the Parasympathetic Nervous System	Effects of the Sympathetic Nervous System
Rest and Digest	*Fight or Flight*
Slow heartbeat	Increase heartbeat
Constrict airways	Relax airways
Increase activity in digestive system	Decrease activity in digestive system
Increase urine output	Decrease urine output
Constrict pupils	Dilate pupils
	Secrete adrenaline

The effects of massage can reduce or manage pain in clients with injuries ranging from acute to chronic. If a muscle or a group of muscles is **hypertonic**, having increased or abnormally high muscle tone, and/or is riddled with trigger points (discussed below), then compressions and deep strokes can increase blood flow into the area, allowing the muscle fibers to relax and start to straighten and lengthen. Clients can extend the benefits of massage through a series of stretches and/or self-care exercises recommended by their massage therapist or doctor.

When in Doubt, Refer Out: If a client is experiencing his or her first or worst headache, the therapist should refer out to a specialist, as the headache could be symptomatic of a larger issue. Additionally, if a client is experiencing any type of unusual or idiopathic symptoms, and is unsure of the origin, it is a good idea for the therapist to halt treatment and refer the client to a physician.

Not only can massage reduce pain and promote relaxation, it also can decrease recovery time after an intense workout or surgery, promote tissue regeneration, increase joint mobility and muscle flexibility, reduce spasms and cramping, release endorphins, and stretch atrophied, weak, or tight muscles. Pre- or post-workout, massage is a great alternative therapy that allows athletes to maximize their performance output.

In the 1800s Hawaiian kings and queens would receive *lomilomi* massages specifically on their abdomens during luaus so they could digest more quickly and consume more of the feast. *Lomilomi* translates into *massage* (sometimes also *rub-rub*) and is a type of gentle massage using long strokes with lots of rocking motions incorporated to help the client achieve a sense of relaxation.

Furthermore, massage can also:

+ promote good posture
+ improve sleep quality

- ✦ provide greater energy
- ✦ enhance concentration
- ✦ reduce fatigue
- ✦ decrease tension headaches and migraines

Perhaps because stress decreases the immune response, massage can increase activity of the immune system by stimulating lymph flow (the body's built-in defense system). Overall, massage can decrease and suppress stress levels.

SPECIAL POPULATIONS

As social creatures, humans seek out positive, compassionate touch, whether a handshake greeting from a colleague or a hug from a friend or family member. Touch—and massage—give the recipient a feeling of general well-being.

Evidence of the connection between touch and well-being goes back to ancient civilizations. Early records in China, dating back thousands of years, mention types of massage and their benefits. Massage benefits both young and elderly, sick and healthy, injured and spry. It offers the same benefits across all ages and stages of health: it increases one's range of motion, circulation, and general sense of well-being, and decreases stress, pain, and tension.

It is important that therapists always perform intakes with their clients to ensure there are no contraindications that would prohibit the bodywork. Specific contraindications include, but are not limited to, severe edema (swelling), inflammation, high blood pressure, congestive heart failure, hypertension, skin damage or lesions, certain types/stages of cancer, and varicose veins. If a client has recently had a major heart attack or stroke, or has recently undergone surgery, the therapist must first receive clearance from the client's physician.

As the baby boomer generation ages in America, **elderly massage** is becoming more common. Many of the aged population are sedentary due to injury, arthritis, balance issues, or circulatory problems. Stimulating, but gentle, massage can achieve results similar to exercise. Additionally, research shows that social connections are a key component to health and happiness in the elderly community. Frequent visits with massage therapists can benefit elderly clients by adding to their support networks.

Aging populations are affected by a number of pathologies, both mental and physical. Gentle massage and joint play can have a positive effect for clients suffering from arthritis. **Synovial fluid** is located within the joint capsules and is released through movement, lubricating the joint and allowing for greater ease of movement for the client.

Massage facilitates both communication and relaxation, so it offers considerable benefits to Alzheimer's patients. Furthermore, the effects of gentle, regular massage encourage clients to sleep more deeply and longer, which allows their bodies to regenerate and repair tissue.

With age, some people develop **varicose veins**—veins that have become large, twisted, and painful. They are most common in the legs but can occur elsewhere in the body. The valves in the veins no longer properly function, causing blood to flow away from the heart and pool in the veins below. If a client has varicose veins, the therapist should work proximal to the site of injury.

Babies also benefit from massage. Massage increases a sense of general well-being and decreases stress across all populations—this goes for infants, too. Because babies do not yet have the ability of speech, parents or therapists should pay close attention to the baby's physical response. Is the baby smiling and cooing during the massage? If so, the massage should be continued. If the baby is fussy and/or unresponsive, the parent or therapist should discontinue the massage and try again another time.

Infant massage can benefit premature babies by encouraging weight gain and growth. Research has found that, for premature and low-weight babies, massage not only can increase their weight, but also can increase bone density and reduce cortisol levels. Additionally, massage may shorten babies' hospital stays and improve cognitive and motor development as they age. When performed by parents, massage can foster baby-parent bonding, in that they are sharing a positive interaction.

Baby massage should be cleared with a physician or licensed healthcare provider, especially if the baby has had any health problems or was recently discharged from the hospital.

Massage can also benefit those with illnesses and/or mental disorders. While it is always important for any practitioner to ask permission from the client, it is also important to have the massage cleared by a client's licensed care provider, such as a doctor or psychiatrist, if a serious mental disorder or incapacitating illness keeps the client from communicating.

Clients with panic disorders or major depression benefit from frequent massage due to its relaxing properties. Some clients with autism can also benefit through positive touch, typically when practiced by someone they are familiar with, such as a family member or their licensed healthcare provider.

Clients with illnesses such as rheumatoid arthritis and fibromyalgia can also benefit from frequent massage. During flare-ups, it is important for a therapist to use gentle strokes when working with a fibromyalgia patient. When a client is not experiencing an episode of inflammation, deeper trigger point work is beneficial through breaking up adhesions and trigger points that were activated during a flare-up. Clients experiencing a flare-up can benefit from light work such as lymphatic drainage, as long as they are comfortable with being touched during their pain episode.

As always, a therapist should clear massage with a client's main healthcare provider if there is an underlying issue that could contraindicate massage.

PRACTICE QUESTIONS

1. What is homeostasis?

   A) the ability of the body to find its way home when lost

   B) the ability of the body to regulate balance

   C) the ability of the body to deregulate balance

   D) the ability of the body to know when not to move

   Answers:

   A) Incorrect. Homeostasis does not navigate.

   B) Correct. Homeostasis regulates balance in the body.

   C) Incorrect. Homeostasis regulates toward balance.

   D) Incorrect. Homeostasis does not control movement.

2. Which of the following is NOT a benefit of receiving massage?

   A) better quality of sleep

   B) increased stress levels

   C) increased range of motion

   D) decreased tension headaches

   Answers:

   A) Incorrect. Massage does promote better sleep quality.

   B) Correct. Massage decreases stress levels.

   C) Incorrect. The effects of massage do increase range of motion on treated muscles and joints.

   D) Incorrect. Massage has been linked to decreased tension headaches in headache sufferers.

Massage Modalities

There are many, many types of massage modalities in use today. The following is a compilation, in alphabetical order, of many of those used in practices, clinics, and spas today. Many incorporate the techniques and logic associated with Swedish massage but others have roots in holistic and osteopathic approaches. Therapists often blend many different techniques from different styles of massage to create their own treatment styles.

AROMATHERAPY MASSAGE

Aromatherapy massage is another practice that builds upon the foundation of Swedish massage. It is the practice of using the natural essential and aromatic oils extracted from all parts of plants, including flowers and herbs. The inhaled scents are intended to have a medicinal effect on a person, both physically and psychologically, by activating and assisting in the natural ability of the body to heal. A diffuser, filled with water, is heated and essential oils are added to circulate the scent through the process of convection. Also, oils can be added to lubricants and massaged into the skin.

The use of essential oils in a massage treatment can have a number of different effects. The oils being used may be calming, like lavender, or stimulating, like cinnamon. Combining well-chosen oils can promote relaxation, reduce stress, and help promote circulation to reduce swelling and pain.

Aromatherapy, like other forms of massage, seeks to achieve a general sense of relaxation and well-being. Aromatherapy massage should be avoided in certain populations, such as those suffering from allergies. It is important for therapists to be trained in aromatherapy before they begin practicing on clients so they know what the specific contraindications for treatment are.

Deep Tissue Massage

Deep tissue massage is not too different from Swedish massage in its use of strokes; the difference comes in the application. Deep tissue massage focuses on the muscles and **fascia**, or **connective tissue** that are deeper (such as rhomboids major and minor or soleus) than the more superficial muscles (such as trapezius or gastrocnemius). In general, it focuses on areas affected by inflammatory medical conditions and injury. In order to reach these deep muscles, therapists must apply more pressure, but to reach the deeper muscles they also must move more slowly so as not to injure the client.

Deep tissue work is usually approached by first warming and relaxing the area and then working deeper into the musculature and fascial layers. The goal is to generate an increased blood flow into the area of focus, separate muscle fibers, and break down adhesions. Techniques are applied in a slow, deliberate manner often using fingers and elbows.

Compressions are often used to warm up the tissue and muscles slowly, layer by layer. Compression strokes are applied without oil in a deep, rhythmic, and slow-pumping action that targets the muscle bellies. The goal of compression strokes is to spread muscle fibers, soften tight muscles, and increase lymphatic flow and circulation within the area being treated. Compressions should not be applied to areas of trauma or in the vicinity of a bony landmark, as into the clavicle or over the patella.

Friction techniques are common, especially cross fiber. The Canadian doctor Therese C. Pfrimmer is primarily credited with the development of deep tissue work in the 1940s. Her book *Muscles . . . Your Invisible Bonds* was originally published in 1977. The Pfrimmer Deep Muscle Therapy® technique is taught and used today.

Clients with chronic pain issues frequently request deep tissue massage. While some clients may say, "You can go as deep as you want," to their therapist, or "I can take the pressure," the therapist should not use this as a green light to beat up a client's tissue. Though a client may say one thing, his muscle and tissues may be saying another. This is where working slowly and deliberately, "listening" to the muscles with the hands, comes into play.

The main goal of deep tissue massage, in addition to promoting relaxation, is to decrease muscle tension in specific areas where the client feels stress. Deep tissue massage accomplishes this by increasing blood flow to the specific area and allowing the adhered muscle fibers to lengthen by direct application and stretch through the manipulation of the connective tissues attached to the muscles.

HOT STONE MASSAGE

Hot stone massage, commonly featured on spa menus, uses heated stones during a massage session. The stones may be placed on specific areas of the body or held in the hand while massaging. This type of massage follows the basic relaxation principles of Swedish massage, but uses specifically placed stones that have been warmed to a high heat temperature on exposed areas of the client's body. Stones are used to warm up the client's tissue by being placed on specific areas, or they are used as an extension of the therapist's hands.

The use of heated stones to promote healing and relaxation is a practice that dates back thousands of years in Native American, Hawaiian, and Asian cultures. The most common stones used are basalt, formed as volcanic lava cools, and river rock. Both become smoothed over time by the natural actions of water, sand, and salt. The heat from the stone is pulled into the muscle, leaving it warm and pliable and inducing an overall state of calmness and well-being. In addition, cold stones, usually marble, may be incorporated into a session. Hot and cold stones can be used in an alternating or localized manner.

Hot stone massage's goal is to melt away tension, quite literally, through heated massage. The heat increases local circulation, which in turn can decrease muscle tonicity. Contraindications of hot stone massage can include acute trauma or injury, skin lesions, high blood pressure, diabetes, or menopause in women (as the warmed stones may trigger a hot flash).

LYMPHATIC DRAINAGE MASSAGE

Lymphatic drainage massage, or manual lymph drainage, is designed specifically to promote healing and decrease edema and pain. It solely addresses the lymphatic system, a superficial, slow-moving system in the body (see chapter 4), and the strokes and techniques used are light, slow, and superficial. Its goal is to assist the movement of lymph toward lymphatic nodes and remap lymph movement in cases where lymph nodes have been removed either surgically or damaged through other treatments such as radiation.

Specialized lymphatic work is proven to increase lymph flow in the superficial capillaries. Light Swedish techniques, stroking and kneading, along with elevation of a limb increase lymph flow. Massage techniques move lymph by mechanically pumping the lymph fluid through lymphatic capillaries by using light touch in pumping and circular motions.

Lymphatic massage can benefit clients recovering from surgery to help reduce swelling and edema. It also can help clients who suffer from fibromyalgia as light techniques might be the only thing tolerable during a flare-up. Additionally, a client who is feeling low on energy or an athlete who just competed in a strenuous exercise can each benefit from lymphatic drainage massage. Furthermore, it may be viewed as an aid to detoxification. While lymph drainage can assist with edema when there is a buildup of interstitial fluid, cases of lymphedema should be immediately referred out to experienced and trained medical providers.

Contraindications to lymphatic drainage massage include, but are not limited to, acute inflammation, malignant tumors, thrombosis, or major heart problems. As always, if either the therapist or client is worried about the ability to use the treatment, a physician or healthcare provider should be contacted before proceeding.

Myofascial Massage (Release)

As mentioned above, fascia is a connective tissue. It covers everything from blood vessels to individual muscle fibers and muscle bellies to organs. Given that it is a connective tissue that surrounds everything, it can sometimes become very adhesive, and therefore restrictive in its movement when a muscle or group of muscles is not working, firing, or moving properly.

Myofascial massage focuses specifically on muscle fascia; *myo* means muscle. This technique addresses fascial restrictions resulting from injury, stress, and repetitive patterns. Myofascial adhesions can build up after acute or chronic trauma. Scar tissue from surgery also causes myofascial adhesions: it accumulates from the overproduction of collagen and resulting lack of mobility, or limited range of motion.

Myofascial massage focuses on penetrating the layers of fascia, from superficial to deep. This massage can be performed on its own, or as a precursor accompaniment to deep tissue massage. Typically, myofascial massage is performed without any lubricant, as skin-on-skin contact promotes the tissue dragging and thus stretching the myofascia. Slow and gentle pressure, superficial stretching, and holding techniques allow the fascia to relax, soften, and release. It should also be performed at a very slow pace, both across and into the skin and muscles, targeting the specific layers of fascia at varying depths.

The goal of myofascial massage is to stretch the fascia, increase local circulation and lymph flow, and increase the treated muscles' abilities to stretch. Its benefits can include an increased stretch response in the muscles, allowing them to reach their end-range motion without pain.

Remember when it was fashionable to tie shirts at the waist to expose the midriff? Think back to those shirts. When the fabric got bunched up to one side and tied up, the rest of the shirt was pulled taut along with it. Now think about fascia and connective tissue. If a muscle is pulled in one direction, it pulls muscles it's connected to in that direction as well! Your job as a massage therapist is to smooth out the tightened fascia so that it does not pull other muscles out of alignment.

PRENATAL MASSAGE

Dating back to shamanism and the early days of midwifery, massage and touch techniques have been used to alleviate stress and pain as a woman's body changes during pregnancy as well as during the labor process. Pregnant women go through a series of physiological changes from the first weeks of gestation as the fetus develops, to sometimes months after the delivery. These changes affect both the muscular system and virtually every organ system. Prenatal massage can be performed on a healthy pregnant woman at any stage of her pregnancy, and often the massage helps the mother to feel more bonded to her baby.

Techniques are generally lighter on the legs, with the goal of moving fluids using effleurage strokes and lymphatic drainage techniques to reduce edema. Positioning is usually adapted to sideline or through additional cushioning designed for pregnancy. There are specific guidelines to follow while performing a prenatal massage in order to ensure that both mother and her developing baby remain safe during and after the treatment.

 While pregnant women benefit from massage, women on bed rest under a doctor's care should not undergo massage therapy.

During pregnancy, the gestation period is broken down into first, second, and third trimesters.

It should be known that the presence of the hormone **relaxin**, typically produced within the first two weeks of pregnancy, affects the composition of collagen in the fascia, ligament, and joint capsules to allow greater elasticity and movement, especially in the abdomen and pelvic region, for delivery. Weight-bearing joints such as the sacroiliac, ankle, and foot joints are more vulnerable as a result, and the treatment should be approached with this knowledge in tow.

The **first trimester** occurs from zero to three months or zero to thirteen weeks, and has the highest risk of miscarriage. During the first trimester, a pregnant woman can have the following symptoms:

+ Nausea and vomiting, which typically occur in the morning of the first ten to fourteen weeks. There are some rare cases where the sickness can last throughout the day, and throughout the duration of pregnancy.
+ Frequent urination, due to the presence of the hormone progesterone, which causes the smooth muscles of the bladder to relax.
+ Constipation, once again due to the presence of progesterone causing the relaxation of the smooth muscle of the intestine.
+ Blood pressure, which often drops in early pregnancy due to progesterone, which relaxes the muscular wall of the blood vessels.

- Growth and tenderness or sensitivity of breast tissue, which begins at this stage and can continue throughout the pregnancy, making certain positions uncomfortable.

- Musculoskeletal changes, which can occur due to the increase of estrogen, progesterone, and relaxin.

- Taste and smell; these can also become hypersensitive throughout the pregnancy.

- Mood swings, exhaustion, and anxiety; these are apt to occur for both partners, due to worry surrounding pregnancy and birth, especially during the couple's first pregnancy.

The **second trimester** occurs from four to seven months, or fourteen to twenty-six weeks. The risk of miscarriage is greatly reduced at this stage in the pregnancy. Throughout this trimester, the woman undergoes several tests and examinations to assess her health, as well as the growing baby's health. Symptoms during the second trimester can include:

- Edema, a common consequence of the retention of fluid, typically resulting from the mechanical obstruction created by the uterus and its contents; this increases venous pressure in the lower limbs, making the woman uncomfortable.

- Hypertension, or, more seriously, preeclampsia, is a major concern for maternal mortality or fetal or neonatal morbidity. Hypertension is when blood flows through blood vessels with a greater force than normal. A symptom of preeclampsia is edema in the face and/or hands. To be sure a pregnant woman does not have preeclampsia, a physician or a midwife should perform tests. Preeclampsia affects seven out of one hundred pregnant women.

- Backache becomes a more common symptom due to the fetus growing within the mother, shifting the mother's center of gravity and pulling her spine forward due to the increased weight gain in her belly. Typically, the lower back is affected more than the upper or midback, but sometimes the postural shift can affect the entire back.

- Varicose veins can develop at any time, but are more likely to develop as the pregnancy advances. This is due to the growing uterus's compression on the lower body veins that sit in the pelvis. While mild varicosities may decrease postpartum, they also may return with greater severity with each subsequent pregnancy.

During the **third trimester**, or the last three months, twenty-seven to forty weeks, many of the symptoms from the first and second trimesters are present, to varying degrees of irritation to the pregnant woman.

- Compression syndromes can become more prevalent. Syndromes like thoracic outlet and carpal tunnel can occur due to edema in the arm and hand. Sciatic nerve compression or piriformis syndrome can cause discomfort down through the leg and ankle.

✦ Fatigue, insomnia, and restlessness are all common complaints made by women in their third trimester. Comfortable positions are often difficult for a pregnant woman to achieve due to her larger belly and the symptoms listed above, causing pain in a number of positions.

It is important for a therapist to be specifically trained in all the changes a woman goes through during pregnancy and how to treat them, as well as how to communicate effectively and compassionately with the mother-to-be. Emotions often run high throughout the pregnancy due to excitement, fear, and/or hormonal changes affecting her general comfort levels. The therapist should bear in mind that the hormonal, emotional, and physical changes the mother-to-be is going through can sometimes throw her into mood swings, and that a relaxation-focused therapeutic massage may be just the thing she needs to return her to homeostasis.

Prenatal massage usually involves focused training and a genuine interest in addressing the needs of pregnant women. The therapist should provide a relaxing treatment through massage techniques and by varying bolstering techniques in order to achieve optimum comfort for the woman. Follow-up may include postnatal massage, which treats the aches and pains associated with nursing, lifting, stress, and hormonal adjustments.

Sports Massage

Again, many of the techniques utilized in Swedish massage are adapted for use in sports massage. Sports massage is designed to help athletes perform to their best ability. The treatment enhances performance, prevents injury, and rehabilitates if an injury has occurred. The iliotibial (IT) band, Achilles tendon, rotator cuff, and hamstrings are some common areas of focus.

Typically sports massage is applied before or after an athletic event. It may be used pre-event to stimulate circulation and warm up soft tissue and joints using a vigorous approach. Post-event it may be used to aid the cooldown process, address aches and pains, and encourage the removal of metabolic waste that has built up during the event. Sports massage may also be used for maintenance between events and workouts to focus on healing injuries, stretching, joint mobilization, and general body maintenance.

In addition to the Swedish massage techniques used in sports massage, compressions and stretching are also incorporated. The goal of sports massage is to address and treat any areas that are either in pain or not achieving their full range of motion.

When performed in a pre- or post-event setting, the client generally remains clothed rather than draped with sheets on a table. Post-event massage is common in long-distance races as well as amateur and professional sports leagues—more often at the professional level. When performed at a spa, the client will disrobe to his level of comfort and lie on a table with sheets to be draped throughout the treatment.

Jack Meager, born in 1923, is considered a pioneer in the field of sports massage. He spent fifteen years developing his technique and methodology. In 1998 he wrote the text *Sports Massage: A Complete Program for Increasing Performance and Endurance in Fifteen Popular Sports.*

> 🔍 Massage therapists should understand performance-related injuries like strains and sprains. A **strain**, or a *pulled muscle*, is when a muscle or tendon is torn. Strains often result from the sudden overstretching or intense contraction of a muscle. Muscle injuries usually heal in four to ten weeks. In contrast, a **sprain** is a ligament injury—usually a tear—and is often caused by trauma to a joint. Depending on its severity, a sprain causes sudden pain, rapid swelling, and even disability of movement. Sprains can take weeks to months to heal. Both strains and sprains should be treated immediately with RICE (rest, ice, compression, and elevation) to decrease pain and swelling for two to three days following the injury.

SHIATSU MASSAGE

Shiatsu massage is a combination massage that incorporates both Japanese and Chinese medicine traditions. Shiatsu technique relies on pressure applied by the therapist's fingers, thumbs, hands, elbows, knees, or feet to specific points on the client's body during the treatment. The specific points are blocked areas along a client's meridian channels (or energy lines, discussed in more detail in chapter 4). The blocked areas are released through deep pressure, allowing the meridian points to be realigned and balanced.

Shiatsu points are called Tsubo (vital) points; the Tsubo points are based more on anatomic locations and structures. Shiatsu also incorporates techniques defined by terms such as *shaking, hooking, plucking, patting,* and *brushing.* The theory of shiatsu incorporates the belief that when the palm presses against the Tsubo point, negative ions in the palm react with the positive calcium ions in the bloodstream. This exchange causes an increase in the calcium component in the bloodstream, in turn decreasing the potassium component that interferes with blood flow. The result is an increase in blood flow.

Additionally, shiatsu massage focuses on rotating and stretching limbs and joints to further increase mobility and circulation.

The goal of shiatsu massage is to work pressure points along clients' meridians to balance their *qi* (otherwise known as energy). Just like any massage, it should be used by a healthy individual with no preexisting conditions that could become complicated or compromised by the treatment.

THAI MASSAGE

Thai massage combines aspects of massage, stretching, energy flow, and a genuine client-centered intent by the practitioner that elevates the practice from a mechanical process to an intuitive flow. It is a massage that combines acupressure with assisted yoga positions, and does not use a lubricant. As a result, a client remains clothed during the treatment. Also, Thai massage is most commonly practiced on a mat on the floor. Pillows, towels, or other types of bolsters may be used by the practitioner throughout the treatment. The massage aspect of it includes pressure, rolling, squeezing, and rocking.

The benefits of Thai massage include increased range of motion and overall flexibility, decreased tension headaches, and increased balance, both energetically and physically. Because of the nature of Thai massage and its assisted movements, it is not encouraged for populations unable to sit on the floor for extended periods of time. Therapists who have a concern as to whether their client can receive Thai massage should perform intake with the client and consult their client's healthcare provider if needed.

TRIGGER POINT THERAPY

Overuse, repetition, poor posture, and trauma result in adhesions in myofascial points. As a result, soft tissue becomes tender and stiff, affecting function and range of motion. These hyperirritable spots, or *knots*, in taut bands of muscles, are **trigger points**. Associated pain can radiate out, affecting other areas of the body.

Imagine a string or a strand of yarn. The piece of fabric has a specific length, but if that length gets knotted up, then it shortens. This is exactly what happens within the muscle fibers when a trigger point is present. An active trigger point not only may result in pain, but also in limited range of motion within the affected muscles.

The goal of **trigger point therapy** is to locate trigger points and manipulate the tissue using compression techniques to deactivate the trigger point response. The compressions may be done with a finger, elbow, or tool. This is an interactive practice where the therapist relies on the client's feedback related to pain and pain sensation over a period of minutes before release.

There are a number of different types of trigger points. First, there are **active trigger points**, which are trigger points that are painful both at rest and with movement. These trigger points are not as common. They do, however, often send out typical pain patterns, so when a client complains of a persistent pain in a specific area, a well-versed

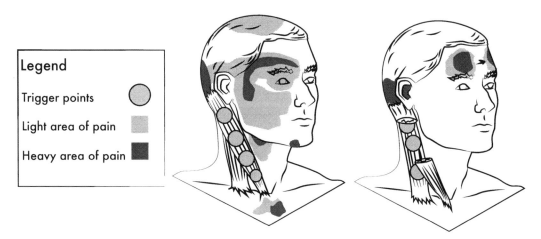

Figure 6.2. Sternocleidomastoid Trigger Points

massage therapist will know that she should check in a specific muscle for an origination point, or in this case, an active trigger point. It is a good idea for therapists to have visual guides handy as references for clients: "Here is the trigger point, and here is the pain pattern it follows."

Certain trigger points can cause headaches. For example, in Figure 6.2, the trigger points in the anterior sternocleidomastoid (SCM) muscle produce a referral pattern that can result in a headache arcing around the eye or the top of the head. Additionally, posterior SCM trigger points can result in referral patterns causing a headache above the eyes or behind the ears.

Second, the most common, **latent trigger points**, only produce pain when they are palpated. These trigger points may exist for years after the initial injury, and produce the same pain patterns as active trigger points, but only when they are palpated.

It is not wholly understood why trigger points persist in muscle tissue, meaning that they are **idiopathic**, or without a known cause. However, it is thought that either direct trauma, overuse of a muscle, or one muscle overcompensating for another bring them into being.

A client's day-to-day activity may reveal why he is being plagued by trigger points. It is important for the therapist to ask questions about the client's activity level, posture during the day and at night during sleep, and items the client regularly carries—from children to bags—in addition to other factors that may play a part in his pain.

Trigger points can be reduced or eliminated through massage. By warming up the tissue and then going in—more specifically, by stripping through the taut bands of muscles—massage can alleviate the pain symptoms. After the muscle fibers begin to relax, or soften, under the massage therapist's fingers, the therapist should perform some relaxing effleurage strokes before stretching the tissue, allowing the muscle fibers to realign. It is important for a therapist to stay within the client's comfort level and not cross her pain threshold, which could cause the client's muscle to guard against the therapist, and maybe even spasm in response.

> **?** During a deep tissue massage, a therapist is working on a client's upper back because of a reported shoulder issue. A band of muscle fibers continues to "kick" the therapist out when she tries to increase pressure. What is happening? How should the therapist continue the treatment?

Pressure on the skin through touch or massage triggers Pacinian corpuscles, or receptors found deep in the skin, that receive pressure stimulation. These **Pacinian corpuscles** send a signal to the vagus nerve in the brain, which slows the heart down and decreases blood pressure. Additionally, touch releases the hormone **oxytocin**, sometimes referred to as the *cuddle hormone* because it increases the recipient's feelings of empathy and general well-being. Oxytocin is a neuropeptide, or a neuronal-signaling molecule that influences activity of the brain, related to decreasing stress and increasing empathy and bonding. (Massage also releases neurotransmitters dopamine and serotonin, which play a part in rest and digestion, too.)

Al Pacino is a deep, physical actor, just like Pacinian corpuscles are deep pressure sensors located in skin.

In addition to the body's biological response to massage, the manipulation of soft tissues allows for increased range of motion, decreased muscle tension and adhesions, and greater spatial awareness. Massage recipients often comment on their increased body awareness during and after massage. **Proprioception** is the ability to sense one's body in relation to the space and objects around it.

? A fifty-two-year-old client, Rose, is worried that her company might fire her in the next round of layoffs and has not been sleeping due to the subsequent stress. Seeing her mother in pain, Rose's daughter bought her a massage. How, specifically, can Rose benefit?

OTHER MODALITIES

Following is a brief overview of more specialized modalities:

Acupressure is a technique that is rooted in Traditional Chinese Medicine. It is like acupuncture but, instead of needles, it relies on the fingers, palms, elbows, and feet to apply pressure to points along energy pathways. The goal is to release muscular tension, promote circulation, and free stagnant *qi* to restore health and balance.

Animal massage generally focuses on dogs (canine massage) and horses (equine massage). Equine massage, especially, is quite old, dating back to the ancient and medieval civilizations of Rome, Greece, Egypt, and Arabia, where horses were prized and used in warfare. Animal anatomy is very similar to human anatomy and animals develop many of the same ailments as humans as they age. Also, sporting events and competitions that involve animals frequently incorporate animal massage into care and treatment routines.

Ashiatsu means *foot pressure*. It is an ancient form of East Asian bodywork. Its original focus was on energy channels. Today, it is valued also because the weight of the body together with the feet provide deep and controlled compression as well as mimicking many of the same Swedish massage strokes as the hands on the body. In the mid-1990s, Ruthie Piper Hardee developed the Ashiatsu Oriental Bar Therapy®, which greatly contributed to the popularity and growth of ashiatsu in the United States.

Chair massage is a practice using a chair designed to place a client in a comfortable seated position. This massage is performed through clothes. A full-body chair massage can be quite effective when performed by an experienced practitioner. Chair massage is generally used to promote the benefits of massage and generate new business. Chair massage services are often found at public gathering places, as a workplace employee benefit, and at sporting competitions.

Champissage™ is derived from the Indian Ayurvedic practice of *champi*, meaning head massage. It includes massage of the shoulders, upper arms, neck, scalp, face, and ears to balance energy.

Craniosacral therapy is a light-touch method of assessing and enhancing the craniosacral system made up of the membranes and cerebrospinal fluid that surround the brain and spinal column. It was developed by osteopath John E. Upledger at Michigan State University, where he performed academic research and served as a professor of biomechanics. Craniosacral work is performed using techniques that allow the body to heal itself naturally. It is a noninvasive treatment that is safe for all ages.

Esalen® massage was developed in the 1960s at the Esalen Institute in Big Sur, California. It integrates many traditional Swedish massage strokes in a slow and flowing manner with the intent to affect, calm, and heal the body, mind, and spirit.

Four-handed massage is a type of treatment generally found as a spa service, and involves two massage therapists massaging in sync with each other. The value is that a great sense of relaxation is induced as the overstimulation to the nervous system results in surrender, release, and ultimate relaxation.

Geriatric massage focuses on the elderly, who experience pain and discomfort specifically as a result of aging and associated medical conditions. These sessions usually incorporate light effleurage strokes and are of a shorter duration than a standard massage. Adaptive positioning, draping, and bolstering are usually required. Vessel and musculoskeletal weakness and frailty, susceptibility to infection, skin dryness and damage, and medications are factors that affect the application of massage. Geriatric massage is usually done in medical care facilities under the direction of a physician.

Healing touch is an energy-based therapeutic approach to healing that clears energy fields in and around the body with the goal of restoring balance and promoting self-healing. This work is used today in many medical care facilities and is safe for all ages and conditions.

Infant massage is usually taught to parents and caregivers, and not performed by a massage therapist. The strokes used are generally very light effleurage and nerve strokes intended to calm, stimulate body systems, and provide a bonding experience. Generally, one or more fingers are used, rather than full-hand contact.

Integrative massage incorporates Swedish as well as other massage and bodywork techniques. The client is assessed as an individual with specific needs and a therapeutic plan is devised based on information obtained during intake. This is a very common approach taken by experienced therapists who have completed many hours of training and hands-on experience beyond massage school.

Lomi lomi, discussed previously, is most closely associated with Hawaiian and Polynesian cultures. It is an ancient and holistic approach to care. The massage aspect of lomi lomi incorporates long, rhythmic, and fluid strokes using the hands and forearms. Other gentle strokes and techniques may be incorporated.

Lypossage is a body-contouring technique that has increased in popularity as a spa service. It uses tapotement, kneading, skin rolling, and effleurage techniques to stimulate the circulatory and lymphatic systems' process of waste removal. It is best known as a treatment that targets and reduces cellulite in a systematic way.

Medical massage is an emerging area of massage therapy that focuses on medically diagnosed conditions. Rather than full bodywork, it focuses on specific areas and problems under the supervision of or prescription by a physician and costs are generally covered by insurance.

Neuromuscular therapy combines the treatment of muscle and nerves. The goal is to determine the nerve involved in soft tissue malfunctions that are causing pain, treat the problem, and retrain the signals sent out by the nerve. This therapy may be incorporated into a medical treatment plan overseen by a physician.

Oncology massage is an advanced training that addresses the needs of those who are in cancer treatment, as well as appropriately addressing the results of cancer treatments that have affected the body's lymphatic drainage system and soft tissue.

Orthopedic massage addresses issues of the musculoskeletal system. Muscle-release techniques, stretches, and mobilization of joints are the focus of this type of treatment.

Polarity therapy was developed by Dr. Randolph Stone, who died in 1981. As an osteopath, chiropractor, and naturopathic doctor, he spent much of his career learning about different forms of holistic and homeopathic treatments that he combined into a therapy that incorporates energy pathways, diet, exercise, and communication to rebalance and heal the minds and bodies of patients.

Raindrop technique uses therapeutic-grade essential oils applied in a sequence along the spine. The treatment oils are high in antioxidants and are absorbed into the body, reducing inflammation caused by viruses and bacteria along the spine. The oils are dropped from six inches above the spine and massaged into the body using light finger strokes as well as massaging the oil into the bottoms of the feet. The principal single oils used are basil, cypress, marjoram, oregano, peppermint, thyme, and wintergreen.

Reflexology, also known as zone therapy, is the belief that areas of the feet, hands, and ears respond reflexively to pressure applied. The theory is that areas or zones map to organs and systems of the body, and that using techniques that apply pressure to those particular areas can alleviate and prevent associated ailments.

Reiki is an energy treatment that uses the hands lightly touching or held just above the body. Reiki practitioners progress through different levels of training and attunements where they learn sacred symbols used during treatments. The goal is to balance areas of the body where energy flow is either too strong or too weak, thus bringing the body into balance and enhancing its own healing ability. While it is not associated with any religion or religious dogma, it may be considered a spiritual practice by both the practitioner and the recipient.

Rolfing®, developed by biochemist Ida P. Rolf, is a soft tissue manipulation technique designed to realign the body. Formally referred to as structural integration and commonly referred to as Rolfing, it is done over ten sessions. It is believed to address pain resulting from physical and emotional trauma.

Tui na addresses chronic pain related to musculoskeletal conditions using vigorous techniques. It is rooted in Traditional Chinese Medicine and related techniques are used in conjunction with tui na.

Visceral manipulation was developed by an osteopath named Jean-Pierre Barral. Viscera, found surrounding internal organs, are manipulated using gentle manual techniques with the goal of releasing restrictions that cause dysfunction.

Watsu®, meaning water shiatsu, is a water-based treatment that incorporates shiatsu techniques while the practitioner supports the client; both are immersed in a pool of warm water. The practitioner cradles, moves, and stretches the client in order to promote healing and relaxation in a nurturing, meditative, and heart-centered manner. This form of therapy was developed by the Zen shiatsu practitioner Harold Dull in the early 1980s.

Zero balancing, developed by Dr. Fritz Frederick Smith in the early 1970s, is a technique that incorporates energy flow and body structures. Finger pressure and gentle traction relax and realign the body with a focus on joints that affect posture and movement. It clears blocked energy pathways, allowing healing and structural realignment.

PRACTICE QUESTIONS

1. What is a trigger point?

   A) the ball of the foot

   B) a hypoirritable spot in a muscle

   C) a bone in the thumb

   D) a hyperirritable spot in a taut band of muscle

   Answers:

   A) Incorrect. A trigger point is not a specific area.

   B) Incorrect. The correct term is *hyperirritable*; the prefix *hypo–* is not used.

   C) Incorrect. A trigger point is not a bone.

   D) Correct. This is the correct definition of a trigger point.

2. Which of the following is a physical response to the sympathetic nervous system?

   A) contract the bladder

   B) stimulate saliva production

   C) increase heart rate

   D) increase stomach digestion

   Answers:

   A) Incorrect. The sympathetic nervous system relaxes the bladder.

   B) Incorrect. The sympathetic nervous system decreases saliva production.

   C) Correct. The sympathetic nervous system increases heart rate.

   D) Incorrect. The sympathetic nervous system decreases stomach digestion.

3. What type of massage is considered the foundation of many other types of massage?

   A) Swedish massage

   B) sports massage

   C) deep tissue massage

   D) prenatal massage

   Answers:

   A) Correct. Swedish massage is a common practice in the West; many other types of massage are rooted in this modality.

   B) Incorrect. Sports massage uses Swedish techniques such as rocking or compressions.

   C) Incorrect. Deep tissue massage incorporates Swedish techniques in its treatment approach.

   D) Incorrect. Prenatal massage is similar to Swedish massage, but the therapist needs special training and certification in order to perform it on a client.

4. What feel-good hormone can touch release in the recipient?

   A) cortisol

   B) relaxin

   C) oxytocin

   D) dopamine

   Answers:

   A) Incorrect. Cortisol is a stress hormone.

   B) Incorrect. Relaxin is a hormone released in pregnant women to prepare their bodies to deliver.

C) Correct. Oxytocin is known as the *cuddle hormone*, promoting a feeling of well-being.

D) Incorrect. Dopamine plays a role in starting motion.

5. What is the term for veins whose valves are not functioning properly and therefore not returning blood to the heart?

A) valvular veins

B) varicose veins

C) lymphatic beds

D) spider veins

Answers:

A) Incorrect. *Valvular veins* is not a real term.

B) Correct. Varicose veins develop when veins' valves do not close properly, causing a backflow and pooling of blood in the veins. They are unsightly and sometimes uncomfortable for clients.

C) Incorrect. Lymphatic beds, or capillary beds, are where blood changes over from ingoing to outgoing properties.

D) Incorrect. Spider veins are a cosmetic issue that can sometimes be a precursor to varicose veins.

6. Which of the following massage modalities does NOT use compression?

A) acupressure

B) shiatsu

C) healing touch

D) trigger point

Answers:

A) Incorrect. Acupressure uses pressure applied to energy pathways.

B) Incorrect. Shiatsu is a Japanese modality similar to acupressure.

C) Correct. Healing touch is a form of energy work that does not use pressure.

D) Incorrect. Trigger point work focuses on myofascial points using compressions.

7. Which of the following modalities is water based?

A) zero balancing

B) hot stone therapy

C) Watsu

D) Esalen

Answers:

A) Incorrect. Zero balancing is a modality that incorporates energy flow and body structures.

B) Incorrect. Stones may be heated in water but this modality is not water based.

C) Correct. *Watsu* means water shiatsu and is a water-based treatment.

D) Incorrect. Esalen is a modality developed in the 1960s that does not incorporate water.

8. Which of the following is considered a light-touch modality?

A) ashiatsu

B) Rolfing

C) sports massage

D) craniosacral

Answers:

A) Incorrect. Ashiatsu is a technique to provide deep pressure using the feet.

B) Incorrect. Rolfing is soft tissue manipulation.

C) Incorrect. Sports massage may incorporate techniques that are deep and vigorous.

D) Correct. Craniosacral is considered a light touch modality safe for all ages.

Hydrotherapy (Hot and Cold Therapies)

Long before the term *massage* was formally used, the relationship between touch and bodywork treatments and water existed. Shamanistic practices often involved applications of heat and cold in some **hydrotherapeutic** form—for example, sweat lodges; saunas where water was poured over hot stones; steam; cold water in streams, rivers, and lakes; and natural mineral springs. In many cultures, water sites, whether artificial or natural, became communal gathering places to heal, rest, and cleanse. The histories of Turkey, Greece, Rome, East Asia, and Persia all reveal traditions of systematic and ritualistic uses of bath sites for hygiene and healing. Most of these places included some form of bodywork, whether with the hands, feet, or tools, to promote healing, purification, stimulation, and relaxation. As massage and bodywork spread throughout Europe and to North America, bathhouses, sanitariums, and resorts became attractions for those seeking health and wellness using water-based techniques and therapies.

Hydrotherapy uses water in any of its forms (solid, liquid, or gaseous) to achieve therapeutic benefits. Hydrotherapy can be used in conjunction with any type of massage treatment. Applied before the treatment, heat can increase the fascia's flexibility and allow the therapist easier access into the client's tissue. It can also be used after vigorous treatments, such as friction techniques during a trigger point treatment, to decrease the inflammation response through administering ice massage or applying a cold pack.

The use of water in treatment affects the body depending on temperature, moisture, mineral content, and pressure. The greater the temperature difference, the greater the effect on the body. Temperatures can range from freezing, at 32 degrees Fahrenheit, to boiling, at 212 degrees Fahrenheit. The temperature used will depend on type, length, and application being performed. Effects vary depending on the length of time applied and the degree of temperature used. Hydrotherapy may be used on the entire body, as in a hot or cold bath, or applied to a specific area, as in a hot or cold pack. Regardless of the hydrotherapy applied, a client should rest for at least the same duration as the treatment to allow the body time to return to homeostasis.

Moisture creates a humid, steamy environment. Mineral baths, whether natural or artificial, generally contain varying levels of minerals that are beneficial for their anti-bacterial, circulatory, detoxifying, pain-alleviating, relaxing, and moisturizing effects. Pressure is generally in the form of jets of water in hydrotubs, whirlpools, and showers.

The physiological effects of hydrotherapy occur as the client's body tries to return to a state of homeostasis. Heat causes an increase in blood flow and muscle relaxation; when cold therapy is used, physiological effects include vasoconstriction and reduced pain.

In a spa environment, the transfer of heat is referred to as **thermotherapy**. If there is a difference in temperature between two areas, heat will always move to the area with the lower temperature. Heat can travel from its source to another area in three ways: **conduction**, **convection**, and **radiation**. Conduction is the transfer of heat between substances that are in direct contact with each other. The better the conductor (such as a heating pad), the more rapidly heat will be transferred. When the body comes in contact with a higher temperature, it will absorb that heat. Convection occurs when heated water molecules rise up into a cooler space and convert to a gas form that circulates in the environment surrounding the heat source. An easy example of conduction and convection is immersion into a hot bath or shower. The body will immediately begin to absorb the heat generated by the water using conduction and, at the same time, the heated water molecules will rise up, creating a steamy, humid environment using convection. Radiation is another method of heat transfer that results without the need for liquid. For example, a lightbulb radiates heat.

Additionally, hydrotherapy can produce reflexive effects. Examples include heat on one limb increasing the blood flow in the contralateral limb, or moist heat applied to the abdomen causing decreased intestinal activity. A therapist should always consider the weight of a treatment pack when applying it to affected areas—for example, a heavy pack would not feel as comfortable as a lighter one on an area affected by bursitis.

Some examples of hydrotherapy applications are found in Table 6.2.

Table 6.2. Hot and Cold Hydrotherapy Applications

Hydrotherapy	Examples of Applications
Hot	compresses, arm and foot baths, hydrocollators, Thermophore, wax (or paraffin) baths, hot stone massage
Cold	compresses, arm and foot baths, ice packs, ice massage, cold stone massage

Compresses can be cold or hot, whichever will achieve a positive effect in the treatment. Towels are immersed in water of the chosen extreme temperature, wrung out, and applied to the client's skin on the affected area. The compress is then covered with another towel used as insulation. The therapist should check on the compress to make sure it is holding its temperature, and change it should the temperature rise or drop. After the application is finished, the therapist should remove the compress and dry the client's skin.

Arm and foot baths also can be hot or cold, depending on need. The forearms are immersed in water up to the elbows, or the feet just past the ankles. Immersion times up to thirty minutes are indicated within temperatures that the client can withstand. Heat will increase blood flow to the areas, while cold will decrease blood flow and reduce localized swelling. After the water treatment, the client's limbs should be dried before further work.

Ice packs are gel-filled plastic packs that are kept in a freezer until they are needed, and can be found in both spas and therapeutic settings. Before application, the therapist must wrap the pack in a towel so as not to injure the client's skin; then another towel is wrapped around to insulate the pack before application to the client's skin. The pack should be applied for twenty-five to thirty minutes, and its purpose is to decrease inflammation from friction treatments, activity, or sustained injury.

Ice massage is typically used in therapeutic settings. Water is frozen in a paper cup. To use, the therapist peels away the top edge to expose the ice while gripping the base of the cup; this is easier than handling an ice cube. The ice is then rubbed over the client's skin in a circular manner. Depending on the type of treatment that occurred beforehand, the duration of the applied ice will vary. Ice massage is commonly used with friction treatment, between rounds of aggressive friction work to break up adhesions or scar tissue in the connective tissue. Ice massage can also be used after trigger point therapy as a distraction before the stretch.

Hydrocollators are one of the most common types of heat therapy practiced in spas and therapeutic settings. They are gel-filled packs in metal tanks containing temperature-controlled water. Hydrocollator packs should be wrapped in towels to avoid burning the client. Additionally, hydrocollator packs should not be left on for more than ten minutes.

Stone massage was mentioned earlier. The goal of hot stone massage is to reduce muscle tonicity and increase circulation through the hot stone application. Therapists can either place and rest the stones on the client's body, or massage with the stones as an extension of their hands. In addition to hot stone massage, cold stone massage also can be used as a treatment to restrict blood flow and reduce inflammation.

Thermophore, like a hydrocollator, is a heat pad, but Thermophore is moist heat and its pad typically comes in different sizes with a control setting for the client. Duration of the application is up to ten minutes, and the client should never lie on the Thermophore pack.

Wax (paraffin) baths are a common feature found on larger spas' menus. Therapists can apply the wax by repeatedly dipping the client's hands or feet into the bath, dipping strips of cheesecloth in the wax and then applying them to the client's skin, or dipping a brush in the wax and "painting" over the client's body or a specific area. Regardless of application method, the therapist should then wrap the waxed areas in plastic wrap and cover them with a towel to conserve the heat. The wax can be left on for up to twenty minutes, then removed in preparation for the rest of the massage.

Hot Therapy

When heat is applied locally, tissue temperature increases: local vasodilation—increased blood flow to the skin surface—occurs, and blood flow to the affected muscles increases, too. Increased blood flow triggers the removal of metabolic waste. Increased temperature also stimulates the immune system, which detects the increase as a threat to the body. The heat directly increases metabolism, oxygen, and nutrient supply, as well as sweat production.

Heat can also benefit joints by warming tendons and cartilage, allowing them to move and extend with greater ease. It softens connective tissue after a trigger point treatment on the area. Perceived pain may lessen as a result of decreased nerve firings. As exposure time increases, the body, through the homeostatic process, attempts to bring itself back into a balanced state, causing vasoconstriction and perspiration, having a detoxifying effect.

Hot therapy is common in treating chronic issues, or spasmodic muscle fibers and groups. Using hot therapy permits the massage therapist to work deeper into the muscle in a shorter amount of time. For example, if a client is exhibiting frozen shoulder symptoms, the muscles are cold and may be contracting. A hot pack on the shoulder warms the tissue and increases blood and lymph flow to the area, while the therapist works into the client's lower back, making for a treatment that is both efficient and beneficial to the client.

As with all massage and body treatments, certain conditions may determine if heat is safe. Absolute and local contraindications of using heat treatments are an acute injury or illness, autoimmune disease or disorder, contusions, cardiac conditions, high or low blood pressure, prosthetics or implanted medical devices (pacemakers and intravenous lines), obesity, skin problems (rashes, abrasions, or blisters), pregnancy, and conditions that hinder sensation (such as some geriatric conditions and diabetes). It is always best to err on the side of caution. You should not hesitate to ask a client to seek out a physician's approval for any type of heat application.

Therapists should always check the heat in order to prevent injury to the client through prolonged exposure.

COLD THERAPY

Cyrotherapy is another word for cold therapy. Cold is a natural anti-inflammatory, causing vasoconstriction that decreases blood flow and cell metabolism for a period of up to twenty minutes. After that, the vessels will begin to dilate again in order to bring the body back into a balanced state by returning blood circulation. Local vasoconstriction allows the cold to penetrate deeper into the tissue as the warm blood flowing to the area decreases. Lower temperatures increase blood viscosity and, as a result, reduce bleeding. Generally, cold therapy reduces edema, inflammation, swelling, and bleeding. With a prolonged cold application, cell metabolism and leukocyte migration also decrease, reducing inflammation as a result. When used locally, cold therapy lowers the temperature of the skin, muscle, and joint to which it is applied.

To better understand how cold therapy works, think of inflammation like a traffic jam. There is a blockage of some sort in the road—in this case, an injury that red blood cells and lymph are running to clean up. However, as a result there is so much congestion that nothing is moving. With all the blood and lymph rushing to the area, heat and swelling increase. A cold therapy application comes in like a traffic cop, closing down lanes—in this case, vasoconstriction occurs—while the accident gets cleaned up and repaired with the blood and lymph that are already there. When the ice is removed, traffic can flow again at its normal pace. Should swelling and heat build up again, then ice should be reapplied. It is best for ice to be applied immediately up to forty-eight hours after the injury to help the healing process.

Pain is decreased with cold application, either because cold is a counterirritant, or because cold blocks pain transmission. Muscle spasms also can decrease due to reduced muscle spindle firing. Collagen flexibility is decreased with cold application. Brief cold applications can have a stimulating effect because the body is trying to regain homeostasis, and begins working harder to achieve that balance. Some studies have shown that when cold was applied to clients with chronic inflamed joint disease, their pain and stiffness decreased, while their range of motion increased.

The most common methods of cold application include cold packs, cold stone treatments, and immersion. Aside from cold stone therapy, most cold applications are used in clinics where sports massage is provided, such as physical therapy facilities, and in full-service spas, where cold plunge pools and showers are available.

It is important that a therapist not place the cold application directly on the client's skin, so as not to introduce frostbite.

Use this mnemonic device to remember cold therapy application stages: When it is cold outside, you need to **C**lean **T**he **B**aby's **N**ose (cold, tingling, burning, and numbness).

Cold therapy often is not as well received as heat therapy, but once the client gets used to it, this therapy can reduce pain and spasms. Typical cold therapy application is twenty to thirty minutes; during the application, a client should experience the following stages in this order: a sensation of cold, tingling or itching, aching or burning, and finally numbness. The therapist should advise the client that these stages are normal and to be expected. The therapist should also ask the client to speak up if the client reaches the numbness stage early so that the application can be removed.

Like hot therapy, cold therapy also has certain contraindications. While cold therapy is often welcome in warmer months, it can be too uncomfortable for some clients in colder weather. If a client who is already cold receives cold therapy, the application will further decrease the client's body temperature and could lead to other complications. Raynaud's disease and other circulatory insufficiencies also contraindicate cold therapy applications.

CONTRAST THERAPY

Contrast therapy is typically performed in the subacute or chronic stages of an injury. A warm or hot application is followed by a cool or cold application for a number of rounds. Hot and cold therapy applications may be repeated for several rounds for a greater effect on the local circulation. Contrast therapy always starts with a hot application and always concludes with a cold application. The ratio for application is 3:1, or three minutes of heat followed by one minute of cold. The greater the difference in temperature, the greater the effects will be on local circulation.

Contrasting hot and cold therapies causes alternating vasodilation and vasoconstriction of blood flow. This type of therapy helps to decrease edema and increase tissue healing by forcibly moving metabolites through the blood.

Contrast therapy can be achieved through the use of hot and cold packs, or hot and cold foot and arm baths. Self-care can be performed at a local bathhouse with hot and cold pools.

Therapists should be aware of contrast therapy contraindications. Clients with acute conditions and injuries should avoid contrast therapy. Additionally, clients with vascular pathologies (heart issues) should also avoid contrast therapy treatment, as should clients who are sensitive to drastic temperature changes.

? Why should contrast therapy be avoided in the acute stage? What happens in the acute stage of an injury that would not benefit from extreme transitions from hot to cold?

In spa environments, massage therapists may find themselves providing treatments that incorporate massage with other applications such as **body wraps** and **scrubs**. Body wrapping is generally used to relax and detoxify the body by increasing body temperature, resulting in sweating. Body scrubs, using salts and sugar, incorporate friction to stimulate and exfoliate. These treatments may begin and end with a vigorous or relaxing massage. Most spas will have signature treatments that are taught to employees on-site.

A therapist should never leave the treatment room while a client is undergoing hydrotherapy, especially if it is hot. A client should never be left unattended, not only to prevent liability against the therapist, but also for the client's well-being. A therapist should check in with the client and monitor the client's skin under the heat or cold, ensuring the temperature is not too extreme and won't cause burning or other damage.

PRACTICE QUESTIONS

1. What does the mnemonic device *Clean The Baby's Nose* stand for?

   A) Cold, Tingling, Burning, Numbness

   B) Cool, Twinging, Blistering, Numbness

   C) Cold, Twitching, Burning, Numbness

   D) Cold, Tingling, Burning, Nerve damage

   Answers:

   A) **Correct.** Cold, tingling, burning, and numbness are the client's responses to cryotherapy.

   B) Incorrect. The client should not feel twinging and should definitely not blister from cryotherapy.

   C) Incorrect. The client should not twitch from the cryotherapy treatment.

   D) Incorrect. The client should definitely not experience nerve damage from proper cryotherapy application. Therapists should review contraindications and perform thorough intake with clients before treatment.

2. When using contrast therapy, what is the ratio for heat-to-cold duration?

   A) 2:1

   B) 3:3

   C) 1:3

   D) 3:1

   Answers:

   A) Incorrect. There needs to be a 3:1 application in order to produce greater benefits.

   B) Incorrect. Cold therapy should be applied for a shorter amount of time so as not to erase the benefits of hot therapy.

C)   Incorrect. Heat is applied longer than cold is.

      D)   **Correct.** A three-minute heat application to a one-minute cold application should be used.

3.   What are the benefits of cryotherapy?

      A)   vasodilation

      B)   vasoconstriction

      C)   increased inflammation

      D)   increased lymph flow

Answers:

A)   Incorrect. Vasodilation occurs with heat application.

B)   **Correct.** Vasoconstriction occurs with cold therapy.

C)   Incorrect. Cold therapy decreases inflammation.

D)   Incorrect. Cold therapy decreases lymph flow to the area.

4.   Which of the following is NOT a benefit of hot therapy?

      A)   vasodilation

      B)   vasoconstriction

      C)   increased blood flow and lymph flow

      D)   decreased nerve firings

Answers:

A)   Incorrect. Vasodilation is a benefit of hot therapy.

B)   **Correct.** Vasoconstriction occurs with the application of cold therapy.

C)   Incorrect. Hot therapy increases blood and lymph flow to the area.

D)   Incorrect. Hot therapy decreases nerve firings of the area applied.

5.   When should therapists leave the room when using hot therapy?

      A)   after ten minutes

      B)   only if they really have to go to the bathroom

      C)   never

      D)   after the first application

Answers:

A)   Incorrect. Therapists should never leave the room during hot therapy applications.

B)   Incorrect. Therapists should take care of personal needs before and after treatments, and they should never leave the client alone during the treatment.

C) Correct. Therapists should always be in the room during a treatment.

D) Incorrect. Therapists should stay in the room and continue the treatment after the first application.

6. Steam is the result of what scientific process?

A) radiation

B) conduction

C) convection

D) thermotherapy

Answers:

A) Incorrect. Radiation is the transfer of heat without the need for a liquid.

B) Incorrect. Conduction is the transfer of heat between substances in direct contact with each other.

C) Correct. Convection occurs when heated water molecules rise up into a cooler space and convert into steam.

D) Incorrect. *Thermotherapy* is a general term for heat transfer, not a specific type.

7. A hydrocollator pack is usually filled with what?

A) water

B) ice

C) herbs

D) silicon

Answers:

A) Incorrect. A hydrocollator pack is immersed in a bath of water for heating, not filled with water.

B) Incorrect. A hydrocollator pack is immersed in a bath of water for heating, not filled with ice.

C) Incorrect. A hydrocollator pack is not used for herbal treatments or applications.

D) Correct. A hydrocollator pack is filled with a granular substance, usually silicon.

8. Cold treatments are referred to as what specific type of therapy?

A) cryotherapy

B) hydrotherapy

C) thermotherapy

D) neuromuscular therapy

A) **Correct.** Cryotherapy is the use of cold for treatments or applications.

B) Incorrect. *Hydrotherapy* is a general term for a treatment or application using water.

C) Incorrect. Thermotherapy is the use of heat for treatments or applications.

D) Incorrect. Neuromuscular therapy is a modality that combines the treatment of muscles and nerves.

PART II: Practice

SEVEN: Practice Test One

READ THE QUESTION CAREFULLY AND CHOOSE THE MOST CORRECT ANSWER.

1. How long should a massage therapist keep a client's records?

    A) one month

    B) ten days

    C) three years

    D) ten years

2. What is the name of the circulatory system function that delivers nutrients and oxygen to tissues and organs and also collects cell waste from interstitial fluids?

    A) hypophyseal

    B) diastolic

    C) capillary exchange

    D) hepatic portal

3. A professional organization provides all of the following services except one. Which one?

    A) legal representation for members

    B) a code of ethics

    C) legislative updates affecting the profession

    D) public awareness

4. The book *The Art of Massage* was published by whom?

    A) Douglas O. Graham

    B) John Harvey Kellogg

    C) Aulus Cornelius Celsus

    D) Pehr Henrik Ling

5. Which of the following is NOT a benefit of massage?

    A) decreased cortisol levels

    B) increased heart rate

    C) increased oxytocin levels

    D) decreased sympathetic nervous system firings

6. Filtrate is a fluid in the urinary system. Which of the following is *true* about filtrate?

    A) Ninety-nine percent is urinated out of the body.

    B) One percent is retained by the body.

    C) Filtrate primarily consists of toxic waste.

    D) Most filtrate is reabsorbed.

7. What are the two primary lymphatic structures?

   A) spleen and vermiform appendix

   B) afferent and efferent lymphatic vessels

   C) right lymphatic duct and thoracic duct

   D) bone marrow and the thymus

8. Which cranial nerve is related to tongue movement?

   A) trochlear

   B) facial

   C) olfactory

   D) hypoglossal

9. Which of the following is a set of limits that defines and maintains a relationship?

   A) nonverbal cues

   B) licenses

   C) designations

   D) boundaries

10. What does the acronym *SOAP* stand for in SOAP notes?

   A) Subjective Obtain Act Plan

   B) Subjective Objective Assessment Plan

   C) Sound Off All Parties

   D) Subjective Objective Ask Plan

11. Who or what is amma?

   A) the first formal written record of Chinese medical practices

   B) the Yellow Emperor of China

   C) a system of manual and energy techniques

   D) a Greek word for rubbing

12. Which of the following is a skin condition resulting from rapid replication of epithelial cells?

   A) mole

   B) wart

   C) eczema

   D) psoriasis

13. Who should NOT receive a full-body massage?

   A) a client with fibromyalgia

   B) a lonely client

   C) an angry client

   D) a client with hypertension

14. When therapists receive telephone calls from potential clients, they should do what?

   A) be present and enthusiastic

   B) explain the fee schedule first

   C) relate their skills and abilities

   D) explain their hours up front so they can establish boundaries at the outset

15. Which is the yang organ of digestion that peaks from 9 p.m. to 11 p.m.? Its element is fire, and it has twenty-three acupressure points.

   A) triple warmer

   B) pericardium

   C) stomach

   D) bladder

16. Which of the following is NOT a principle of massage?

   A) deep-superficial-deep

   B) general-specific-general

   C) peripheral-central-peripheral

   D) proximal-distal-proximal

17. What term did Hippocrates use to classify phlegm, blood, yellow bile, and black bile?

   A) Hellenic

   B) anatripsis

   C) systematic principles of diagnosis

   D) the four humors

18. Each of the following options list two things a state may require or specify, except one. Which one?

   A) hours of education, US citizenship

   B) designation, license renewal requirements

   C) accepted exam, liability insurance

   D) CPR training, certificate of health

19. Bolus and chyme are associated with which body system?

   A) reproductive

   B) endocrine

   C) urinary

   D) digestive

20. What should be included in the S of a SOAP note?

   A) symptoms the client talks about

   B) things the therapist sees on the client

   C) signs of injury

   D) scheduling issues

21. What is fascia?

   A) Fascia is a muscle that lies just under the dermis.

   B) Fascia is a connective tissue that only covers bones.

   C) Fascia is a connective tissue that covers everything from blood vessels to muscles.

   D) Fascia is a ligament sheath.

22. Regarding burns, which statement is NOT correct?

   A) A first-degree burn is considered relatively minor.

   B) A third-degree burn results in the most pain.

   C) A fourth-degree burn may be diagnosed if the damage reaches tendon and bone.

   D) A second-degree burn may require a skin graft.

23. Inspiration occurs when the pressure within what structures falls below the atmospheric pressure?

   A) maxillary sinus

   B) nasal cavity

   C) alveolar sacs

   D) bronchioles

24. What stages does the client's body go through when receiving a cold treatment?

   A) burning, tingling, cold, numbness

   B) numbness, cold, tingling, burning

   C) cold, burning, tingling, numbness

   D) cold, tingling, burning, numbness

25. If self-disclosure during massage sessions moves from a client sharing information that is pertinent to the massage to revealing personal information that is unrelated to the massage, what might be the outcome?

   A) The therapist-client bond becomes stronger.

   B) The therapist begins to consider pursuing a new career as a psychologist.

   C) The client will keep coming back because the therapist is such a good listener.

   D) The therapist begins to feel resentful and burned out.

26. Which of the following is NOT true about Pehr Henrik Ling?

A) He was a Swedish physician.

B) He opened the Swedish Royal Central Institute of Gymnastics.

C) He created the Swedish movement cure.

D) He is considered the father of physical therapy.

27. What happens to the body in the parasympathetic nervous system?

A) decreased heart rate, increased digestion, inhibited saliva

B) increased heart rate, decreased digestion, decreased saliva

C) decreased heart rate, relaxed bladder, increased digestion

D) decreased heart rate, increased digestion, contracted bladder

28. What is NOT one of the best ways to become competent in a modality?

A) taking a weekend workshop

B) understanding the relationship between anatomy and physiology and the modality

C) familiarizing oneself with evidence-based studies

D) a genuine belief the therapy will do no harm

29. What should be included in the O of a SOAP note?

A) obtuse information

B) oblique pain

C) observed information

D) obvious information

30. Which statement is NOT true about chakra balancing?

A) Chakras are energy channels that function separately.

B) Chakras' energy channels are located along the midline.

C) Colors associated with chakras are formed by vibrational frequencies and wavelengths.

D) Chakra energy channels are associated with organs, systems, and anatomical locations.

31. If a therapist is almost 100 percent certain a coworker is gathering personal information from client files, what should he do?

A) He should approach the coworker and ask her what the heck she is doing.

B) Do nothing. It is not up to the therapist to police his coworkers.

C) He should call the state board and report his suspicions.

D) He should tell his supervisor what he thinks his coworker is doing and why he came to that conclusion.

32. What is an inflammatory bowel disease that affects the large intestine and rectum sections of the colon?

A) ulcerative colitis

B) Crohn's disease

C) celiac disease

D) goiter

33. Which of the following is NOT true of an effleurage stroke?

A) It is a gliding stroke.

B) It distributes lotion.

C) It assesses muscle tone and tightness.

D. Techniques include tapping and plucking.

34. What is a blood-borne pathogen?

   A) an infectious microorganism in human blood that can cause disease

   B) an infectious microorganism in plants

   C) a deadly pathogen in the air that gets in blood

   D) anything that carries germs

35. Which of the following terms is NOT related to proprioceptive neuromuscular facilitation (PNF) treatment?

   A) slow twitch

   B) spiral-diagonal

   C) hold-relax stretch

   D) contract-relax stretch

36. Peyer's patches and tonsils are most closely associated with which body system?

   A) immune

   B) digestive

   C) lymphatic

   D) endocrine

37. If a client arrives for a massage drunk, the therapist can refuse to massage based on what?

   A) personal safety

   B) contraindications

   C) improper hygiene

   D) revulsion to the smell of alcohol

38. All but one of the following massage modalities were developed by osteopaths. Which one?

   A) polarity therapy

   B) visceral manipulation

   C) zero balancing

   D) Watsu

39. Who benefits from massage?

   A) everyone

   B) only babies

   C) everyone but babies

   D) everyone but the elderly

40. What are the two types of myofibrils?

   A) actin and myosin

   B) troponin and tropomyosin

   C) ADP and ATP

   D) epimysium and perimysium

41. If a client writes on an intake form that she had cancer treatment years ago and fully recovered, what is a logical question?

   A) "Did you ask your doctor if it is okay to get a massage?"

   B) "Did you have any lymph nodes removed in the course of treatment?"

   C) "Do you have a family history of cancer?"

   D) "Was your recovery difficult for you and your family?"

42. What should be included in the *A* of a SOAP note?

   A) actions of the client

   B) actions of the therapist

   C) a new idea about the client's issue

   D) a recommendation for a new therapist

43. What is the name of the sphincter that is located at the junction of the stomach and small intestine?

   A) lower esophageal

   B) sphincter of Oddi

   C) ileocecal

   D) pyloric

44. All of the following EXCEPT one are concepts and terminology found in a professional code of ethics. Which one?

   A) a commitment to competence

   B) honesty and integrity

   C) annually renewing membership to maintain a professional license

   D) confidentiality of client information

45. What happens to the body in the sympathetic nervous system?

   A) increased heart rate, constricted airways, decreased digestion

   B) increased heart rate, relaxed airways, secretion of epinephrine

   C) increased heart rate, contracted bladder, increased digestion

   D) increased heart rate, increased digestion, relaxed airways

46. Which statement is NOT correct?

   A) Lymphatic trunks feed into the right lymphatic duct and the thoracic duct.

   B) The cisterna chyli collects lymph draining from the abdomen and lower body.

   C) The vermiform appendix is the most important secondary lymphatic structure.

   D) The spleen has only afferent lymphatic vessels.

47. What is the importance of keeping and maintaining SOAP notes?

   A) to instruct on how to clean laundry

   B) to know how to better treat other clients

   C) to keep for a therapist's scrapbook

   D) to list clients' issues and track their progress

48. In massage therapy, when is NOT getting informed consent okay?

   A) when a client runs late for an appointment, for the purpose of giving a client as much hands-on massage time as possible

   B) when a client gets weekly massages and it is just not necessary anymore

   C) never

   D) when a client is deaf

49. If a client begins to cry and discloses that he has been really depressed and is considering suicide, what is the therapist's obligation?

   A) A massage therapist is bound by rules of confidentiality and cannot disclose this threat.

   B) The therapist should end the massage immediately and call 911.

   C) The therapist should listen attentively and be empathetic.

   D) When the massage is over, the therapist should immediately call the National Suicide Prevention Lifeline and ask for advice and guidance.

50. Which type of joint is classified as slightly movable?

   A) synarthrotic

   B) diarthrotic

   C) synovial

   D) amphiarthrotic

51. Which of the following is a corticosteroid?

   A) Januvia®

   B) Metformin

   C) prednisone

   D) lisinopril

52. A modality of massage and bodywork that includes balancing energy flow, attunements, and sacred symbols is called what?

A) Reiki

B) craniosacral

C) lomi lomi

D) raindrop technique

53. What is a benefit of percussion?

A) to feel the beat

B) to warm up muscles

C) to stimulate muscles

D) to cause the client to bleed

54. Legally, who can provide massage in a professional setting?

A) anyone

B) a licensed massage therapist

C) a licensed esthetician

D) a sports coach

55. There are two types of immune responses, innate and adaptive. Which body system is most closely associated with the adaptive response?

A) digestive

B) integumentary

C) lymphatic

D) respiratory

56. Continually attempting to engage with the therapist socially is a sign of what psychological occurrence?

A) transference

B) dual relationship

C) contraindication

D) sexual misconduct

57. The autonomic nervous system is broken down into which two subcategories?

A) brain and spinal cord

B) central and peripheral nervous systems

C) parasympathetic and sympathetic

D) somatic and brain

58. In traditional Chinese medicine, which element represents late summer and nurturing?

A) water

B) earth

C) metal

D) wood

59. Transference may trigger what?

A) a nonverbal cue from a client

B) a job promotion

C) countertransference

D) a written warning from a supervisor to an employee

60. What should be included in the *P* of a SOAP note?

A) patient information

B) palliative care

C) plans for future treatments

D) performance review

61. What is NOT the description of a trigger point?

A) a hyperirritable spot in a taut band of muscle

B) a tense area that radiates pain when activated

C) an area of discomfort otherwise known as a knot

D) a hyperirritable spot near the tendon of a muscle

62. If a new client arrives for an appointment, the therapist should do what?

   A) shout from another room that she is busy with a client so the newcomer will think she has a busy practice

   B) greet the client with a hug and tell her that she has come to the right place

   C) give the client a form to fill out and tell her you will return in five or ten minutes

   D) greet the client courteously, give her the intake form, and tell her you will be available if she has any questions

63. What does "being safe" mean for a massage therapist?

   A) looking both ways before crossing the street

   B) planning an evacuation in the event of emergency

   C) identifying and controlling hazards and risks

   D) identifying and addressing pain

64. What is the term used to identify a muscle that opposes a movement?

   A) synergist

   B) antagonist

   C) prime mover

   D) fixator

65. Which of the following is true about shamans?

   A) Illness and disease were believed to be caused by shamans.

   B) Shamans were considered to be evil.

   C) Shamans were considered to be healers in their tribes.

   D) Only male members of tribes were shamans.

66. What is hydrotherapy?

   A) therapy using firemen's hoses

   B) therapy on a table in a pool

   C) therapy using water in any of its forms to achieve therapeutic effect

   D) therapy using no water

67. The clavicle articulates with the manubrium forming what joint?

   A) glenohumeral

   B) sternoclavicular

   C) acromioclavicular

   D) acetabulofemoral

68. Which of the following is NOT true of a contraindication?

   A) A contraindication implies that no massage may be performed.

   B) Pitted edema is a site-specific contraindication.

   C) An aneurysm is a condition that would not benefit from a Swedish massage.

   D) A client with a medical condition that is in an acute state should not receive a massage.

69. What is effleurage?

   A) Effleurage is to knead.

   B) Effleurage is to glide, stroke, or touch lightly.

   C) Effleurage is to use friction deep in the muscle belly.

   D) Effleurage is to stroke in a deep, rhythmic, and slow manner.

70. How do trigger points develop?

   A) shooting a gun

   B) repetitive activity or injury

   C) blood flow to the area backs up

   D) standing for long periods of time

71. A fifteen-year-old boy who is on the soccer team at school comes to a therapist for a massage with parental consent. During the massage the client grimaces when the therapist massages his upper arm. The therapist expresses concern and asks if the pressure is okay. The client replies that in the locker room after a game his coach grabbed his arm and told him his mistake cost the game. What should the massage therapist do?

   A) The therapist should tell the boy she is sorry about what happened.

   B) She feels really bad, but what can she do? It is up to his parents to deal with this issue.

   C) The therapist should avoid the area and, when the massage is complete, communicate with the parents about what their son disclosed and then follow up with a call to social services.

   D) The therapist should excuse herself from the massage and contact social services immediately.

72. The brain's hypothalamus prompts which part of the pituitary gland to release, and inhibit its release of, hormones?

   A the cortex

   B) the anterior lobe

   C) the posterior lobe

   D) the medulla

73. What is kneading?

   A) Kneading is to stroke gently.

   B) Kneading is to pick up the muscle and pull away from the body.

   C) Kneading is to pick up the muscle and move in a circular, squeezing compression.

   D) Kneading is to squeeze the AC joint.

74. Which of the following refers to an outward bulge in a vein, artery, or the heart itself caused by weakening of the vessel wall usually due to hypertension?

   A) arteriosclerosis

   B) aneurysm

   C) hernia

   D) decubitus ulcer

75. Erector spinae muscles consist of three columns of muscles. Which three are they?

   A) external oblique, internal oblique, transverse abdominis

   B) iliocostalis, longissimus, spinalis

   C) external intercostals, internal intercostals, serratus posterior inferior

   D) lateral pterygoid, medial pterygoid, masseter

76. What is percussion?

   A) It is performed with the idea to shake the client.

   B) It is performed with the idea of client as drum skin.

   C) Performed lightly or heavily, it helps to wake up the sleeping client.

   D) Performed lightly or heavily, it helps to stimulate muscles or loosen mucus.

77. A therapist has an arrangement with an accountant to provide massages in exchange for accounting services. What is this type of arrangement called?

   A) trading

   B) bartering

   C) inappropriate

   D) risky

78. Synapses, Schwann cells, and the sodium-potassium pump are most closely associated with which system?

   A) reproductive
   B) nervous
   C) urinary
   D) muscular

79.. Which of the statements pertaining to the Ayurvedic approach is NOT true?

   A) Most illness begins during the digestive process.
   B) People should avoid caustic environments.
   C) Ingesting more liquids than solids is necessary.
   D) Adapting seasonally is important.

80. What is a contraindication to pregnancy massage?

   A) any work in the first trimester
   B) the pregnant woman is going into labor
   C) any work in the second trimester
   D) the pregnant woman is on bed rest under a doctor's care

81. Which of the following is NOT a type of massage?

   A) sports massage
   B) lymphatic drainage massage
   C) acrobatic massage
   D) Swedish massage

82. What Swedish massage technique is described as similar to wringing out a wet rag?

   A) vibration
   B) raking
   C) friction
   D) tapotement

83. What is a potential benefit of a social media dual relationship?

   A) finding a new friend with common social interests
   B) discovering a client is going to the same concert as the therapist and maybe meeting up
   C) a client discovering the therapist is a member of the state massage board
   D) a client finding out the therapist's sister is dating someone she used to date and getting filled in on his bad behavior

84. What is a hydrocollator?

   A) a heat therapy of gel-filled packs stored in a hot water tank
   B) water treatment
   C) hot therapy used with stones
   D) a cold therapy applied with towels

85. Alpha and beta cells are most closely associated with which body system?

   A) endocrine
   B) integumentary
   C) nervous
   D) reproductive

86. Which layer of the epidermis is held in place by a basement membrane?

   A) stratum basale
   B) stratum lucidum
   C) stratum corneum
   D) stratum spinosum

87. Which of the following is NOT caused by a virus?

   A) HIV
   B) acne
   C) herpes simplex
   D) shingles

88. Who is considered the "father" of medicine?

    A) Herodicus
    B) Johann Mezger
    C) Hippocrates
    D) Asclepius

89. A therapist's friend refers a coworker for a massage. Once the therapist starts massaging the coworker regularly, the friend starts asking questions about where he lives, his age, and if he has a girlfriend. What should the therapist do?

    A) give all the details
    B) respond with anger and disgust that the friend would ask those questions
    C) tell the client
    D) tell the friend the therapist appreciates the referral but does not disclose personal information about clients

90. Why should a therapist work proximal-distal-proximal when massaging a limb?

    A) It helps to pump and flush the blood and lymph flow without backups.
    B) It helps to keep the therapist focused.
    C) It helps to keep the client awake during treatment.
    D) The principle has been passed down, but has lost its meaning.

91. What is referred to as the anatomical pacemaker?

    A) the sinoatrial node
    B) the atrioventricular node
    C) the heart's conduction system
    D) the sphygmomanometer

92. The sliding filament theory is associated with which body system?

    A) muscular
    B) skeletal
    C) nervous
    D) digestive

93. What is a proper height for a massage table?

    A) three feet above the ground
    B) at the therapist's shoulders
    C) whatever the therapist finds comfortable for work
    D) wherever the client feels comfortable

94. A therapist-client role presents itself as a what?

    A) mutual relationship
    B) fair balance of power
    C) business agreement
    D) role and power differential

95. What is homeostasis?

    A) the ability of the body to regulate equilibrium or balance across all systems
    B) the ability of the body to destroy equilibrium or balance across all systems
    C) the ability of the body to stay awake for twenty-four hours
    D) the ability of the body to ignore headaches

96. Which is an example of a convergent muscle?

    A) biceps brachii
    B) extensor digitorum longus
    C) rectus abdominis
    D) pectoralis major

97. The first time a client comes to a therapist for a massage she complains about lower back pain she has had for months. How should the therapist communicate when inquiring about this pain?

A) "Oh, you probably have an issue with a lumbar vertebra putting pressure on the sciatic nerve. I can fix that."

B) "Have you spoken with a doctor about this pain?"

C) "You have such large breasts. This is probably contributing to your lower back pain."

D) "I bet you sit all day at a computer."

98. What is the importance of working centripetally?

A) to encourage bone growth

B) to encourage the body to metabolize

C) to encourage blood flow back to the heart

D) to encourage the bladder to contract

99. How many times can sheets be reused before washing?

A) once

B) twice

C) never

D) all day

100. Arterioles, capillaries, and venules are most closely associated with which body system?

A) circulatory

B) lymphatic

C) integumentary

D) nervous

1. A) Incorrect. A client's records should be kept for ten years.

B) Incorrect. Ten days is not long enough to keep a client's records.

C) Incorrect. Three years is seven years too short for keeping a client's records.

D) Correct. A therapist should keep a client's records for ten years.

2. A) Incorrect. The hypophyseal is a portal system between the hypothalamus and anterior pituitary for the purpose of hormone exchange.

B) Incorrect. Diastolic is a measure obtained when the ventricle relaxes.

C) Correct. Capillary exchange is a circulatory system function performed by capillaries.

D) Incorrect. The hepatic portal is a system that dumps collected blood into the liver, allowing it to extract glucose, fat, and proteins.

3. **A) Correct.** Providing legal representation to individual members is not a role of a professional organization.

B) Incorrect. A code of ethics establishes consistency in how members practice.

C) Incorrect. Professional organizations are a valuable source of information regarding pending legislation related to the profession.

D) Incorrect. Communicating with the public can enhance and promote a profession.

4. A) Incorrect. Douglas O. Graham is best known for his publication entitled *A Practical Treatise on Massage: Its History, Mode of Application and Effects, Indications & Contra-Indications.*

B) Correct. Kellogg's *The Art of Massage* was published in 1895.

C) Incorrect. Aulus Cornelius Celsus was a Roman physician who wrote *De Medicina.*

D) Incorrect. Pehr Henrik Ling died in 1839.

5. A) Incorrect. Massage does decrease cortisol (stress) levels.

B) Correct. Massage decreases heart rate and encourages relaxation.

C) Incorrect. Massage does increase oxytocin levels.

D) Incorrect. Massage does decrease sympathetic nervous system (fight-or-flight) firings.

6. A) Incorrect. Ninety-nine percent of filtrate is reabsorbed and put back into circulation.

B) Incorrect. One percent of filtrate is toxic waste and is removed from the body.

C) Incorrect. Filtrate contains many things that can be used by the body.

D) Correct. Most filtrate is reabsorbed.

7. A) Incorrect. The spleen and vermiform appendix are secondary lymphatic structures.

B) Incorrect. Afferent vessels feed lymph into lymph nodes, and efferent vessels transport lymph out of lymph nodes.

C) Incorrect. The right lymphatic and thoracic ducts drain lymph.

D) Correct. Bone marrow produces B lymphocytes that stay in the marrow and mature and T lymphocytes that travel to the thymus and then mature.

8. A) Incorrect. The trochlear nerve is related to eye movements.

B) Incorrect. The facial nerve is related to expressions, taste, and the production of saliva.

C) Incorrect. The olfactory nerve is related to smell.

D) Correct. The hypoglossal is related to tongue movement.

9. A) Incorrect. Nonverbal cues are expressions and reactions that suggest a positive or negative reaction.

B) Incorrect. A license is given to someone who has met requirements and standards.

C) Incorrect. A designation is a formal title given after requirements are met.

D) Correct. In massage, boundaries are established by present rules, values, and morals.

10. A) Incorrect. *Obtain* and *act* are not the *O* and *A* of SOAP notes.

B) Correct. *SOAP* stands for *Subjective Objective Assessment Plan.*

C) Incorrect. This is not what SOAP notes stands for.

D) Incorrect. The *A* in the acronym stands for *assessment,* not *ask.*

11. A) Incorrect. The Nei Ching is the formal written record of Chinese medical practices.

B) Incorrect. Huang Ti was known as the Yellow Emperor of China. The Nei Ching was written during his period of rule.

C) Correct. Amma is considered the forerunner of the practice of massage and bodywork.

D) Incorrect. Hippocrates used the word *anatripsis* to refer to the technique of rubbing.

12. A) Incorrect. A mole is formed by an excessive amount of melanin.

B) Incorrect. A wart is a small tumor that arises from the epidermis and is viral in nature.

C) Incorrect. Eczema is believed to be tied to an internal systemic immune system dysfunction and its response to irritants and stress.

D) Correct. Psoriasis appears as pink and red scaly patches.

13. A) Incorrect. Clients with fibromyalgia can benefit from different types of massage depending on their pain cycle.

B) Incorrect. A lonely client would benefit from massage's social aspect and touch component.

C) Incorrect. Angry clients can benefit from massage, which reduces stress levels and increases feel-good hormones.

D) Correct. A client with hypertension (or high blood pressure) is at risk from a full-body massage because of the increased blood flow massage encourages.

14. **A) Correct.** The perception that you are listening and interested is important.

B) Incorrect. This is an insulting way to begin a conversation.

C) Incorrect. Let the client inquire about skills and abilities first.

D) Incorrect. This will sound dismissive and aggressive.

15. **A) Correct.** The triple warmer has an upper, middle, and lower warmer section.

B) Incorrect. The pericardium is a yin organ of circulation that peaks from 7 p.m. to 9 p.m., its element is fire, and it has nine acupressure points.

C) Incorrect. The stomach is a yang organ of digestion that peaks from 7 a.m. to 9 a.m., its element is earth, and it has forty-five acupressure points.

D) Incorrect. The bladder is a yang organ of digestion that peaks from 3 p.m. to 5 p.m., its element is water, and it has sixty-seven acupressure points.

16. **A) Correct.** The principle of massage is superficial-deep-superficial.

B) Incorrect. General-specific-general is a principle of massage.

C) Incorrect. Peripheral-central-peripheral is a principle of massage.

D) Incorrect. Proximal-distal-proximal is a principle of massage.

17. A) Incorrect. The term *Hellenic* refers to a period in ancient Greece (also known as the *Classical Period*) when scientific study, art, philosophy, and literature flourished.

B) Incorrect. *Anatripsis* was the term Hippocrates used to define rubbing.

C) Incorrect. Hippocrates did not use this term to classify bodily fluids.

D) **Correct.** Hippocrates referred to phlegm, blood, yellow bile, and black bile as the four humors.

18. A) **Correct.** A state may regulate hours of education required, but the federal government, not states, determines eligibility to practice a profession based on legal status in the United States.

B) Incorrect. A state can establish what title a massage therapist may use and license renewal requirements.

C) Incorrect. A state can determine which exam or exams a massage therapist must pass in order to obtain a license to practice. Also, some states require proof of liability insurance before a therapist can be licensed.

D) Incorrect. Most states require CPR training, and some may require a certificate of health from a physician.

19. A) Incorrect. There is no relationship at all.

B) Incorrect. There is no relationship at all.

C) Incorrect. There is no relationship at all.

D) **Correct.** A bolus is formed in the oral cavity, and chyme is a semifluid mass formed in the stomach.

20. A) **Correct.** Anything clients mention about their condition should be listed under S.

B) Incorrect. Things the therapist notices about the client should be listed under O.

C) Incorrect. Signs of injury would be listed in the O section.

D) Incorrect. Scheduling issues would not be included in SOAP notes.

21. A) Incorrect. Fascia is not a muscle.

B) Incorrect. Periosteum is a bone covering, not fascia.

C) **Correct.** Fascia is a connective tissue that covers everything from blood vessels to muscles.

D) Incorrect. Fascia is not a ligament sheath.

22. A) Incorrect. A first-degree burn only affects the epidermis.

B) **Correct.** If nerve damage results from a third-degree burn, pain will be diminished or nonexistent.

C) Incorrect. If burned skin results in damage to all three layers of skin and tendon and bone beneath, then a fourth-degree burn may be diagnosed.

D) Incorrect. Second-degree burns penetrate the dermis and may require a skin graft.

23. A) Incorrect. The maxillary is one of four sinuses in the upper respiratory system.

B) Incorrect. The right and left nostrils pull inhaled air into the nasal cavity.

C) **Correct.** The movement of air into and out of the lungs is because of a pressure gradient between the lungs and the atmosphere. Inspiration occurs when the pressure within the alveolar sacs falls below the atmospheric pressure, resulting in air entering the lungs.

D) Incorrect. The two bronchi branch into bronchioles that spread through each lung.

24. A) Incorrect. That is not the correct response order.

B) Incorrect. That is not the correct response order.

C) Incorrect. That is not the correct response order.

D) **Correct.** The client would feel cold, tingling, burning, and numbness during cold therapy.

25. A) Incorrect. There is no professional correlation between too much self-disclosure and the strengthening of the therapist-client bond.

B) Incorrect. While there is nothing wrong with pursuing a career as a psychologist, this thought has nothing to do with being a professional massage therapist.

C) Incorrect. Assuming this is a valid reason for a client to keep coming back diminishes the therapist's skills, training, and dedication.

D) **Correct.** Clients revealing too much personal information about themselves and their lives can become a huge burden for the therapist.

26. A) **Correct.** Pehr Henrik Ling was not a physician.

    B) Incorrect. He did open the Swedish Royal Central Institute of Gymnastics.

    C) Incorrect. The Swedish movement cure combined medical gymnastics, exercise, and massage.

    D) Incorrect. He is considered the father of physical therapy.

27. A) Incorrect. Saliva increases in the parasympathetic nervous system.

    B) Incorrect. Heart rate decreases and saliva production increases in the parasympathetic nervous system.

    C) Incorrect. The bladder contracts in the parasympathetic system.

    D) **Correct.** Heart rate decreases, digestion increases, and the bladder contracts in the parasympathetic nervous system.

28. A) **Correct.** Taking a weekend workshop in a new modality does not guarantee competence.

    B) Incorrect. Understanding the effect of a modality on human anatomy and physiology is valuable.

    C. Incorrect. Familiarizing yourself with evidence-based studies aids communicating the benefits of a modality.

    D) Incorrect. A genuine belief in a therapy will motivate a therapist to commit to and practice the application.

29. A) Incorrect. Unclear information should be clarified and filed accordingly.

    B) Incorrect. If the oblique muscles are in pain, that would be listed in the *S* section.

    C) **Correct.** Anything the therapist observes in the client's behavior is listed in the *O* section.

D) Incorrect. Obvious information would have to be specifically stated and filed in the proper category.

30. A) **Correct.** Chakra energy channels function separately and together.

    B) Incorrect. There are seven chakras along the midline.

    C) Incorrect. Colors are an important aspect of chakra balancing.

    D) Incorrect. Body systems and functions are associated with chakras.

31. A) Incorrect. Approaching and accusing a coworker on one's own can have negative outcomes.

    B) Incorrect. If he is conscientious regarding ethical responsibilities, he should do something.

    C) Incorrect. The therapist has a strong suspicion but no actual proof.

    D) **Correct.** This is the best course of action and something management should address.

32. A) **Correct.** Ulcerative colitis may be considered an autoimmune disorder, but it is a chronic condition.

    B) Incorrect. Crohn's disease can affect any part of the gastrointestinal tract.

    C) Incorrect. Those who suffer from celiac disease experience intestinal inflammation when exposed to gluten, damaging and destroying intestinal villi and interfering with the digestion of nutrients.

    D) Incorrect. A goiter is an enlargement of the thyroid gland.

33. A) Incorrect. *Effleurage* is a French word that means to glide.

    B) Incorrect. Initial effleurage strokes allow the distribution of lotion.

    C) Incorrect. Effleurage strokes should sense muscle tone and tightness.

    D) **Correct.** Tapping and plucking are forms of tapotement.

34. **A)** **Correct.** A blood-borne pathogen lives in blood and can be transferred through bodily fluids.

B) Incorrect. A blood-borne pathogen lives in human blood, not in plants.

C) Incorrect. A blood-borne pathogen does not live in the air.

D) Incorrect. Almost anything can carry germs; blood-borne pathogens are specifically microorganisms that cause disease and live in human blood.

35. **A)** **Correct.** Slow twitch fibers are related to muscle energy use; the term is not used in PNF.

B) Incorrect. Spiral-diagonal is a primary tenet of PNF.

C) Incorrect. Hold-relax is a type of PNF stretch.

D) Incorrect. Contract-relax is a type of PNF stretch.

36. A) Incorrect. While these structures may contribute to the innate immune response, they are not formal structures of the immune system.

B) Incorrect. Peyer's patches are located in the small intestine to monitor intestinal bacteria and tonsils are located in the throat, but neither are part of the functions of digestion.

C) **Correct.** These are both secondary lymphatic structures.

D) Incorrect. There is no relationship at all.

37. **A)** **Correct.** An intoxicated client can put a massage therapist's personal safety at risk.

B) Incorrect. A contraindication is related to the assessment of a client's health.

C) Incorrect. An intoxicated client does not necessarily have improper hygiene.

D) Incorrect. A therapist should never massage a drunk client, regardless of the therapist's personal feelings about alcohol.

38. A) Incorrect. Polarity therapy was developed by osteopath Randolph Stone.

B) Incorrect. Visceral manipulation was developed by an osteopath named Jean-Pierre Barral.

C) Incorrect. Zero balancing was developed by an osteopath named Fritz Frederick Smith.

D) **Correct.** Watsu was developed by Harold Dull, a practitioner of Zen shiatsu.

39. **A)** **Correct.** Everyone can benefit from massage.

B) Incorrect. While babies do benefit from massage, they are not the only ones.

C) Incorrect. Infant massage is an important practice.

D) Incorrect. Elder massage is increasingly common.

40. **A)** **Correct.** Actin are thin filaments and myosin are thick filaments.

B) Incorrect. Troponin and tropomyosin are protein molecules that cover actin filaments.

C) Incorrect. ADP and phosphate molecules attach to myosin heads, and ATP results when ADP and phosphate molecules are energized.

D) Incorrect. Epimysium is a connective tissue that surrounds a muscle and perimysium is a connective tissue that surrounds bundles of fascicles.

41. A) Incorrect. Cancer in the distant past does not imply the need for a doctor's clearance.

B) **Correct.** If lymph nodes were removed, adapting a massage in a localized area may be necessary.

C) Incorrect. This has nothing to do with a pre-massage assessment.

D) Incorrect. This is a personal question and has nothing to do with a pre-massage assessment.

42. A) Incorrect. The client's actions would be listed in the O section.

B) **Correct.** Any action or technique the therapist applied should be listed in the A section.

C) Incorrect. New ideas should be listed in the *P* section.

D) Incorrect. A recommendation for a new therapist should be listed in the *P* section.

43. A) Incorrect. The lower esophageal sphincter is located at the junction of the esophagus and the stomach.

B) Incorrect. The sphincter of Oddi is located at the junction of the ileum and accessory organ ducts.

C) Incorrect. The ileocecal sphincter is located at the junction of the small intestine and the colon.

D) Correct. The pyloric sphincter is located at the junction of the stomach and small intestine.

44. A) Incorrect. Competence is an important aspect of providing a professional service.

B) Incorrect. Honesty and integrity are qualities expected from a professional.

C) Correct. Professional licensing does not hinge on status of membership in any particular organization.

D) Incorrect. Maintaining client confidentiality is a professional requirement.

45. A) Incorrect. Airways relax in the sympathetic nervous system.

B) Correct. Heart rate increases, airways relax, and epinephrine is secreted in the sympathetic nervous system.

C) Incorrect. The bladder relaxes and digestion decreases in the sympathetic nervous system.

D) Incorrect. Digestion decreases in the sympathetic nervous system.

46. A) Incorrect. Once lymph has been cleansed, lymphatic trunks route the fluid back to the venous bloodstream.

B) Incorrect. The cisterna chyli does collect lymph draining from the abdomen and lower body.

C) **Correct.** The vermiform appendix is a secondary lymphatic structure, but its modern purpose is not known.

D) Incorrect. The spleen only receives lymph and stores platelets and lymphocytes.

47. A) Incorrect. SOAP notes are a clinical form of recordkeeping, not a laundry how-to list.

B) Incorrect. SOAP notes are for individual clients.

C) Incorrect. SOAP notes are to be kept in a client's file in the treatment office.

D) Correct. SOAP notes track the progress of a client's pain and relief.

48. A) Incorrect. Saving time when a client has arrived late is not an excuse for failing to get informed consent.

B) Incorrect. It does not matter how long a client has been seeing a therapist or the number of massages the client gets; informed consent must be obtained before each massage session begins.

C) Correct. A massage therapist must always get informed consent before a massage.

D) Incorrect. A client's deafness is not an excuse. A therapist must get informed consent using sign language, written discussion, establishing the client is a skilled lip-reader, or having a mutually agreed-upon interpreter in the room to assist with the exchange of dialogue.

49. A) Incorrect. In this case, the therapist has a moral and ethical responsibility to disclose.

B) Incorrect. Abruptly ending a massage to call 911 can further affect the client's mental state at a time when he is clearly distraught.

C) Incorrect. While this is something to do in the moment, it is not one's only obligation.

D) Correct. Contacting an organization that is equipped to respond to public concerns and reports is the best option.

50.

A) Incorrect. Synarthrotic joints are immovable.

B) Incorrect. Diarthrotic joints move freely.

C) Incorrect. Diarthrotic joints may be referred to as synovial joints.

D) Correct. Amphiarthrotic joints are slightly movable.

51.

A) Incorrect. Januvia® is an oral medication used to treat type 2 diabetes.

B) Incorrect. Metformin is also used to treat type 2 diabetes.

C) Correct. Prednisone may be used to treat allergic disorders, arthritis, blood disorders, breathing disorders, cancer, eye problems, immune system disorders, lupus, psoriasis, eye problems, and ulcerative colitis.

D) Incorrect. Lisinopril is an ACE inhibitor that treats hypertension and congestive heart failure.

52.

A) Correct. The goal of Reiki is to balance areas of the body where energy flow is either too strong or too weak, thus bringing the body into balance and enhancing its own healing ability.

B) Incorrect. Craniosacral work is a light-touch method of assessing and enhancing the craniosacral system.

C) Incorrect. Lomi lomi incorporates long, rhythmic, and fluid strokes using the hands and forearms.

D) Incorrect. Raindrop technique uses essential oils applied in a sequence along the spine to reduce inflammation caused by viruses and bacteria.

53.

A) Incorrect. This is false.

B) Incorrect. While percussion helps to warm up muscles, it is not its main benefit.

C) Correct. Percussion stimulates muscle firings.

D) Incorrect. Nothing should be performed with harming a client in mind.

54.

A) Incorrect. A massage therapist must have taken and passed courses and exams in order to practice professionally.

B) Correct. A massage therapist must have taken and passed courses and exams in order to practice professionally.

C) Incorrect. Even if licensed in another profession, an individual may not practice massage therapy without having passed courses and exams for licensure specifically in massage.

D) Incorrect. Sports coaches may not legally practice massage without having passed certain courses and exams in order to be licensed therapists.

55.

A) Incorrect. The digestive system responds innately using mechanical processing and chemical digestion.

B) Incorrect. The integumentary system responds innately to invaders.

C) Correct. The adaptive response by the lymphatic system is slow and highly selective.

D) Incorrect. The respiratory system responds innately using cilia, sneezing, and coughing.

56.

A) Correct. Transference may occur in a client-therapist relationship where there is a perceived imbalance of power.

B) Incorrect. A dual relationship may involve a type of social relationship with a client outside of the client-therapist relationship, but it is not a psychological occurrence.

C) Incorrect. A contraindication is a condition that affects the treatment plan of a massage therapist.

D) Incorrect. A client continually attempting to engage with a therapist socially does not imply sexual misconduct.

57.

A) Incorrect. The brain and spinal cord make up the central nervous system.

B) Incorrect. These are the two distinct divisions of the nervous system.

C) Correct. The parasympathetic relaxes and the sympathetic stimulates.

D) Incorrect. The somatic nervous system is part of the peripheral nervous system division and the brain is part of the central nervous system.

58. A) Incorrect. Water represents winter, birth, and death.

    B) Correct. Earth does represent late summer and nurturing.

    C) Incorrect. Metal represents autumn and accumulation.

    D) Incorrect. Wood represents spring and growth.

59. A) Incorrect. A nonverbal cue may be an indicator of discomfort or relaxation.

    B) Incorrect. Transference has no relationship to job titles.

    C) Correct. A client's unconscious needs may trigger a therapist's unconscious needs.

    D) Incorrect. Transference has nothing to do with workplace violations.

60. A) Incorrect. Patient information should be listed on the intake form or in the S section.

    B) Incorrect. Palliative care should be listed under the S section.

    C) Correct. Future treatment plans and homework should be listed in the P section.

    D) Incorrect. A performance review does not belong in the SOAP notes.

61. A) Incorrect. This is the definition of a trigger point.

    B) Incorrect. This is a definition of a latent trigger point.

    C) Incorrect. Trigger points are also known as knots.

    D) Correct. A trigger point is not necessarily near the tendon of a muscle.

62. A) Incorrect. This is rude and gives the client the perception of an unprofessional environment.

    B) Incorrect. This is unprofessional and disrespectful of personal boundaries.

C) Incorrect. The therapist should stay available while the client completes the intake form in case she has any questions.

    D) Correct. This is professional and client centered.

63. A) Incorrect. While a person should always exercise caution when crossing the street, this does not apply to professional safety for the massage therapist.

    B) Incorrect. Exit routes should be clearly marked in the professional setting, but there is a better answer here.

    C) Correct. Knowing what hazards and risks are present, and keeping them under control, is the definition of "being safe."

    D) Incorrect. Identifying and addressing pain is to be done in treatment; it is not the same as "being safe."

64. A) Incorrect. A synergist muscle assists movement.

    B) Correct. The antagonist muscle opposes movement.

    C) Incorrect. The prime mover is the main muscle in a movement and contracts the most.

    D) Incorrect. A muscle acting as a fixator provides stability to a muscle movement.

65. A) Incorrect. Shamans were believed to use magical abilities to get rid of illness and disease.

    B) Incorrect. Shamans were viewed as healers who could fight off evil.

    C) Correct. Shamans were respected and honored as healers.

    D) Incorrect. A tribal shaman could be male or female.

66. A) Incorrect. This is not hydrotherapy.

    B) Incorrect. This is not hydrotherapy.

    C) Correct. This is the correct definition of hydrotherapy.

    D) Incorrect. This is not hydrotherapy.

67.

A) Incorrect. The scapula articulates with the humerus forming the glenohumeral joint.

B) Correct. The clavicle articulates with the manubrium forming the sternoclavicular joint.

C) Incorrect. The scapula articulates with the clavicle forming the acromioclavicular joint.

D) Incorrect. The hip articulates with the femur forming the acetabulofemoral joint.

68.

A) Incorrect. Some medical conditions are contraindicated for massage that promotes circulation, but clients with these conditions may still benefit from a less intensive and noninvasive modality of massage.

B) Correct. Pitted edema is a condition that is an absolute contraindication for massage.

C) Incorrect. Someone who has a diagnosed aneurysm should not receive a Swedish massage.

D) Incorrect. Someone in an acute state of an illness or injury should not receive a massage.

69.

A) Incorrect. Petrissage is to knead.

B) Correct. Effleurage strokes are performed at the beginning of the treatment.

C) Incorrect. Friction occurs by working into the muscle belly to break up adhesions.

D) Incorrect. Compressions involve stroking in a deep, rhythmic, and slow manner.

70.

A) Incorrect. While repetitively shooting a gun could lead to trigger points, it is not a main development.

B) Correct. Trigger points develop from injury and repetitive activity.

C) Incorrect. This could be a definition of inflammation or varicose veins.

D) Incorrect. This could be a cause of swollen limbs, varicose veins, or general soreness.

71.

A) Incorrect. This may be good in the interim but it is not all the therapist should do.

B) Incorrect. The therapist doesn't know if he informed his parents about what happened.

C) Correct. This is the best course of action to assure that his parents know and that a state agency is aware.

D) Incorrect. This action would most likely scare and upset the client.

72.

A) Incorrect. The cortex is one of the two layers of the adrenal glands.

B) Correct. The anterior lobe makes up 75 percent of the pituitary gland.

C) Incorrect. The pituitary gland's posterior lobe stores and releases hormones produced by the hypothalamus.

D) Incorrect. The medulla is one of the two layers of the adrenal glands.

73.

A) Incorrect. Effleurage is to stroke gently.

B) Incorrect. That is not the correct definition and might injure a client.

C) Correct. Kneading is performed in circular, squeezing compressions in muscles and tendons.

D) Incorrect. Squeezing the AC joint could harm the client.

74.

A) Incorrect. Arteriosclerosis is a hardening of arteries and a reduction in arterial elasticity as the result of a buildup of calcium deposits.

B) Correct. An aneurysm that ruptures causes hemorrhaging with a high risk of fatality.

C) Incorrect. A hernia is a protrusion of an organ or other internal body material through the membrane that encases it.

D) Incorrect. A decubitus ulcer, also referred to as a pressure ulcer or bedsore, is primarily the result of pressure preventing blood flow to an area.

75.

A) Incorrect. These muscles are part of the abdominal group.

B) **Correct.** Each column contains three muscles.

C) Incorrect. These muscles assist with inhalation and exhalation.

D) Incorrect. These muscles are involved in moving the mandible.

76. A) Incorrect. Vibrations, not percussion, shake the client.

B) Incorrect. This definition is false.

C) Incorrect. Though percussion may awaken a sleeping client, that is not its intention.

D) **Correct.** Percussion, or tapotement, can help to loosen mucus and stimulate muscles.

77. A) Incorrect. A therapist may trade massages with another massage therapist, but that is an informal trade of one massage for another massage.

B) **Correct.** Bartering is a commonly used way of exchanging services and is an accepted form of doing business under federal tax code.

C) Incorrect. There is nothing inappropriate about bartering as long as services are fair and balanced and properly documented.

D) Incorrect. Bartering is no riskier than an exchange of a service for a cash payment.

78. A) Incorrect. None of these terms is associated with reproduction.

B) **Correct.** All of these terms are related to nervous system functions.

C) Incorrect. None of these terms is associated with the urinary system.

D) Incorrect. While the muscular system relies on the nervous system for movement, none of these terms is associated with the system.

79. A) Incorrect. Most illness begins during digestion is the core belief of Ayurveda.

B) Incorrect. Practitioners of Ayurveda should create a healthy environment and avoid caustic ones.

C) **Correct.** Ingestion of liquids and solids should be balanced.

D) Incorrect. Adapting to seasonal changes is important.

80. A) Incorrect. Unless contraindicated by a doctor's note, a pregnant woman benefits from massage.

B) Incorrect. Some pregnant women choose to have their massage therapist present to help them relax.

C) Incorrect. Unless contraindicated by a doctor's note, a pregnant woman benefits from massage.

D) **Correct.** If a pregnant woman is on bed rest under a doctor's care, it is best not to massage her.

81. A) Incorrect. Sports is a type of massage therapy.

B) Incorrect. Lymphatic drainage is a type of massage therapy.

C) **Correct.** Acrobatic is not a type of massage therapy.

D) Incorrect. Swedish is a type of massage therapy.

82. A) Incorrect. Vibration is rapid, rhythmic, and maintains constant contact.

B) Incorrect. Raking is a type of effleurage.

C) **Correct.** Grasping and moving one hand clockwise and the other hand counterclockwise is a form of friction.

D) Incorrect. Wringing is not a form of tapotement.

83. A) Incorrect. A therapist may end up jeopardizing the therapist-client relationship by bringing social interests into the massage room.

B) Incorrect. A therapist may end up jeopardizing the therapist-client relationship by injecting herself into a client's social activities.

C) **Correct.** Learning more about a therapist's involvement in and commitment to the practice of massage may help a client better appreciate the therapist's experience and professionalism; the client may even refer other people to the therapist for massage.

D) Incorrect. Communicating negative information to a client about her sister's personal relationship will put the therapist in an awkward and unwelcome position.

84. A) **Correct.** A hydrocollator is a hot water tank filled with gel packs.

B) Incorrect. A hydrocollator is a water tank, but it is specifically used for hot therapy.

C) Incorrect. A hydrocollator is not a hot stone treatment.

D) Incorrect. A hydrocollator is not a cold therapy.

85. A) **Correct.** Alpha and beta cells are located in the pancreas and produce glucagon and insulin.

B) Incorrect. There is no relationship at all.

C) Incorrect. There is no relationship at all.

D) Incorrect. There is no relationship at all.

86. A) **Correct.** The stratum basale layer is the deepest of the five epidermis layers. It is also referred to as the stratum germinativum.

B) Incorrect. The stratum lucidum may not be present in all people or only in the hands and feet.

C) Incorrect. The stratum corneum only contains dead cells that flake off continuously.

D) Incorrect. The stratum spinosum is nicknamed the *prickly layer*.

87. A) Incorrect. HIV literally stands for *human immunodeficiency virus*.

B) **Correct.** Acne is a bacterial infection.

C) Incorrect. Herpes simplex is a virus that can be transmitted orally or sexually.

D) Incorrect. Clinically, shingles may be referred to as varicella zoster virus.

88. A) Incorrect. Herodicus is considered the father of sports medicine.

B) Incorrect. Johann Mezger is considered the founder of modern massage.

C) **Correct.** Hippocrates believed in observation, logical thought, and systematic principles of diagnosis.

D) Incorrect. Asclepius is known as the god of medicine and healing.

89. A) Incorrect. This is totally inappropriate and unethical.

B) Incorrect. The friend may not be aware of the confidentiality standards by which the therapist needs to abide.

C) Incorrect. There is no point in embarrassing or angering the client. Also, this response crosses boundaries.

D) **Correct.** This is the best answer. The therapist should state firmly and directly that he does not disclose personal information about a client.

90. A) **Correct.** Proximal-distal-proximal pumps blood out from the body, encouraging circulation throughout the limb, and then flushes it back toward the heart.

B) Incorrect. While working proximal-distal-proximal may help keep the therapist focused, that is not the reason to use this technique.

C) Incorrect. The client may not remain awake during treatment.

D) Incorrect. The principle does have meaning.

91. A) **Correct.** Cardiac muscle cells send out signals to begin the cardiac cycle. The sinoatrial node is the first to receive them.

B) Incorrect. The atrioventricular node receives the signals from the sinoatrial node.

C) Incorrect. The heart's conduction system has many components that keep the heart beating.

D) Incorrect. A sphygmomanometer is a device that measures blood pressure.

92. A) **Correct.** The sliding filament theory of muscle contraction is key to skeletal muscle movement.

B) Incorrect. The musculoskeletal system works together but this theory is associated with the muscular system.

C) Incorrect. There is a neuromuscular junction that creates a relationship between the muscular and nervous systems, but the sliding filament theory is related to muscle fiber movement.

D) Incorrect. Smooth muscle does surround organs of digestion, but this theory is not related to the digestive process.

93. A) Incorrect. The proper working height can vary depending on the treatment, the therapist's comfort, and the size of the client.

B) Incorrect. This is probably too high for a therapist to perform an effective treatment.

C) **Correct.** The height depends on the therapist's comfort level when performing the massage.

D) Incorrect. The height is dependent on what is comfortable for the therapist, not the client.

94. A) Incorrect. Mutual implies equal.

B) Incorrect. In this relationship, the therapist has more power than the client does.

C) Incorrect. While this is an agreement to provide a service for a fee, it is not how the role is defined.

D) **Correct.** A client views the therapist as a professional with skills and knowledge that exceed her own.

95. **A)** **Correct.** Homeostasis means achieving balance in the body.

B) Incorrect. Homeostasis means achieving balance in the body.

C) Incorrect. Homeostasis means achieving balance in the body.

D) Incorrect. Homeostasis means achieving balance in the body.

96. A) Incorrect. The biceps brachii is a fusiform muscle.

B) Incorrect. The extensor digitorum longus is a unipennate muscle.

C) Incorrect. The rectus abdominis is a parallel muscle.

D) **Correct.** The pectoralis major is a convergent muscle.

97. A) Incorrect. This borders on diagnosis and implies the therapist can assure a remedy.

B) **Correct.** If a client has had a pain for a long time, the therapist should inquire if she has seen a medical doctor to get an assessment of the condition.

C) Incorrect. Drawing attention to a client's breast size and implying their size is the cause of chronic lower back pain is unprofessional.

D) Incorrect. This may be an indication of a cause of lower back pain but this response sounds dismissive and condescending.

98. A) Incorrect. Bone growth is not directly affected by centripetal work.

B) Incorrect. Metabolism is not directly affected by centripetal work.

C) **Correct.** Working toward the heart helps to encourage blood flow back to the heart.

D) Incorrect. Bladder contraction is not directly affected by centripetal work.

99. A) Incorrect. Sheets should be washed after each client.

B) Incorrect. Sheets should never be used on more than one client.

C) **Correct.** The rule is one set of sheets per one client.

D) Incorrect. The sheets need to be changed and cleaned after each client.

100. **A)** **Correct.** Arterioles, capillaries, and venules are blood vessels in the circulatory system.

B) Incorrect. While there are lymphatic capillaries, arterioles and venules are not vessels used in the lymphatic system.

C) Incorrect. These terms are not associated with the integumentary system.

D) Incorrect. These terms are not associated with the nervous system.

EIGHT: Practice Test Two

READ THE QUESTION CAREFULLY AND CHOOSE THE MOST CORRECT ANSWER.

1. Which is an example of a convergent muscle?

   A) biceps brachii

   B) extensor digitorum longus

   C) rectus abdominis

   D) pectoralis major

2. The exchange of gases between the blood and body tissues is referred to as what?

   A) internal respiration

   B) external respiration

   C) vital capacity

   D) pulmonary ventilation

3. A profession is defined as which of the following?

   A) an acceptable application of services

   B) a group of individuals who share the same occupation and perform the functions of the occupation in a consistent, moral, legal, and ethical manner

   C) a commitment to moral reasoning and character

   D) a code of conduct

4. Which of the following is NOT a contraindication for massage in a specific population?

   A) hypertension

   B) contagious disease

   C) open, infected surface wound

   D) general fatigue

5. Which of the following is NOT accurate about Avicenna?

   A) He was the first person in history who combined sports with medicine.

   B) He wrote about massage, exercise, and the value of hydrotherapies.

   C) He endorsed the use of friction techniques after athletic events.

   D) He valued touch and grooming in the care of horses.

6. How can therapists work most efficiently?

   A) use only their forearms

   B) call a friend to work with them

   C) use proper body mechanics

   D) quit

7. The first time a client comes to a therapist for a massage he complains about pain in his left shoulder he has had for six months. How should the therapist communicate when inquiring about this pain?

   A) "You should work on strengthening your upper body."

   B) "Oh, you probably have bilateral instability in your shoulder. I can fix that."

   C) "What did your doctor say when you discussed this with her?"

   D) "I bet you only sleep on your left side."

8. The endocrine system is made up of a group of what?

   A) gonads

   B) exocrine glands

   C) lymph nodes

   D) ductless glands

9. What type of massage is performed in small, circular movements, targeting deeper layers of muscles bound with adhesions or trigger points?

   A) effleurage massage

   B) friction massage

   C) cross-fiber friction massage

   D) lymphatic drainage massage

10. A general description of massage used by most United States agencies that regulate its practice usually includes a version of all the following but one. Which one?

    A) the manipulation and mobilization of soft tissue

    B) enhancement of muscle tone and circulation

    C) promotes relaxation

    D) physical therapy

11. Why should clients with hypertension NOT receive massage?

    A) Clients with hypertension are usually angry.

    B) Clients with hypertension have high blood pressure and massage can force movement of blood, leading to injury.

    C) Clients with hypertension are sensitive to touch.

    D) Clients with hypertension have high blood pressure and massage can cut off blood flow.

12. Which of the following is NOT one of OSHA's basic universal precautions?

    A) wearing sterile vinyl or latex gloves during treatment

    B) labeling and double-bagging contaminated waste

    C) washing hands after eating, drinking, or blowing one's nose

    D) wiping down massage equipment at the end of the day

13. The epiphyseal plate and periosteum are associated with which body system?

    A) reproductive

    B) skeletal

    C) muscular

    D) digestive

14. Which is a true statement?

    A) The left and right atrium are inferior to the left and right ventricle.

    B) The tricuspid valve is located between the right atrium and the right ventricle.

    C) The bicuspid valve is one of two semilunar valves.

    D) Semilunar valves connect the atrium chambers to their adjacent arteries.

15. Which is NOT true about the study of ethics?

   A) It is a relatively new field of study.

   B) It addresses rights and wrongs in societies.

   C) In helps to define rules of medical treatment and research.

   D) It looks at how discrimination affects group behavior.

16. An individual is seated on the floor with her legs extended. She extends her ankles until her toes point. Which term describes this action?

   A) dorsiflexion

   B) plantar flexion

   C) abduction

   D) eversion

17. What is NOT true about oocytes?

   A) Oocytes are immature eggs in females.

   B) An oocyte matures into an ovum inside an ovarian follicle.

   C) Oocytes are produced throughout a female's reproductive years.

   D) As females age, the quality and genetic stability of each oocyte begins to degrade.

18. Boundaries are most at risk of being crossed under which circumstance:

   A) when a client has come to a therapist exclusively for more than a year

   B) when a therapist goes to a client's home to perform a massage

   C) when a therapist works out of his home

   D) when the client is a coworker

19. Which of the following is NOT a type of skin cancer?

   A) cystic fibrosis

   B) basal cell carcinoma

   C) squamous cell carcinoma

   D) malignant melanoma

20. Which of the following is NOT true of a petrissage stroke?

   A) It is a superficial technique.

   B) It is a kneading technique that releases soft tissue.

   C) It may be referred to as *milking*.

   D) It involves lifting, squeezing, and rolling.

21. What is vasodilation?

   A) Blood vessels enlarge, increasing blood pressure.

   B) Blood vessels enlarge, decreasing blood pressure.

   C) Blood vessels dilate, increasing blood pressure.

   D) Blood vessels narrow, decreasing blood flow.

22. What is vasoconstriction?

   A) Blood vessels narrow, decreasing blood flow.

   B) Blood vessels expand, increasing blood flow.

   C) Blood vessels expand.

   D) Blood vessels narrow, increasing blood flow.

23. Which of the following should therapists NOT do to their nails?

   A) keep them short and filed

   B) keep them unpolished

   C) chew them short

   D) wash them regularly

24. A healthy client sees a massage therapist frequently, usually for a relaxation massage. When the client arrives for an appointment, she requests a deep tissue massage. What should the response be?

A) "Oh, I really think we should stick with what is working."

B) "No way. You will be in so much pain tomorrow."

C) "Well, there is no reason why we cannot do that, but I do want you to be aware that you will most likely have some soreness in the next day or two. Are you comfortable with that?"

D) "Why didn't you say so sooner? I could have been doing that all along."

25. Which of the following is NOT a sign of transference?

A) overt adoration of the therapist

B) lingering after the massage, keeping a therapist engaged in conversation

C) asking for special considerations

D) always leaving a big tip

26. Regarding traditional Chinese medicine's five steps, all of the following are true EXCEPT one. Which one?

A) They are an assessment tool.

B) They include observation of demeanor.

C) They involve asking ten questions.

D) They involve determining someone's dosha.

27. Therese C. Pfrimmer is credited with what type of massage modality?

A) Esalen

B) polarity therapy

C) deep tissue

D) visceral manipulation

28. What is the most appropriate stage of healing during which to apply cross-fiber treatment?

A) acute

B) subacute

C) chronic

D) pre-injury

29. Which of the following should therapists eat before going to work?

A) a heavy, spicy meal

B) nothing, to preserve hygiene

C) a big, fibrous meal

D) a balanced, nutritious meal

30. When signals travel down axons, what is it called?

A) nerve impulse conduction

B) saltatory

C) continuous

D) the reflex arc

31. In the lymphatic system, when a new invader is recognized by a t-cell, it communicates instructions to which cell?

A) b-cell

B) plasma cell

C) memory cell

D) an antibody-producing machine

32. How should a massage therapist treat a trigger point?

A) effleurage, kneading, lymphatic draining, effleurage

B) effleurage, kneading, friction, stretching, effleurage

C) kneading, friction, kneading, effleurage

D) effleurage, stretching, kneading, friction

33. George and Charles Taylor were brothers who are most noted for what?

A). introducing Champissage to the United States

B) bringing the Swedish massage cure to the United States

C) inventing what is known today as Kellogg's Corn Flakes

D) developing sports massage

34. Clients may refuse a massage when they arrive based on which of the following?

A) The therapist is older or younger than expected.

B) A client may refuse a massage without having to state why.

C) The therapist is wearing a yarmulke.

D) The therapist is wearing a wedding ring.

35. Which of the following is NOT true about pathology?

A) The term is of Greek origin.

B) It literally means the study of physiology.

C) A pathologist studies how a disease progresses.

D) It is an approach that determines the cause, development, effect on cells, and consequences of disease.

36. Which of the following is NOT true when performing strokes?

A) Massage therapists should keep their hands relaxed, but firm.

B) Massage therapists should bend their hands at a 45-degree angle.

C) Massage therapists should keep their hands rigid and stiff.

D) Massage therapists should hold their fingers together.

37. *Arrector pili* and *keloid* are terms most closely associated with which body system?

A) endocrine

B) integumentary

C) respiratory

D) muscular

38. Which meridian channel is paired with the heart?

A) small intestine

B) pericardium

C) liver

D) spleen

39. During a massage session, a client starts to passionately relay the horrible day she had at work. How should the massage therapist respond?

A) "You think you had a bad day, let me tell you about mine."

B) "Oh my gosh, I can't believe that happened!"

C) "It seems like this massage came at a good time. It's great you have this chance to relax."

D) "You really should be quiet! Your talking is probably disturbing other massages that are in session."

40. Which of the following statements is NOT true regarding thermotherapy?

A) Short-term exposure to heat results in vasodilation.

B) Someone with diabetes would greatly benefit from thermotherapy.

C) Extended exposure to heat causes vasoconstriction.

D) A hydrocollator may be used to heat packs filled with silicon.

41. Which of the following is NOT a type of tapotement/percussion?

A) pincement

B) clapping

C) hacking

D) kneading

42. Focusing attention on a client from arrival to departure is a sign of being what?

A) aggressive

B) client centered

C) passive

D) suspicious

43. According to the US Department of Labor's Occupational Outlook Handbook, 2016 – 17 Edition, what does a massage therapist NOT do?

A) relieve pain

B) improve circulation

C) heal emotional scars

D) relieve stress

44. An individual extends his arms horizontally and rotates them from the shoulders, making circles. Which term describes this action?

A) circumduction

B) pronation

C) inversion

D) rotation

45. What is the yang organ of digestion that peaks from 5 a.m. to 7 a.m.?

A) lung

B) stomach

C) spleen

D) large intestine

46. Which of the following muscles inserts on the greater trochanter?

A) piriformis

B) tensor fasciae latae

C) biceps femoris

D) psoas major

47. Chronic obstructive pulmonary disease (COPD) is a collection of chronic lung conditions. Which of the following is NOT considered part of COPD?

A) asthma

B) bronchitis

C) emphysema

D) migraine

48. Which statement is most correct regarding what happened after the fall of the Roman Empire?

A) Medical education was spread across the globe.

B) Hydrotherapy became a treatment enjoyed by all instead of just soldiers and the wealthy citizens of Rome.

C) Massage and touch were important for the care of the sick and dying.

D) Women were denied the right to provide care to those who were sick and dying.

49. If a client tells a therapist he was doing a job in someone's home and stole a credit card he saw on a desk, the therapist should do what?

A) ask the client to buy her lunch

B) tell the client the therapist did the same thing once and never got caught

C) contact the police

D) avoid responding as it's none of her business

50. How can therapists produce more force in their treatment?

A) push harder on the client

B) keep their back foot grounded and use a fist or elbow

C) use their feet

D) punch the client

51. Oocytes and gametes are associated with which body system?

A) immune

B) integumentary

C) reproductive

D) respiratory

52. Smell, taste, vision, and hearing are related to what kind of sense?

A) afferent

B) efferent

C) special

D) Wernicke's

53. What is a benefit of effleurage?

A) releasing trigger points

B) warming up the tissue with long, fluid strokes

C) high stress

D) spreading muscle fibers with deep, squeezing strokes

54. What type of treatment uses water in any of its forms to achieve therapeutic benefits?

A) effleurage

B) hydrotherapy

C) hot stone

D) ice massage

55. Sexually fantasizing about a client may be a sign of what?

A) countertransference

B) sexual misconduct

C) unethical workplace behavior

D) client-centeredness

56. What does the prefix *brady–* refer to?

A) small

B) slow

C) vessels

D) the lungs

57. Which of the following is a classification of a boundary related to massage?

A) competence

B) character

C) education

D) personal

58. Which of the following best describes the relationship between the federal government and massage?

A) The federal government regulates massage licensing requirements.

B) The federal government provides grants and loans.

C) The federal government requires all massage therapists to take HIV/AIDS courses.

D) The federal government oversees the content of all massage licensing exams.

59. Which meridian channel terminates in front of the ear at the temporomandibular joint?

A) heart

B) large intestine

C) small intestine

D) kidney

60. Skeletal bones go through a remodeling process throughout the lifetime. What role do osteoclasts play in this process?

   A) They form new bone.

   B) They become embedded in the bone matrix.

   C) They break down bone.

   D) They signal to the endocrine system to release calcitonin.

61. What role does the pancreas play in the digestive system?

   A) It produces bile.

   B) It stores bile.

   C) It produces an enzymatic juice that breaks down carbohydrates, fats, and proteins.

   D) None. It is an organ of the endocrine system.

62. A client who regularly sees a massage therapist always leaves a tip significantly below average. The therapist finds she is adding a few more minutes to each massage and making exceptions to her schedule to accommodate the client, hoping the tip will improve. What might this indicate?

   A) transference

   B) poor massage technique

   C) countertransference

   D) a struggling client who just cannot afford a better tip

63. What is the best way to ensure a good tax year, without an audit?

   A) paying a bookie to wipe one's record clean

   B) moving to Canada

   C) having a family member in the IRS

   D) proper bookkeeping with incomes and expenses listed clearly

64. What is an embolism?

   A) a thickening of arterial walls

   B) a pain in the chest resulting from insufficient blood flow to the heart

   C) a blood clot or gas bubble

   D) when spinal disk material protrudes beyond the vertebrae

65. What is a contraindication for using hot therapy?

   A) spastic muscles

   B) trigger points

   C) hypertension

   D) bound fascia

66. What does the word root *opia* refer to?

   A) sight

   B) breathing

   C) kidneys

   D) pain

67. Which part of the small intestine is where most of the nutrients are absorbed?

   A) ileum

   B) jejunum

   C) duodenum

   D) cecum

68. What is the value of using a self-assessment technique?

   A) It is a good way to determine if rates should be increased.

   B) It is a good way to prepare for a meeting with a supervisor.

   C) It is a good way to analyze a moment during a massage that blurred a boundary.

   D) It is a good tool for assessing if new staff should be added.

69. What is a contraindication for using cold therapy?

   A) returning the body to homeostasis

   B) reducing pain

   C) decreasing inflammation

   D) Reynaud's disease

70. What does the acronym *RICE* stand for?

   A) Rest, Ice, Compression, Elevation

   B) Rest Instantly, Constantly Evaluate

   C) Rest, Injure, Contact, Emergency

   D) Run, Ice, Cold, Exercise

71. If a regular client states to a therapist, "my cancer has returned," what should the therapist do?

   A) Make an excuse to step out of the room so the client does not see the therapist crying.

   B) Inform the client it is unlikely that the massages have triggered the return of the cancer.

   C) Empathetically and delicately share with the client that professionally a massage is not recommended without medical clearance.

   D) Use the massage time to provide emotional support and comfort.

72. Which of the following statements is NOT correct about proprioceptors?

   A) Proprioceptors are only found in muscles.

   B) They are important in muscle memory and hand-eye coordination.

   C) Muscle spindles and Golgi tendon organs are two types of proprioceptors.

   D) They communicate speed, angles, and balance to the central nervous system.

73. Which of the following is NOT required for independent contractors?

   A) filing a W-2

   B) filing a W-9

   C) saving a percentage of each paycheck

   D) filing their own taxes

74. Which of the following terms is NOT related to the sliding filament theory of muscle contraction?

   A) cross bridge

   B) recovery stroke

   C) vasodilation

   D) action potential

75. When clients show up for a scheduled appointment, they are giving what?

   A) implied consent to perform massage

   B) voluntary consent to perform massage

   C) informed consent to perform massage

   D) absolute consent to perform massage

76. Which of the following cannot be used as a tool during massage?

   A) elbow

   B) thumb

   C) forearm

   D) ninja star

77. What is the common name for eponychium?

   A) a hair strand

   B) fingernail

   C) cuticle

   D) hair follicle

78. What should therapists NOT bring to a job interview?

A) a good work ethic

B) a wrinkly outfit

C) their resume

D) their license

79. The concept of the energy body has its roots in which type of medicine?

A) Western

B) allopathic

C) Eastern

D) complementary and alternative

80. What is the name of the lid-like piece of cartilage that covers the trachea?

A) alveoli

B) epiglottis

C) hyaline cartilage

D) bronchi

81. What is sports massage?

A) a game that is played for therapeutic benefits

B) a technique that helps athletes perform to their best ability

C) deep compressions along bony ridges

D) light strokes to encourage lymph flow

82. Which of the following is NOT an example of a reprimand in the workplace?

A) a letter from the board in the state in which the therapist practices

B) verbal

C) written

D) immediate termination

83. Which meridian channel is considered the root of life and stores essence?

A) heart

B) gallbladder

C) kidney

D) liver

84. What is NOT an effect of effleurage?

A) pliable tissue

B) increased blood flow

C) high levels of stress

D) relaxation

85. In what population does the hormone relaxin release its highest levels?

A) babies

B) the elderly

C) pregnant women

D) teenagers

86. The horizontal plane of the body is also referred to as which of the following?

A) midsagittal

B) coronal

C) transverse

D) sagittal

87. Employers have the right to expect their employees to do all of the following EXCEPT

A) refrain from lewd and foul language in the workplace.

B) dress in clean, modest, and professional attire.

C) perform massages free of charge on days the employer is fundraising for a local charity.

D) refrain from negative talk about coworkers.

88. Which of the following would NOT be considered a massage business workplace violation?

A) using a company computer without permission

B) using the onsite washing machine and dryer to do personal laundry

C) refusing to stay after hours to massage a walk-in client

D) gathering client information for a side business unrelated to massage

89. Why do massage therapists need insurance?

A) Accidents happen, but risk can be avoided.

B) People are terrible and looking to make money.

C) Without liability insurance, they have to pay taxes.

D) They want to sue their clients.

90. Which of the following best describes a type of bony landmark referred to as a ramus?

A) It is formed by two diverging lines.

B) It is a prominent elevation.

C) It is an opening or canal.

D) It is an arm or branch of a bone.

91. Which of the following statements is NOT true?

A) There are twelve cranial nerves.

B) There are twenty-four vertebrae in a human adult's vertebral column.

C) There are ten pairs of ribs.

D) There are twenty-six bones in a human foot.

92. Which of the following drugs is potentially addictive?

A) Crestor®

B) Vyvanse®

C) Lyrica®

D) Coumadin®

93. Which of the following best describes a type of bony landmark referred to as a foramen?

A) It is a bulge.

B) It guides and limits motion.

C) It is a hole in a bone for nerves or vessels to pass through.

D) It is a narrow, slender projection.

94. What is NOT a benefit of lymphatic drainage massage?

A) It reduces swelling and edema.

B) It assists in surgery recovery.

C) It releases trigger points.

D) It increases energy.

95. Which may be the repercussion of an employee talking about a really obese client in the break room of a place of business?

A) None. It is okay as long as the conversation is with a coworker the therapist is friends with outside of work.

B) Management informs the therapist he will no longer be allowed to massage that client.

C) The therapist may receive a written warning of termination by his employer.

D) The therapist tells the staff member who schedules the appointments he will buy her dinner if she does not schedule the therapist with that client again.

96. What is the purpose of a business plan?

    A) to show the best way to make the most money

    B) to beg investors for money

    C) to clearly outline realistic business goals

    D) to show clients that the therapist is a serious professional

97. The pectineus is part of which muscle group?

    A) lateral rotators

    B) quadriceps femoris

    C) hamstring

    D) adductor

98. In traditional Chinese medicine's five elements theory, what nourishes wood?

    A) earth

    B) water

    C) metal

    D) fire

99. What is proprioception?

    A) the ability to sense one's body in relation to space

    B) the ability to move better

    C) the ability to become aware of something through the senses

    D) the ability to sense pain

100. Which of the following bones is roughly shaped like a cube and, generally, is as wide as it is long?

    A) irregular

    B) sesamoid

    C) short

    D) long

1. A) Incorrect. The biceps brachii is a fusiform muscle.

   B) Incorrect. The extensor digitorum longus is a unipennate muscle.

   C) Incorrect. The rectus abdominis is a parallel muscle.

   D) Correct. The pectoralis major is a convergent muscle.

2. **A) Correct.** Internal respiration is the exchange of gases between the blood and body tissues.

   B) Incorrect. External respiration occurs between the alveoli and blood capillaries.

   C) Incorrect. Vital capacity refers to the greatest volume of air that can be pulled into the lungs.

   D) Incorrect. Pulmonary ventilation relates to inspiration and expiration.

3. A) Incorrect. A code of ethics describes an acceptable application of services.

   B) Correct. Massage therapists, accountants, and psychologists each make up groups of people that are examples of professions.

   C) Incorrect. Moral reasoning and character are part of ethical behavior.

   D) Incorrect. A code of conduct is a written statement of guiding principles and expectations related to day-to-day responsibilities, procedures, and professional conduct, as well as the repercussions of infractions.

4. A) Incorrect. Hypertension may often contraindicate work.

   B) Incorrect. A contagious disease may often contraindicate work.

   C) Incorrect. An open and infected surface wound may often contraindicate work.

   D) Correct. General fatigue is not a contraindication to receiving work.

5. **A) Correct.** Herodicus, a fifth-century BCE Greek doctor, was the first known historical medical figure to link sports with medicine.

   B) Incorrect. Avicenna did write about massage, exercise, and the value of hydrotherapies.

   C) Incorrect. Avicenna did endorse the use of friction techniques.

   D) Incorrect. Avicenna believed valued horses benefited from touch and grooming after physical activity.

6. A) Incorrect. Using only forearms can lead to issues for both the therapist and the client.

   B) Incorrect. Unless providing a specific treatment that calls for two therapists, a massage therapist is an independent worker and should not need a partner during treatment.

   C) Correct. Proper body mechanics allow a therapist to work efficiently without working hard.

   D) Incorrect. Quitting is not a good work practice!

7. A) Incorrect. Drawing attention to a client's physique is unprofessional.

   B) Incorrect. This borders on diagnosis and implies the therapist can assure a remedy.

   C) Correct. If a client has had a pain for a long time, the therapist should inquire if he has seen a medical doctor to get an assessment of the condition.

   D) Incorrect. This may be an indication of a cause of shoulder pain but this response sounds dismissive and condescending.

8. A) Incorrect. Gonads are found in the reproductive system.

   B) Incorrect. Exocrine glands have ducts and do not feed directly into the bloodstream.

   C) Incorrect. Lymph nodes are found in the lymphatic system.

   D) Correct. Ductless glands secrete hormones in the endocrine system.

9.
A) Incorrect. Effleurage strokes are long and fluid, warming up tissue and promoting relaxation.

B) Incorrect. Friction massage uses the therapist's digits to work into adhesions in the direction of muscle fibers.

C) Correct. Cross-fiber friction uses superficial layers to work out adhesions in deeper layers of tissue.

D) Incorrect. Lymphatic drainage massage is very light work that pumps and moves lymph flow.

10.
A) Incorrect. Skin, fascia, tendons, ligaments, and muscles are classified as soft tissue.

B) Incorrect. Massage is considered to enhance muscle tone and circulation.

C) Incorrect. Massage is believed to promote relaxation.

D) Correct. In the United States, physical therapy is usually viewed as a separate profession.

11.
A) Incorrect. Clients with hypertension aren't necessarily angry people.

B) Correct. Massage can increase blood flow when blood vessels are already pressed to their limit, and this could lead to harm for the client.

C) Incorrect. Clients with hypertension are not necessarily supersensitive.

D) Incorrect. Massage does not cut off blood flow.

12.
A) Incorrect. Wearing gloves during treatment can help prevent the spread of disease.

B) Incorrect. Labeling and double-bagging contaminated waste is a basic precaution.

C) Incorrect. Washing hands is a great way to prevent disease from spreading.

D) Correct. Equipment should be wiped down after each massage treatment, between clients.

13.
A) Incorrect. There is no relationship at all.

B) Correct. The periosteum is a connective tissue used to build and maintain bones and the epiphyseal plate is the growth place on long bone.

C) Incorrect. There is no relationship at all.

D) Incorrect. There is no relationship at all.

14.
A) Incorrect. The left and right atrium are *superior* to the left and right ventricle.

B) Correct. The tricuspid valve is one of two atrioventricular valves.

C) Incorrect. The bicuspid valve is one of two atrioventricular valves.

D) Incorrect. Semilunar valves connect the *ventricle* chambers to their adjacent arteries.

15.
A) Correct. The study of ethics extends back thousands of years.

B) Incorrect. The core of ethics is establishing what is morally right and wrong.

C) Incorrect. The practice of medicine and medical research are guided by ethics.

D) Incorrect. Discrimination against an individual or groups of individuals is an ethical concern.

16.
A) Incorrect. Dorsiflexion is a flexion of the foot in which the toes face upward towards the ceiling.

B) Correct. Plantar flexion is an extension of the ankle.

C) Incorrect. Abduction is movement away from the body, such as moving the arms to a horizontal position.

D) Incorrect. Eversion is the elevation of the lateral edge of the foot.

17.
A) Incorrect. Females are born with oocytes.

B) Incorrect. Every month several oocytes may mature into ovum but only one is released.

C) Correct. What a female is born with is her only supply.

D) Incorrect. As a female ages, the possibility of pregnancy lessens.

18.
A) Correct. The longer a massage therapist has been massaging a client, the higher the risk of boundaries

becoming blurred and crossed due to the strong and trusting relationship between the two individuals.

B) Incorrect. A massage therapist working in someone's home will likely be more protective of boundaries.

C) Incorrect. A massage therapist who practices at home should be more alert regarding boundaries.

D) Incorrect. A massage should always be conducted professionally and within boundaries, regardless of the relationship with the client.

19. **A)** **Correct.** Cystic fibrosis is a genetic disorder.

B) Incorrect. Basal cell carcinoma is a type of skin cancer.

C) Incorrect. Squamous cell carcinoma is a form of skin cancer.

D) Incorrect. Malignant melanoma is a type of skin cancer.

20. **A)** **Correct.** It is a technique that usually follows effleurage and is deeper and more aggressive than effleurage.

B) Incorrect. *Petrissage* is a French term that refers to kneading.

C) Incorrect. *Petrissage* may be referred to as a milking technique.

D) Incorrect. *Petrissage* does involve lifting, squeezing, and rolling of the skin and underlying fascia.

21. A) Incorrect. This would be cause for concern.

B) **Correct.** In vasodilation, blood vessels widen, allowing blood more room to travel and thus lessening pressure.

C) Incorrect. This is the same as answer A.

D) Incorrect. This is vasoconstriction.

22. **A)** **Correct.** Vasoconstriction occurs when the blood vessel walls narrow, giving blood less room to travel, thus increasing its pressure.

B) Incorrect. This is vasodilation.

C) Incorrect. This is part of vasodilation.

D) Incorrect. This is not a condition.

23. A) Incorrect. A therapist's nails should be short and filed.

B) Incorrect. A therapist's nails should be unpolished.

C) **Correct.** Therapists should not chew their nails.

D) Incorrect. Therapists should wash their hands and nails regularly.

24. A) Incorrect. The client has the right to request a different kind of massage. Implying the therapist knows better when the client has no contraindications for deep tissue massage is not advisable.

B) Incorrect. This is a condescending and dismissive response.

C) **Correct.** In this case, the therapist should remain open to the client's request while informing her of potential outcomes and side effects; this allows the client to make an informed and voluntary decision.

D) Incorrect. This response sounds aggressive and may offend or embarrass the client.

25. A) Incorrect. Overt adoration of the therapist and her or his skills can suggest transference.

B) Incorrect. Not being able to disconnect from the therapist after the service is complete can suggest transference.

C) Incorrect. Wanting special treatment from a therapist may suggest transference.

D) **Correct.** Showing financial appreciation for a therapist's work is not a sign of transference.

26. A) Incorrect. The five steps are used as an assessment tool.

B) Incorrect. Observation of demeanor is one of the five steps.

C) Incorrect. Described as the ten questions, it is one of the five steps.

D) **Correct.** Doshas are related to Ayurveda.

27.

A) Incorrect. Esalen massage was developed in the 1960s at the Esalen Institute in Big Sur, CA.

B) Incorrect. Polarity therapy was developed by Dr. Randolph Stone.

C) Correct. Therese C. Pfrimmer is credited with developing deep tissue techniques. Her Pfrimmer Deep Muscle Therapy is still taught today.

D) Incorrect. Visceral manipulation was developed by an osteopath named Jean-Pierre Barral.

28.

A) Incorrect. The tissue is still repairing in the acute stage. Vigorous treatment could further damage it.

B) Correct. The initial healing process is complete and the adhesions are still forming, allowing the perfect, pliable window to start treatment.

C) Incorrect. While therapists can perform cross-fiber treatment in chronic stages, it is best to start the treatment earlier in the healing process.

D) Incorrect. This is not a stage of healing.

29.

A) Incorrect. A heavy meal can slow down a therapist and make him sleepy.

B) Incorrect. Therapists should eat something before their shifts so they have energy. A small, nutritious meal will not interfere with personal hygiene.

C) Incorrect. A big meal with lots of fiber can produce negative effects in a small treatment room.

D) Correct. A therapist should eat a filling, nutritious meal that gives her energy to work.

30.

A) Correct. Nerve impulses are conducted down myelinated and unmyelinated axons.

B) Incorrect. The term *saltatory* means a nerve conduction down a myelinated axon.

C) Incorrect. The term *continuous* means a nerve conduction down an unmyelinated axon.

D) Incorrect. The reflex arc is a neural pathway that controls the reflex response.

31.

A) Correct. B-cells receive instructions from t-cells.

B) Incorrect. B-cells mature into plasma cells.

C) Incorrect. A memory cell recognizes a specific invading organism immediately.

D) Incorrect. Plasma cells may informally be referred to as *antibody-producing machines*.

32.

A) Incorrect. This treatment may aggravate a trigger point more.

B) Correct. This treatment includes warming up the tissue, working deeply to release the trigger point, stretching the taut muscle, and easing out of the tissue.

C) Incorrect. This treatment may aggravate a trigger point more.

D) Incorrect. This treatment may aggravate a trigger point more.

33.

A) Incorrect. Champissage is a type of scalp massage that was derived from the Ayurvedic *champi*, meaning head massage.

B) Correct. After studying the Swedish massage cure in Europe, they returned to the United States to practice and published the first textbook on the subject.

C) Incorrect. John Harvey Kellogg and his brother co-invented what we know today as Kellogg's Corn Flakes.

D) Incorrect. Jack Meager is considered the pioneer of sports massage.

34.

A) Incorrect. A client may not refuse a massage based on the therapist's age. Furthermore, a business cannot accept age discrimination as a reason not to charge a client who arrives for a scheduled massage.

B) Correct. Clients are not required to disclose why they decided to cancel the massage after they met the therapist.

C) Incorrect. A client may not refuse a massage based on the therapist's religion. Furthermore, a business cannot accept religious discrimination as a reason not to charge a client who arrives for a scheduled massage.

D) Incorrect. A client may not refuse a massage based on the therapist's marital status. Furthermore, a business cannot accept marital status of a therapist as a reason not to charge a client who arrives for a scheduled massage.

35. A) Incorrect. Pathology is a Greek term.

B) **Correct.** Pathology literally means the study of disease, not physiology.

C) Incorrect. A pathologist does study the progression of a disease.

D) Incorrect. Pathology is an approach that strives to determine the cause, development, the effect on cells, and consequences of a disease.

36. A) Incorrect. The therapist's hands should be relaxed and firm.

B) Incorrect. As long as the therapist's wrists are not bent at a 90-degree angle, this is fine.

C) **Correct.** Therapists' hands should not be rigid and stiff.

D) Incorrect. The therapist's fingers should stay together to perform fluid strokes.

37. A) Incorrect. There is no relationship at all.

B) **Correct.** Arrector pili are small muscles that hold hair follicles in place and keloid is a type of scar formed on the skin.

C) Incorrect. There is no relationship at all.

D) Incorrect. While arrector pili are muscles, they only serve a purpose in the integumentary system.

38. **A)** **Correct.** The heart is a yin organ and the small intestine is a yang organ.

B) Incorrect. The pericardium is paired with the triple warmer.

C) Incorrect. The liver is paired with the gallbladder.

D) Incorrect. The spleen is paired with the stomach.

39. A) Incorrect. This response moves the session away from being client-centered and opens the door to crossing boundaries.

B) Incorrect. This response sounds like it is encouraging the client to keep talking.

C) **Correct.** This response is client centered and also a polite hint to the client to refocus on the intent of the session.

D) Incorrect. This is an overly aggressive and rude response.

40. A) Incorrect. Short-term exposure to heat results in vasodilation, which increases blood flow.

B) **Correct.** Someone with diabetes may have a problem sensing temperature variations.

C) Incorrect. Extended exposure to heat causes vasoconstriction and perspiration in order to return the body to a state of homeostasis.

D) Incorrect. A hydrocollator contains heated water in which packs are immersed to heat. They are most commonly used in chiropractic offices and physical therapy clinics.

41. A) Incorrect. Pincement is a light type of tapotement/percussion.

B) Incorrect. Clapping is a heavy type of tapotement/percussion.

C) Incorrect. Hacking is a heavy type of tapotement/percussion.

D) **Correct.** Kneading is not a type of tapotement/percussion.

42. A) Incorrect. Aggressive behavior is intimidating and overbearing.

B) **Correct.** Being client centered is an important role for a massage therapist.

C) Incorrect. Being passive with a client may result in the therapist being taken advantage of or boundaries to be crossed.

D) Incorrect. Being attentive to paying clients does not suggest a therapist is suspicious of them.

43. A) Incorrect. It states, "With their touch, therapists relieve pain."

B) Incorrect. It states, "With their touch, therapists . . . improve circulation."

C) Correct. Healing emotional scars is not included in the handbook.

D) Incorrect. It states, "With their touch, therapists . . . relieve stress."

44. A) Correct. In circumduction, circular movement occurs distally while the joint stays fixed.

B) Incorrect. Pronation is medial rotation of the forearm.

C) Incorrect. Inversion is the elevation of the medial edge of the foot.

D) Incorrect. Unlike circumduction, rotation is not a complete circle.

45. A) Incorrect. The lung is a yin organ of circulation that peaks from 3 a.m. to 5 a.m.

B) Incorrect. The stomach is a yang organ of digestion that peaks from 7 a.m. to 9 a.m.

C) Incorrect. The spleen is a yin organ of circulation that peaks from 9 a.m. to 11 a.m.

D) Correct. The large intestine is a yang organ of digestion that peaks from 5 a.m. to 7 a.m.

46. **A) Correct.** The piriformis is a lateral rotator of the hip and inserts on the greater trochanter.

B) Incorrect. The tensor fasciae latae inserts on the iliotibial tract.

C) Incorrect. The biceps femoris inserts on the head of the fibula.

D) Incorrect. The psoas major inserts on the lesser trochanter.

47. A) Incorrect. An asthma attack causes coughing, wheezing, and difficulty breathing.

B) Incorrect. Bronchitis occurs when the bronchial tubes are inflamed and mucus production increases.

C) Incorrect. Emphysema occurs when the alveoli in the lungs are severely damaged or destroyed.

D) Correct. A migraine occurs when cranial blood vessels dilate.

48. A) Incorrect. After the fall of the Roman Empire, medical knowledge was not widely valued in Europe.

B) Incorrect. Baths were viewed as glorification of the body and were banned.

C) Correct. The concept of massage and touch was viewed as valuable to the Christian rituals of care for the sick and dying.

D) Incorrect. Women were primarily responsible for care under the authority of the church.

49. A) Incorrect. This response is unethical.

B) Incorrect. This disclosure is unethical and indicates societal misbehavior.

C) Correct. A client disclosed a crime and the therapist has a legal obligation to report to the police knowledge of a crime.

D) Incorrect. Not responding to the client's disclosure during the massage is fine, but does not mean the therapist should not report the crime.

50. A) Incorrect. Pushing into a client is not pleasant for the client or the therapist.

B) Correct. In order to produce more force, tools like the fist or elbow can be used, while the therapist grounds more in the back foot.

C) Incorrect. It is not common to use feet in a standard table treatment.

D) Incorrect. Punching the client is always unacceptable.

51. A) Incorrect. There is no relationship at all.

B) Incorrect. There is no relationship at all.

C) Correct. Oocytes are immature eggs and gametes are eggs and sperm.

D) Incorrect. There is no relationship at all.

52. A) Incorrect. An afferent nerve sends information to the brain.

B) Incorrect. An efferent nerve receives motor signals from the brain.

C) Correct. The special senses perceive stimuli from the external environment through smell, taste, vision, and hearing.

D) Incorrect. The Wernicke's area is a part of the temporal lobe important for recognizing speech and interpreting words.

53. A) Incorrect. Trigger point release is deeper work that comes after effleurage strokes.

B) Correct. Effleurage warms up tissue with long, fluid strokes.

C) Incorrect. Effleurage should produce decreased stress.

D) Incorrect. Compression spreads muscle fibers with deep, squeezing strokes.

54. A) Incorrect. Effleurage does not use water, specifically.

B) Correct. Hydrotherapy is a treatment that uses water in any of its forms to achieve therapeutic benefits.

C) Incorrect. Hot stone massage does not use water, specifically.

D) Incorrect. Ice massage is a type of hydrotherapy, but it only uses one form of water.

55. **A) Correct.** Fantasizing about a client is one of the signs of countertransference.

B) Incorrect. If no action beyond the fantasy is taken, it is not sexual misconduct.

C) Incorrect. It is not unethical workplace behavior unless the therapist discusses this fantasy with the client or a coworker or physically acts upon it.

D) Incorrect. Client-centeredness is focusing on the client in a professional manner.

56. A) Incorrect. The prefix *micro*– means small, as in microorganism.

B) Correct. The prefix *brady*– means slow, as in bradycardia, a slow pulse rate.

C) Incorrect. The prefix *angio*– refers to vessels. For instance, an angioplasty is a procedure that widens obstructed arteries or veins.

D) Incorrect. The prefix *pulmo*– refers to the lungs. For example, the pulmonary artery moves de-oxygenated blood from the heart to the lungs.

57. A) Incorrect. Working competently is part of scope of practice.

B) Incorrect. Someone's character can be good, bad, or questionable, but is not a boundary.

C) Incorrect. Education may factor in to intellectual boundaries, but it is not a boundary itself.

D) Correct. Personal boundaries are formed by an individual's upbringing, his or her own beliefs and comfort levels, and his or her life circumstances.

58. A) Incorrect. Individual states regulate massage licensing requirements.

B) Correct. The federal government provides grants and loans to massage students.

C) Incorrect. Individual states determine if HIV/AIDS courses are required.

D) Incorrect. The federal government has no oversight of massage licensing exams.

59. A) Incorrect. The heart meridian channel terminates on the radial side of the little finger.

B) Incorrect. The large intestine meridian channel crosses underneath the nose and terminates on the other side of the midline.

C) Correct. The small intestine meridian channel terminates in front of the ear at the TMJ.

D) Incorrect. The kidney meridian channel terminates at the clavicle.

60.
A) Incorrect. Osteoblasts form new bone.

B) Incorrect. Osteoblasts get embedded in bone matrix and then become identified as osteocytes.

C) Correct. Osteoclasts break down bone for remodeling.

D) Incorrect. It is calcitonin that signals to the osteoclasts to begin breaking down bone.

61.
A) Incorrect. The liver produces bile.

B) Incorrect. The gallbladder stores bile.

C) Correct. The enzymatic juice produced by the pancreas is delivered to the duodenum.

D) Incorrect. The pancreas is used by both the digestive and endocrine systems.

62.
A) Incorrect. Transference is a behavior directed from the client onto the therapist.

B) Incorrect. If the therapist's other clients leave average or above-average tips, then this is not the issue.

C) Correct. The therapist is personalizing the situation too much by assuming she is doing something wrong.

D) Incorrect. If the client can afford to see a massage therapist regularly and pay for the session, then the client can afford a better tip.

63.
A) Incorrect. This is illegal and not encouraged.

B) Incorrect. Avoiding tax law is a punishable offense.

C) Incorrect. Family favors are illegal.

D) Correct. Keeping a list of incomes and expenses is the best way to have a good tax year.

64.
A) Incorrect. Atherosclerosis is thickening of arterial walls.

B) Incorrect. Angina pectoralis is pain in the chest resulting from insufficient blood flow to the heart.

C) Correct. An embolism moves throughout the circulatory system, potentially lodging in the heart, lungs, or brain.

D) Incorrect. This describes a herniated disk is when spinal disk material protrudes beyond the vertebrae.

65.
A) Incorrect. Spastic muscles can benefit from hot therapy.

B) Incorrect. Trigger points can benefit from hot therapy.

C) Correct. If the blood vessels are narrowed, hot therapy would only increase the volume of blood pressuring the walls, putting the client at risk.

D) Incorrect. Bound fascia can benefit from hot therapy.

66.
A) Correct. The word root *opia* refers to vision. For example, myopia is a condition in which the patient has trouble seeing distant objects.

B) Incorrect. Breathing is described using the suffix *–pnea* as in apnea, the cessation of respiration, or the prefix *pneu–* as in pneumonia.

C) Incorrect. The word root that refers to the kidneys is *renal*. For instance, the adrenal glands are located above the kidneys: *ad–* (above) and *renal* (kidneys).

D) Incorrect. The word root for pain is *algia*, as in neuralgia.

67.
A) Incorrect. The ileum contains clusters of lacteals to enhance fat absorption.

B) Correct. The jejunum is the second section of the small intestine.

C) Incorrect. The duodenum is where enzymes and bile produced by accessory organs are received.

D) Incorrect. The cecum is part of the colon.

68.
A) Incorrect. Rate increases are determined using financial assessment tools.

B) Incorrect. A meeting with a supervisor does not imply the need for self-assessment.

C) Correct. A self-assessment technique is a good way to methodically think through a problematic situation and establish what to do if it occurs again.

D) Incorrect. Bringing on new staff involves a business assessment.

69. A) Incorrect. Cold therapy can promote homeostasis.

B) Incorrect. Cold therapy can reduce pain.

C) Incorrect. Cold therapy can reduce inflammation.

D) Correct. Reynaud's disease and other circulatory issues contraindicate cold therapy.

70. **A) Correct.** *RICE* stands for Rest, Ice, Compression, Elevation.

B) Incorrect. This is not the correct meaning of this acronym.

C) Incorrect. Here, *RICE* has a different meaning.

D) Incorrect. This is not the correct answer choice.

71. A) Incorrect. The therapist should stay professional and client centered.

B) Incorrect. This would be rude, unprofessional, and insensitive.

C) Correct. The therapist must obtain clearance and treatment recommendations from a physician.

D) Incorrect. The therapist should know this is a contraindication for massage without medical clearance.

72. **A) Correct.** Proprioceptors can be found in the inner ear, synovial joints, skeletal framework, tendons, and muscle.

B) Incorrect. Development of muscle memory and hand-eye coordination are related to proprioceptors.

C) Incorrect. Muscle spindles sense muscle stretching and Golgi tendon organs sense muscle tension.

D) Incorrect. Because of communication to the CNS, movements are coordinated.

73. **A) Correct.** A W-2 is for employees, not independent contractors.

B) Incorrect. A W-9 is the form for independent contractors' taxes.

C) Incorrect. Independent contractors should save a percentage of each check, since they will have to pay their own taxes.

D) Incorrect. Independent contractors have to file and pay their own taxes each year.

74. A) Incorrect. A cross bridge is formed when myosin heads and actin attachment sites connect.

B) Incorrect. A recovery stroke is when myosin heads move back into a resting position.

C) Correct. Vasodilation occurs when the diameter of a blood vessel lumen enlarges.

D) Incorrect. Communication between a muscle and the central nervous system results in an action potential.

75. **A) Correct.** Scheduling an appointment and showing up implies a client is consenting to receiving a massage.

B) Incorrect. Voluntary consent is when a client has willingly, and not under duress, agreed to receive a massage based on a two-way conversation with the therapist.

C) Incorrect. Informed consent is based on a client's voluntary agreement to massage after a therapist has reviewed the intake form with the client, gathered additional details, and recommended a treatment.

D) Incorrect. There is no such term as *absolute consent* in massage therapy.

76. A) Incorrect. The therapist's elbow can be used as a tool during massage.

B) Incorrect. The therapist's thumb can be used as a tool during massage.

C) Incorrect. The therapist's forearm can be used as a tool during massage.

D) Correct. The ninja star should not be used as a tool during massage, or anywhere outside of a ninja battle.

77. A) Incorrect. A hair strand is anatomically known as a hair shaft.

B) Incorrect. What is usually called the fingernail is actually the nail plate.

C) **Correct.** The eponychium provides a waterproof seal over the nail matrix and root.

D) Incorrect. A hair follicle is a small tube-shaped crater in the epidermis.

78. A) Incorrect. Therapists should show off their good work ethic.

B) **Correct.** A therapist should arrive wearing clean, unwrinkled clothing.

C) Incorrect. Therapists should bring a copy of their resume to an interview.

D) Incorrect. Therapists should bring their license, or a copy, to an interview.

79. A) Incorrect. Western medicine is rooted in science and evidence-based approaches.

B) Incorrect. Allopathic medicine is synonymous with Western medicine practices.

C) **Correct.** Many Eastern medicine practices are thousands of years old.

D) Incorrect. Complementary and alternative medicine (CAM) is relatively new in Western medicine approaches to care. Treatment plans may incorporate nontraditional therapies and techniques.

80. A) Incorrect. Alveoli are located in the lungs.

B) **Correct.** The epiglottis keeps food and liquid from entering the trachea.

C) Incorrect. Hyaline cartilage keeps the trachea from collapsing and blocking air flow.

D) Incorrect. The trachea bifurcates into the right and left bronchi.

81. A) Incorrect. This is not sports massage.

B) **Correct.** Sports massage is designed with athletes and their performance in mind.

C) Incorrect. This would be painful and ill-advised in any treatment.

D) Incorrect. While lymph work may be a component of a certain sports massage, this definition is incorrect.

82. A) **Correct.** Employment reprimands should come directly from someone who is in a position of authority in the workplace.

B) Incorrect. A workplace reprimand for a minor infraction may be in the form of a verbal warning.

C) Incorrect. A workplace reprimand for a minor or major infraction may be in the form of a written warning.

D) Incorrect. An employer may terminate employment on the spot if the infraction was a serious violation of workplace rules of conduct.

83. A) Incorrect. The heart meridian channel governs the mind and spirit.

B) Incorrect. The gallbladder meridian channel ensures the smooth flow of chi and governs decision-making.

C) **Correct.** The kidney channel is considered the root of life and stores essence.

D) Incorrect. The liver channel is often considered the second heart.

84. A) Incorrect. Effleurage warms up tissue, making it more pliable during later stages of massage.

B) Incorrect. Effleurage increases blood flow.

C) **Correct.** Performed correctly, effleurage should lower stress levels.

D) Incorrect. Effleurage encourages relaxation.

85. A) Incorrect. Babies do not receive relaxin's highest levels.

B) Incorrect. The elderly do not receive relaxin's highest levels.

C) **Correct.** Pregnant women receive relaxin's highest levels, especially during the first two weeks of pregnancy.

D) Incorrect. Teenagers do not receive relaxin's highest levels.

86.

A) Incorrect. The midsagittal (median) plane runs vertically down the midline of the body, dividing it equally into right and left sections.

B) Incorrect. The coronal (frontal) plane passes through the body, dividing it into anterior and posterior sections.

C) Correct. The transverse plane passes horizontally through the body, dividing it into superior and inferior sections.

D) Incorrect. The sagittal plane passes through the body parallel to the midsagittal plane.

87.

A) Incorrect. It is a common rule in the workplace for employees to avoid using lewd or foul language.

B) Incorrect. An employer may legitimately expect employees to adhere to a standard dress code.

C) Correct. An employer cannot insist or require that employees work for free, regardless of the reason.

D) Incorrect. Speaking negatively about a coworker is unprofessional and bad for morale.

88.

A) Incorrect. Using a company computer without permission from a supervisor would be a workplace violation, unless the computer is designated for massage therapists employed by the business.

B) Incorrect. Using a company-owned washer and dryer for personal laundry without permission would be a workplace violation.

C) Correct. An employer cannot insist employees work outside of their officially scheduled and agreed-upon hours.

D) Incorrect. Gathering personal client information for any reason would be a workplace violation.

89.

A) Correct. Insurance helps protect massage therapists and their businesses from risk.

B) Incorrect. Not everyone is ill intentioned and looking to sue, but insurance is a good defense, just in case.

C) Incorrect. Massage therapists have to pay taxes regardless of whether they have insurance.

D) Incorrect. Having insurance does not allow massage therapists to sue their clients; furthermore, this is not a good business practice.

90.

A) Incorrect. An angle is formed by two diverging lines.

B) Incorrect. A crest is a prominent elevation.

C) Incorrect. A meatus is an opening or canal.

D) Correct. A ramus is an arm or branch of a bone. The mandibular ramus is an example.

91.

A) Incorrect. The cranial nerves are numbered using roman numerals one (I) through twelve (XII).

B) Incorrect. A human adult has seven cervical, twelve thoracic, and five lumbar vertebrae, for a total of twenty-four.

C) Correct. There are actually twelve pairs of ribs, not ten.

D) Incorrect. The human foot has seven tarsals, five metatarsals, and fourteen phalanges, for a total of twenty-six bones.

92.

A) Incorrect. Crestor® is a drug that lowers cholesterol and slows the buildup of arterial plaque.

B) Correct. Vyvanse® treats attention deficit hyperactivity disorder (ADHD) in adults and children, as well as binge eating disorder. It can be habit forming.

C) Incorrect. Lyrica® treats diabetic nerve pain, fibromyalgia, spinal cord nerve pain resulting from injury, and persistent nerve pain resulting from having shingles. It is also used as an accompaniment to epileptic drugs.

D) Incorrect. Coumadin® is an anticoagulant, or blood thinner.

93.

A) Incorrect. A protuberance is a bulge.

B) Incorrect. A facet guides and limits motion.

C) **Correct.** A foramen is a hole in a bone for nerves or vessels to pass through. The obturator foramen of the pelvis is one example.

D) Incorrect. A spine is a narrow, slender projection.

94. A) Incorrect. Lymphatic drainage massage can reduce swelling and edema.

B) Incorrect. Lymphatic drainage massage can assist a client in recovery from surgery.

C) **Correct.** Lymphatic drainage massage is a light treatment and does not release trigger points.

D) Incorrect. Lymphatic drainage massage can increase energy.

95. A) Incorrect. This type of conversation is not acceptable at all in the workplace.

B) Incorrect. Management will not consider this appropriate and will want to take further action than disallowing the therapist to perform massages on this client again.

C) **Correct.** The employer will prepare a written explanation of why the behavior was inappropriate and have the therapist sign it.

D) Incorrect. If the therapist's coworker did this, she would be in violation as well.

96. A) Incorrect. Business plans are used to set realistic goals.

B) Incorrect. Business plans should not be used to beg for money; they present investors with an opportunity.

C) **Correct.** A business plan is a model covering all aspects of operations and can be used to obtain loans.

D) Incorrect. A business plan is more for the business's owners and principal lenders.

97. A) Incorrect. Lateral rotator muscles laterally rotate the hip.

B) Incorrect. Quadriceps femoris muscles primarily extend the knee.

C) Incorrect. There are three hamstring muscles.

D) **Correct.** The pectineus originates from the superior ramus of pubis and inserts at the pectineal line of femur. The muscles of the adductor group primarily adduct and medially rotate the hip. The other four muscles in the adductor group are the gracilis and the adductor brevis, longus, and magnus.

98. A) Incorrect. Earth contains metal.

B) **Correct.** Water nourishes wood.

C) Incorrect. Metal collects water.

D) Incorrect. Fire produces earth.

99. A) **Correct.** Proprioception helps with spatial sensation and navigation.

B) Incorrect. Proprioception may help with the ability to move, but it is not the primary definition.

C) Incorrect. Perception is the ability to gain awareness through any of the senses.

D) Incorrect. Nociception is the ability to sense pain.

100. A) Incorrect. Irregular bones do not fit into any classification.

B) Incorrect. Sesamoid bones are small and roundish.

C) **Correct.** Short bones provide support and stability with little movement.

D) Incorrect. Long bones have a length that greatly exceeds their width.

49057872R00148

Made in the USA
Middletown, DE
04 October 2017